Administering the California
Special Needs Trust

Administering the California
Special Needs Trust

*A Guide for Assisting a Person with a Disability
as Trustee of a Special Needs Trust*

Kevin Urbatsch

iUniverse, Inc.
Bloomington

Administering the California Special Needs Trust
A Guide for Assisting a Person with a Disability
as Trustee of a Special Needs Trust

iUniverse books may be ordered through booksellers or by contacting:

iUniverse
1663 Liberty Drive
Bloomington, IN 47403
www.iuniverse.com
1-800-Authors (1-800-288-4677)

Because of the dynamic nature of the Internet, any web addresses or links contained in this book may have changed since publication and may no longer be valid. The views expressed in this work are solely those of the author and do not necessarily reflect the views of the publisher, and the publisher hereby disclaims any responsibility for them.

Any people depicted in stock imagery provided by Thinkstock are models, and such images are being used for illustrative purposes only.
Certain stock imagery © Thinkstock.

ISBN: 978-1-4620-6051-1 (sc)
ISBN: 978-1-4620-6052-8 (ebk)

Printed in the United States of America

iUniverse rev. date: 12/16/2011

CONTENTS

AUTHOR INTRODUCTION

For years, I have made plans for persons with disabilities that included establishing special needs trusts, powers of attorney, advance health-care directives, and limited conservatorships. All too often, once the documents were drafted and the clients left my office, there was little day-to-day guidance I could offer. In order to help my clients, I drafted a relatively short twenty-page (or so) document that discussed some details of managing a special needs trust. While it answered some questions, it also seemed to generate many follow-up questions due to the relative complex nature of special needs trust administration.

Over the years, I have heard a similar type of question from people confused about how special needs trust disbursements would affect the beneficiary's public benefits or whether a trustee was authorized to perform a certain action. It was not only clients but also other attorneys (unfamiliar with public benefit rules) who sought advice on some of the unique issues that arose during special needs trust administration.

It is understandable that clients and attorneys who do not spend every day working on special needs issues are confused due to the complex nature of public benefit administration, but what is more troubling is that many public benefit agency caseworkers often misunderstand the rules governing their own public benefit programs and provide improper advice on how a special needs trust interacts with public benefit programs.

It was imperative that a resource be provided that would allow a trustee to feel more confident in his or her administration. I reviewed the existing publications, and none of them addressed the specific California issues that a special needs trust trustee would see on a day-to-day basis. Sometime in late 2009, I tried expanding my client handout, but as I started working on it, I realized it was going to take a much more thorough treatment to provide the kind of guidance I felt was necessary. Thus, this book was born.

In writing any book, the author needs to decide who the book's audience will be. In this case, I decided my audience is anyone who has taken on the responsibility of administering a California special needs trust. This could be a family member or friend who has never managed any kind of trust, up to and including a national bank trust department, which manages hundreds. Thus, the book provides some of the basics in trust administration, but it also provides a relatively sophisticated level of coverage of all aspects of special needs trust administration.

The law is ever-changing. Public benefit rules change. Tax laws change. Trust laws change. Therefore, if you run into a question that may have a serious impact on the person with a disability's rights or with your role as trustee, it is important that you check my website at www.MyersUrbatsch.com to make sure you are receiving the latest in information about SNT administration. I try to keep track of these changes as they arise and will post the most important changes on my website. Also, I provide a monthly e-newsletter titled the *Special Needs News*, which provides monthly updates and articles on helping trustees and people with disabilities. I encourage you to go to my website and sign up to receive the e-newsletter. Remember though, no book can ever replace the advice from an attorney with experience in special needs trust administration on specific trust administration issues.

For this book, I decided to use a question-and-answer format to address queries as I have received over the years. I have also provided a summary at the end of each chapter that summarizes the chapter's main points. To be fair, I repurposed the summary idea from an excellent publication, titled *Section 8 Made Simple,* published by the Technical Assistant Collaborative, Inc., which I found very helpful in reviewing that area of law. I included footnotes of citations to legal authority, but this was really for my benefit, so I could keep track of any changes in the law and update those things as they arose. I also decided to add a variety of checklists, form documents, and law summaries some of my clients have found helpful over the years. I hope that you find them helpful . . .

If you have any other documents or forms that you have found helpful, please e-mail me at kevin@urbatsch.com and I will include them on my website at www.myersurbatsch.com for the benefit of all. Also, if you have any specific comments, concerns, or questions about this book, please contact me.

Finally, I want to thank you for taking on the responsibility of serving as a special needs trust. It is a challenging but rewarding service you are providing to persons with disabilities, and I hope that you find this book to be a valuable resource.

Kevin Urbatsch

LEGAL DISCLAIMER

This book was written with the intention of providing a resource for trustees of California special needs trusts. It is not, and cannot, be a substitute for actual legal advice between an attorney and client. While the content of this book has been prepared by attorney Kevin Urbatsch, it was done so for informational purposes only and should not be construed as legal advice but rather as this attorney's opinion concerning the law and practice at the time of this book's publication. The material posted in this book is not intended to create a lawyer-client relationship, and readers should not act upon it without seeking professional counsel.

I consider this book the beginning of a dialogue with the readers. If you are aware of an omission, error, or confusing section in this book, please share your knowledge with me. Send your comments to kevin@urbatsch.com.

ACKNOWLEDGMENTS

I would like to thank those individuals who spent their valuable time reviewing chapters and providing feedback. It is nearly certain that any nuggets of wisdom found within these pages are from these selfless souls who agreed (at no charge) to assist the author. Any and all mistakes, omissions, and tortured syntax are solely the responsible of the author.

I wish to thank attorney Susan Katzen for reviewing the entire book and making many necessary modifications and suggestions to it.

The following individuals helped with parts of these chapters:

Chapter 1: Introducing SNT Administration
    Sean Kenney, Esq.—Myers Urbatsch, P.C.
    Roxanne Minott, Esq.
    Dominique Tehrani—Private Professional Fiduciary Candidate
Chapter 2: Avoiding Common Mistakes in Administering SNT
    Sean Kenney, Esq.—Myers Urbatsch, P.C.
    Roxanne Minott, Esq.
    Dominique Tehrani—Private Professional Fiduciary Candidate
Chapter 3: Summarizing Trustee's Legal Responsibilities
    Dominique Tehrani—Private Professional Fiduciary Candidate
Chapter 4: Understanding Public Benefits for Persons with Disabilities
    James Huyck—Public Benefits Consultant/Advocate
    Dominique Tehrani—Private Professional Fiduciary Candidate
Chapter 5: Knowing How SNT Distributions Affect Public Benefits
    Dominique Tehrani—Private Professional Fiduciary Candidate
Chapter 6: Setting the Budget and Making SNT Distribution

ABOUT THE AUTHOR

Kevin Urbatsch is a nationally recognized attorney in estate and settlement planning for persons with disabilities. He is a principal of the estate planning law firm Myers Urbatsch, P.C., located in San Francisco, California. Kevin is a certified specialist in estate planning, trust, and probate law by the California State Bar Board of Legal Specialization.

Kevin is a frequent lecturer to other attorneys, financial professionals, and families of loved ones with special needs. He has lectured before the Academy of Special Needs Planners, National Academy of Elder Law Attorneys, American Association of Justice, Professional Fiduciary Association of California, numerous California bar associations, and not-for-profit groups helping parents and persons with disabilities achieve their full potential.

Kevin has written several books and numerous articles on planning for loved ones with special needs. Kevin is the coauthor of the fourth edition of the Nolo Press book *Special Needs Trusts: Protecting Your Child's Financial Future*, published in 2011. He is also the contributing editor and partial author of CEB's award-winning publication titled *Special Needs Trusts: Planning, Drafting, and Administration*, which is designed to help other estate planning attorneys when planning for persons with disabilities.

Kevin is a charter member of the Academy of Special Needs Planners and a member of the National Academy of Elder Law Attorneys (NAELA); the California Advocates for Nursing Home Reform (CANHR); WealthCounsel, the Bar Association of San Francisco, Probate and Trust Section; and the State Bar of California, Trust and Estate Section.

In May 2011, Kevin won the NAELA's Presidential Recognition Award for his work in special needs planning. In 2010 and 2011, Kevin was named a Northern California Superlawyer. In 2009, Kevin was named KRON-TV's Best of the Bay estate planning attorney for San Francisco and for Northern California.

CHAPTER 1

Introducing Special Needs Trust Administration

This book describes the duties and responsibilities of a California special needs trust (sometimes called a "supplemental needs trust"), or SNT, trustee. A trustee is a person or entity that has the legal responsibility for managing a trust by following the rules set forth in a trust document for the benefit of the beneficiary of the trust. In an SNT, the beneficiary is the person with a disability. Being a trustee is a job, and it can be a difficult one. The person who agrees to be an SNT trustee must understand both the legal duties of being a trustee and the rules of various public benefits programs so the SNT doesn't unintentionally cause the beneficiary to lose his or her benefits.

This book is set up in a question-and-answer format to highlight the different issues that will arise for the SNT trustee.

> **Critical Pointer:** Please keep in mind that the guidelines laid out in this book are far from exhaustive. These guidelines are intended to alert trustees to their duties and to impress upon them the significance of their responsibilities. Please do not hesitate to ask for legal, financial, tax, or other advice, especially if the trustee is not convinced he or she knows the right answer. That advice may cost something in the short run, but the cost can be far less than it takes to fix a mistake later on. Remember that the trust will pay reasonable costs associated with trustees obtaining advice, but trustees could end up paying

out of their own pockets for their failure to secure advice when needed. Use chapter 11 to find help in administering an SNT.

WHAT IS AN SNT?

An SNT is a type of trust designed to provide a person with a disability with assets to enhance his or her quality of life while at the same time allowing that person to remain eligible for needs-based public benefits. The two primary types of public benefit programs that are protected by use of an SNT are Supplemental Security Income ("SSI") and Medicaid (in California we call this program "Medi-Cal").

There are many other reasons why an SNT is valuable:

- protecting the beneficiary from predators who take advantage of minors or vulnerable adults who do not have the capacity to protect themselves;
- providing supplemental lifetime support by purchasing additional items and services that make life more rewarding for the person with a disability;
- providing a system of advocacy to preserve the civil rights of the person with a disability; providing a safe and clean living arrangement so the person with a disability can live in the least restrictive environment;
- providing a system to provide ongoing and safe caregiving services that may also supplement In-Home Supportive Services (IHSS); and
- offering opportunities so the person with a disability can enjoy all social and recreational activities that enhance his or her quality of life.

Critical Pointer: An improperly drafted SNT will cause the beneficiary to lose his or her benefits. There are many ways to draft an improper SNT; it may require payments to the beneficiary or require that payments be used for the beneficiary's support. Thus, before someone agrees to take on the job of trustee, the trustee should have the trust reviewed by an experienced special needs attorney to make sure it was drafted and established correctly.

WHAT IS A SETTLOR, TRUSTEE, TRUST ADVISORY COMMITTEE, OR TRUST PROTECTOR?

In order to understand administration, it is important to know the terms for the different people who may be involved in the administration of the SNT:

- **Settlor, Trustmaker, Grantor, Trustor:** These are different names for the person or entity that created or established the trust. For example, if a parent created a trust for a child with a disability, then the parent would be named the settlor, grantor, trustmaker, or trustor of the trust, depending on the drafting attorney's own convention of use. In California law, the term *settlor* is used; however, there is no difference in treatment if a trust document uses a different name.

- **Trustee:** This is the person responsible for administering the trust once it is established. A trust may also name successor trustees, who would be the persons responsible for managing the trust if the originally named trustee could no longer serve. A trust can have more than one trustee at a time. Be aware that a cotrustee can be held responsible for another cotrustee's breach of a fiduciary duty. Thus, it is important that all cotrustees pay close attention to everything that is done in the administration of the trust. If there is any question or problem, it should be communicated to the other cotrustee or cotrustees immediately. As a general rule, where there are two cotrustees, both have to agree on all matters of trust administration, and where there are three or more cotrustees, the majority rules. In order to minimize the chances of being held responsible for someone else's poor judgment or breach of duty, a cotrustee should be sure to make a written record of any points of disagreement about trust business. In extreme cases, a cotrustee may be required to blow the whistle on other cotrustees' activities.

- **Beneficiary:** This is the person or entity that is to receive the benefit of the trust. The primary beneficiary of a SNT is the person with a disability. There may also be named remainder beneficiaries or sometime contingent beneficiaries; these are the persons who would receive the trust assets once the primary beneficiary either dies or there is a provision in the trust that would cause the assets to go to someone else. For example, an SNT could provide, "I leave my assets to be administered for the benefit of my child with a disability for as long as he is alive, but on his death or upon his no longer being disabled, the assets of the trusts shall be distributed to my grandchildren." In this example, the remainder beneficiaries would be the grandchildren.

Note: There is some confusion on the role of Medi-Cal agency's right of recovery from a first party SNT. This right of recovery does not make the agency a beneficiary of the first party SNT but rather a contingent future creditor of the trust.

- **Trust Advisory Committee**: In some SNTs, there will be a group of persons called a trust advisory committee. Typically, the committee will have the authority to speak on behalf of the beneficiary and make requests for disbursements. They may also have the authority to remove and replace a trustee. Attorneys include committees for a variety of reasons, but primarily to make sure there is a way for someone to oversee the trustee's actions. As with nearly all questions surrounding trust administration, it is very important to read the document to understand what role the committee will serve.
- **Trust Protector:** As with the trust advisory committee, a trust protector is used in some SNTs. The protector will be given a series of responsibilities as spelled out in the trust document. Typically, these include the right to remove and replace trustees and the right to amend the trust if there are changes in the law that will require an amendment to the trust to keep it current.

For further explanations of legal terms used in the trust document please look at the Glossary of Legal Terms at the end of the book.

ARE THERE DIFFERENT TYPES OF SNTS?

Yes, there are two kinds of SNTs, commonly referred to as "first-party" and "third-party" SNTs. The distinguishing feature between the two is who is putting the money into the trust. The difference is set forth as follows:

- A **first-party SNT** is funded with the assets of the person with a disability.
- A **third-party SNT** is typically part of a parent's or grandparent's estate plan for a child with a disability. However, it is not limited to

them; any person other than the person with a disability can fund this type of trust. Such a trust is funded with the assets of a "third party," that is, parents, grandparents, or anyone else other than the person with a disability whom the trust benefits.

For a more complete discussion of the difference between the two types of trusts, see chapter 2.

ARE THE DIFFERENT TYPES OF SNTS TREATED DIFFERENTLY BY AN SNT TRUSTEE?

Yes, the trustee must understand whether he or she is administering a first—or third-party SNT. While many of the duties and responsibilities of the trustee are the same, there are duties and responsibilities that drastically change depending on whether the trust is a first—or third-party trust. Throughout the book, the discussion will indicate if there is a difference in the answer because of the different type of trust being administered.

> **Helpful Hint:** To determine which type of trust is being administered, the trustee needs to find out who provided the original money or assets to the trust. Generally, this is explained in the first few pages of the trust. For example, a trust may state that all funding of the trust is being done by a parent or grandparent, in which case it would be a third-party SNT. Another trust may state that all trust assets have come from the person with a disability, in which case it would be a first-party SNT.

WHY SHOULD I AGREE TO BE AN SNT TRUSTEE?

Administering an SNT on behalf of a person with a disability can be very satisfying. The trustee can make a real difference in that person's quality of life and, sadly, may be the only person fighting for that person's proper care. The level of commitment can vary widely depending on who is the SNT beneficiary. On the most difficult end, there are SNT beneficiaries who are fully dependent on their trustee to make all their decisions and must be protected at all times. On the other end, the person with a disability may have full capacity to manage his or her affairs and only needs a modest amount of attention. In this case, the

SNT is typically established only to keep the person eligible for public benefits. Regardless of the level of commitment, the trustee is doing a great service to this all-too-often neglected member of society.

Correctly administering an SNT is a very important task. If the administration is done incorrectly, the trustee may cause the person with a disability to lose his or her eligibility for public benefits. This results in substantial loss of assets and loss of access to health care. While the loss of financial benefits is important and can be devastating to ongoing care and comfort, the loss of health care can be life threatening. Thus, depending on the circumstance of the SNT, the trustee holds the key to the person with a disability's life, care, and comfort.

HOW DIFFICULT IS IT TO BE AN SNT TRUSTEE?

While it is important and satisfying to administer an SNT, it can also be very difficult. The trust rules and public benefits regulations are highly technical, often unclear, and frequently contradictory. Even small differences in a beneficiary's factual situation can significantly affect the trustee's duties. The most skilled and experienced trustees constantly review the trust document and have a system to keep current with changes in the trust and public benefits laws. The trustee should also understand the beneficiary's disability and know what types of agencies serve this population. Oftentimes, the trustee is asked to pay for services that can be obtained for free from not-for-profit agencies or the government.

Unless the SNT has a very small amount of assets, most SNT trustees retain professionals to assist in the administration, including SNT attorneys, private professional fiduciaries, corporate trust departments, financial advisers, tax professionals, professional caregivers, and public benefits advocates, to name a few.

> **Helpful Hint:** There are numerous resources in this book that will help you stay current with any significant changes in the law, see chapter 11 for a list of websites and other resources for helping the SNT trustee.

WHAT ARE AN SNT TRUSTEE'S DUTIES?

The trustee has a *fiduciary duty* to the SNT beneficiary. A fiduciary duty is the highest duty one person can owe another under the law; it is much like the duty a parent owes to a minor child.

In general, the trust document itself provides a roadmap for the SNT trustee's responsibilities. However, other trustee duties are set forth in California law, which may not be discussed in the trust document at all.

A short summary of the SNT trustee's duties:

- Administer SNT by its terms.
- Loyalty/confidentiality to the SNT beneficiary.
- Deal impartially with SNT beneficiary.
- Avoid conflict of interest(s) with the SNT beneficiary.
- Refuse to require SNT beneficiary to relieve the trustee of liability.
- Take control and preserve SNT property.
- Make SNT property productive.
- Keep SNT property separate from both the SNT trustee's assets and the SNT beneficiary's other assets.
- Enforce claims on behalf of the SNT.
- Defend actions against the SNT.
- Not delegate SNT trustee duties (with some exceptions that are explained in this book).
- Use any special skills the person serving has as SNT trustee.
- Comply with prudent investor rule or other investment standard set forth in document.
- Diversify SNT assets.
- Keep SNT beneficiaries reasonably informed of trust activities.
- Not to undertake role as trustee of an adverse trust interest like investing trust assets in a business that the trustee own separately.
- Reasonably use SNT trustee's discretionary powers, such as deciding what type of disbursements the trust should make.

These duties are listed with appropriate code sections in Appendix B and are further explained briefly below, and in much more detail in chapter 3.

WHERE ARE THE RULES AND LAWS FOR AN SNT TRUSTEE LOCATED?

The SNT trustee's rules are set forth in a variety of places. Primarily, the trustee should review the trust document, which will have most of the information that the trustee will ever need to look up.

Other sources of law concerning trusts include

- California Probate Code
- California case law
- Sources of law concerning public benefits laws include
- United State Code (USC)
- Code of Federal Regulations (CFR)
- Federal case law
- Social Security Administration's Program Operation Manual System (POMS)
- California Welfare and Institutions Code
- Medi-Cal's California regulations (CCR)
- All County Welfare Director's Letters (ACWDL)
- All County Letters (ACL)

These laws are discussed in more detail in chapters 3 and 4, and in chapter 11 a list of website addresses are set forth for each set of laws. This allows a trustee to look up the laws directly.

WHAT PUBLIC BENEFITS PROGRAM RULES WILL AN SNT TRUSTEE NEED TO UNDERSTAND?

A SNT trustee will primarily be concerned with the following types of public benefits:

- **Needs-Based Benefits.** The two "needs-based" programs that are the primary public benefit programs for persons with a disability who are also beneficiary's of an SNT are Supplemental Security Income (SSI) and Medi-Cal, which also pays for the In-Home Supportive Services (IHSS), program which can be very important to many SNT beneficiaries.

However, the trustee should understand how the SNT may (or may not) interact with other public benefits programs, including the following:

- **Entitlement Benefits**. Old Age, Survivors, and Disability Insurance (OASDI), which includes SSDI, Social Security retirement benefits (often referred to as Social Security for short), and Medicare
- **Housing Benefits.** Housing Choice Voucher Program, more commonly known as Section 8 housing
- **Other Benefits.** Regional Center assistance for persons with developmental disabilities, veteran benefits, Healthy Families, catastrophic health-care coverage, CalWorks, and food stamps

Public benefits will be discussed in greater detail in chapter 4.

WILL THE SNT TRUSTEE'S DUTIES CHANGE IF THE PERSON WITH A DISABILITY IS ELIGIBLE FOR ONLY SOME OF THE AVAILABLE PUBLIC BENEFITS BUT NOT ALL?

Yes. Generally, if the SNT beneficiary is an SSI recipient, then the trustee is only responsible for following the SSI rules. The reason that only SSI rules are important is that if the beneficiary is qualified for SSI, he or she automatically receives Medi-Cal. The Medi-Cal rules are then unimportant for continued eligibility. However, if the beneficiary does not qualify for SSI but is still eligible for Medi-Cal, then the SNT trustee must follow the Medi-Cal rules, which can be different from SSI rules. When this happens, we will point this out in the book.

If the only government benefits involved are entitlement programs, such as Social Security Disability Insurance (SSDI), Social Security or Medicare, which have no resource limits, an SNT trustee will operate the trust pursuant to its terms and normal trust laws and will not need to be concerned with violating public benefits laws. There is nothing an SNT trustee can do to ruin eligibility for these entitlement public benefits.

> **Critical Pointer:** It is imperative that the SNT trustee find out exactly which benefits the SNT beneficiary is receiving. The trustee's job can be fundamentally different depending on which benefits the SNT beneficiary is receiving. Many times an SNT beneficiary will not know which public benefits programs

he or she is receiving. It is easy to understand why there is confusion. The Social Security Administration (SSA) manages SSI, SSDI, and Social Security, and the checks come from the same place, so it is easy to be confused. Further, Medi-Cal and Medicare can cover identical types of medical care, and it can be difficult to know which program is covering the beneficiary. See chapter 2 for a discussion on what happens if there is a mix up of the type of public benefits the SNT beneficiary is receiving and chapter 4 to find out how to determine which benefits the beneficiary is receiving.

If the SNT beneficiary is eligible for Section 8 housing, veteran benefits, or any other of the available government benefits, then the SNT trustee must know how these benefits may be affected by the existence of an SNT and whether distributions from the SNT will affect public benefits.

A further discussion of public benefits can be found in chapter 4. For how to make an appropriate SNT distribution and how it will or will not affect public benefits, see chapters 5 and 6.

WHAT TYPE OF DISBURSEMENTS CAN AN SNT TRUSTEE MAKE FOR THE SNT BENEFICIARY?

It is a common misunderstanding that the SNT is very limited in what it can pay for when enhancing the quality of life of a person with a disability. Depending on the SNT terms, the SNT trustee can actually pay for anything that is not illegal or against public policy. This can include a huge variety of items that have no impact on public benefits at all, such as furniture, clothing, vacations, pet expenses, internet, computers, television, and all the things that many people without disabilities take for granted. For a much more complete list, see Appendix M.

Some SNT disbursements, most notably disbursements for food, shelter, or medical care already paid for by Medi-Cal, may affect eligibility for certain types of public benefits. However, the SNT trustee (when the SNT document allows such a disbursement) may still pay for these items if it is in the best interests of the beneficiary. This may reduce (or even eliminate) some public benefit eligibility; however, depending on the circumstances, this may be a good trade-off.

Example: A beneficiary of an SNT wishes to have the SNT trustee pay for a new apartment where the rent is $2,000 per month. The beneficiary is an SSI recipient receiving the maximum amount of SSI ($830 per month as of July 2011 for California). The payment of rent by the SNT trustee will cause a reduction of the monthly SSI check to $585.33 per month in the year 2011. However, this is generally a good trade-off. The SNT beneficiary is able to live in a much nicer and safer apartment and only loses $244.67 per month of SSI. This formula is described in more detail in chapters 4, 5, and 6.

Critical Pointer: It is important to know if the SNT document will allow a trustee to make disbursements that reduce or eliminate eligibility for public benefits. Some SNTs do and some do not. To see whether the SNT allows it, please review chapter 2, which discusses "distribution standards" and provides an explanation for the different types of standards that allow such distributions.

For further discussion on making appropriate distributions, see chapters 5 and 6.

CAN AN SNT TRUSTEE BE RESPONSIBLE IF HE OR SHE MAKES A MISTAKE IN ADMINISTERING AN SNT?

Yes. But the type of actions that will cause the SNT trustee to be held responsible will depend on the terms of the SNT document. If the SNT is silent, then the trustee is liable if the SNT trustee commits a breach of trust. This typically means if the trustee acts (1) in bad faith, (2) knowingly against trust terms or against beneficiary but in good faith, or (3) negligently.

Negligence generally means the failure of the trustee to meet the applicable standard of care of a trustee. A trustee's standard of care will depend on the actions being taken by the trustee. An SNT trustee must do what a prudent person would do in the SNT trustee's situation and act in good faith and with reasonable prudence, discretion, and intelligence. The trustee must use reasonable skill, care, and caution when serving. If the trustee does not use this level of care, he or she will be held responsible for breach of trust. This, however, does not mean the SNT trustee is the insurer for all trust losses.

Whether the trustee's conduct meets the requisite standard of care will be determined by the circumstances as they appear at the time the decision was made, not later, in hindsight. An SNT trustee is also not required to exercise extraordinary care in serving. He or she must exercise ordinary care.

> **Critical Pointer:** Some trustees believe that if they are not being paid that they cannot be held responsible for breaches of trust. This is incorrect. It makes no difference if the trustee is paid or not; he or she will still be fully responsible for any breaches of trust.

Some SNTs have provisions that may limit the trustee's liability. If the SNT document includes a provision that says the trustee's liability is absolutely limited, it may reduce the liability of the trustee to trustee only acts that are

1. intentional breaches of trust, with gross negligence, in bad faith, or with reckless indifference to the interest of the beneficiary, or
2. for any profit that the trustee derives from a breach of trust.

A trust document cannot limit a trustee's liability any further than this. In general, to be held responsible under these provisions, the SNT trustee must be doing something intentional to harm the beneficiary or with such indifference that the trustee should have known that something was being done that would either benefit the trustee at the expense of the SNT or harm the SNT beneficiary.

Some trustees try to limit their liability by forcing beneficiaries to sign agreements that the beneficiary will not sue the trustee for any actions taken by the trustee. These agreements are void, as they contradict public policy under California law.

> **Critical Pointer:** Professional trustees are held to more stringent standards than nonprofessional trustees and are required to apply the knowledge and competence ordinarily possessed by professionals under similar circumstances. Thus, if the SNT trustee is holding him or herself out as an expert in financial matters, he or she will be held to a higher standard of care for the financial performance of the trust than someone who does not hold him or herself out as such an expert.

WHAT ARE THE PENALTIES IF AN SNT TRUSTEE IS RESPONSIBLE FOR A BREACH OF TRUST?

There are a host of penalties that an SNT trustee can receive for a breach of trust. A breach of trust is a violation by the trustee of any duty that the trustee owes a beneficiary. Depending on what happened, an SNT trustee may be held responsible for one or more of the following actions:

- the SNT trustee may be removed and another trustee may be appointed in his or her place;
- SNT trustees may have to pay back from their own assets to the SNT any amount of money that was lost as a result of the wrongful act or give back to the SNT any assets that were wrongfully taken;
- SNT trustees may have to pay a penalty out of their own pocket for their wrongful act, even if no money was lost by the SNT;
- a court may set aside the wrongful act of the SNT trustee as long as someone who is innocent is not harmed;
- SNT trustees may lose or have reduced any money that is owed to them for their services as trustee;
- the court may go after property that was improperly distributed out to someone else;
- in extreme cases, the SNT trustee can be held in contempt of court if the trustee refuses to provide an accounting of his or her actions or if the SNT trustee ignores a court order to perform a certain act; or
- in even more extreme cases, if the trustee ignores a court order, the SNT trustee can be imprisoned until he or she performs the tasks for which he or she had been held in contempt of court.

WHAT RECORDS DOES THE SNT TRUSTEE HAVE TO KEEP?

Trustees have a duty to keep accurate records of trust transactions. Not only is it a legal duty, but it is very prudent to do so. A trustee may be questioned years later by the SNT beneficiary or his or her legal representatives about trust actions. Further, it is not unusual for public benefits agencies, such as the Social Security Administration (SSA) or the Department of Health Care Services (DHCS), to request a review of the trustee's records. Finally, other government agencies, like the IRS, may audit trust tax returns. Without good records, it may be impossible to respond to these requests or remember why disbursements were made.

Records should be thorough, legible, and easily accessible and should provide a cumulative description of the trustee's administration. This can be done by a simple spreadsheet. The trustee should also keep a copy of all receipts.

Without good records, if someone questions the SNT trustee's actions, all presumptions will be made against the SNT trustee as if he or she did something wrong. Further, without proper records, the SNT trustee will be unable to prepare accurate income tax returns for the trust, inviting further liability for violating both state and federal tax law.

> **Example:** One common mistake that SNT trustees make is paying a reimbursement to others for purchases made on the beneficiary's behalf but failing to keep an accurate record of what the underlying purchase was for. For example, trustee reimburses parent of beneficiary $800 for television purchased for beneficiary—a perfectly acceptable transaction. However, trustee only notes that $800 was paid as reimbursement to parents, failing to make sure that it was for a television. Years later, the SSA seeks an explanation of why cash was distributed. If the trustee is not able to adequately explain it, the SSA could take the position that a gift was made and penalize the beneficiary's eligibility for SSI. The better practice is to make a short notation that it was for the purchase of a television and provide a copy of the receipt.

For a further discussion of the recordkeeping requirements of the SNT trustee, see chapter 7.

DOES THE SNT TRUSTEE HAVE TO KEEP THE BENEFICIARY INFORMED OF TRUSTEE'S ACTIONS?

Yes. The SNT trustee has a legal duty to keep a beneficiary reasonably informed about the trustee's administrative decisions and acts and generally to account to beneficiaries on an annual basis. The type of account the SNT trustee must provide will depend on which type of SNT is being administered, for example, court-supervised trust or non-court supervised trust.

In general, if the SNT is not court supervised, the accounting requirement is somewhat relaxed and can be done by sending an annual summary of the trustee's actions by letter to the beneficiaries and their legal representatives.

If the SNT is court supervised, which is generally a first-party SNT established by a court, then there are very formal legal requirements that must be followed, and the court account must be filed in a probate court on a periodic basis, generally one year after the trust is established and every two years thereafter. It is imperative that the trustee review the trust document and the court's order establishing the first-party SNT for direction on whether the trust must file accounts and reports for court approval.

For a further discussion of the accounting requirements of the SNT trustee, see chapter 7.

DOES THE SNT TRUSTEE HAVE TO INVEST THE SNT ASSETS?

Yes. An SNT trustee must always invest SNT assets. However, the type of investments that are authorized depends on whether the trust is a first-party SNT that has been established by a court or a non-court supervised SNT.

Most SNTs are not court supervised, and the trustee's investment powers are derived from the SNT document, which will set forth the investment standard. If the SNT document is silent, the SNT trustee must comply with the Uniform Prudent Investor Act (UPIA), California case law, and the circumstances of the trust and its beneficiaries. All these sources of investment powers are considered in determining whether an investment is proper. In general, the UPIA investment standard of care states,

1. A trustee shall invest and manage trust assets as a prudent investor would, by considering the purposes, terms, distribution requirements, and other circumstances of the trust. In satisfying this standard, the trustee shall exercise reasonable care, skill, and caution.
2. A trustee's investment and management decisions respecting individual assets and courses of action must be evaluated not in isolation but in the context of the trust portfolio as a whole and as a part of an overall investment strategy, having risk and return objectives reasonably suited to the trust.

Kevin Urbatsch

If the SNT is court supervised, the SNT trustee may only invest in a very limited way. The investment standard is identical to that of a court proceeding, called a conservatorship. The conservatorship investment standard authorizes only a short list of approvable investments. However, this limited list can be expanded by court order, so the SNT trustee should look at any court order that set up the trust to see if the investment standard was expanded.

The only duty a trustee may delegate is the investment and management duty. Depending on the size of the SNT and the complexity of the assets, it may be crucial for an unskilled SNT trustee to delegate these functions to an experienced and trusted investment adviser. If a trustee decides to delegate investment or management responsibilities, the trustee must still exercise prudence in (1) selecting the agent, (2) establishing the scope and terms of the delegation of authority, and (3) periodically reviewing the agent's overall performance and compliance with the terms of the delegation.

If SNT trustees decide to maintain these duties, then they can still consult with other professionals, such as financial advisers, real estate brokers, accountants, tax attorneys, and other specialists to aid them in their investment responsibility and protect themselves from potential liability.

For further discussion of the SNT trustee's investment responsibility, see chapter 8.

WHAT IS THE SNT TRUSTEE'S RESPONSIBILITY FOR FILING RETURNS AND PAYING TAXES?

The SNT trustee is responsible for the tax liabilities and reporting for the SNT to both the IRS and the California Franchise Tax Board. The type of reporting and tax payments that will be made will depend on which type of SNT is being administered. The main difference will be whether the SNT is considered by the IRS to be a *grantor trust* or *nongrantor trust*.

> **Helpful Hint:** In general, a third-party SNT will be a nongrantor trust and a first-party SNT will be a grantor trust. However, it is possible that a third-party SNT could be a grantor trust if the parents still have a right to change the terms of the trust. If the SNT trustee is not certain about what type of tax treatment their SNT will receive, it would be best to consult with an SNT attorney or CPA.

For most third-party SNTs, the SNT will be a nongrantor trust. The nongrantor SNT will file separate federal and state tax returns on behalf of the trust and provide a tax form titled a K-1 to the SNT beneficiary for any SNT income that was distributed on behalf of the SNT beneficiary. Generally, it is best if the nongrantor SNT spends any trust income on behalf of the beneficiary. That is because, under IRS rules, trust income that is spent on the beneficiary's behalf is taxed at his or her individual rate, not the trust rate. The beneficiary is often the preferred taxpayer, because

(1) the SNT beneficiary's income tax brackets will be much lower than the trust's tax brackets, and

(2) the SNT beneficiary may have large medical expenses that will qualify as deductions on his or her individual income tax return.

> **Example**: The SNT assets are invested in several funds showing interest earned on the money. For the current year, the interest amounts to $15,000. In the SNT trust accounting, the trustee records that disbursements for the beneficiary's benefit were made out of this income, not the trust principal. When the trust taxes are computed, any money spent from the income for the beneficiary's benefit is taxed at the beneficiary's tax rate. Income that is added to the trust and not disbursed is taxed at the higher trust rate. Thus, it is better tax-wise to distribute income from a "non grantor" SNT.

For the SNT trustee's purpose, the easier tax responsibility is the "grantor trust," or first-party SNT. The IRS income from a first-party SNT is taxed not to the trust, but to the beneficiary with a disability. This is so even if it is retained in the trust.

For a more complete discussion of the SNT trustee's tax responsibilities, see chapter 9.

What Happens When the SNT Beneficiary Dies or the Trust Terminates?

An SNT trustee must continue his or her administration of the trust even though by its terms it has terminated. The three most common events which result in the termination of an SNT are as follows:

1) Death of the beneficiary
2) Exhaustion of trust assets
3) Failure of purpose—for example, if an SNT provision states that if the beneficiary is able to work and pay for his or her own food, clothing, shelter, and medical care, the trust should be terminated

Before acting, the trustee must be satisfied that the event has occurred. For example, if death is the triggering event, the trustee should obtain a copy of the death certificate for the beneficiary.

Upon termination, the trustee's activities are generally divided into three categories:

1) Paying the final expenses of the trust (which may include California's Medi-Cal agency if it is a first-party SNT) and perhaps the expenses of the SNT beneficiary
2) Making a final accounting to the remainder beneficiaries (or the court, if SNT is court supervised)
3) Distributing any remaining assets to the heirs

Before making any payments, the SNT trustee must understand how to prioritize among the claims and debts that may be brought to him or her for payment. As a practical consequence of making the wrong payment, the trustee may be required to pay out of his or her personal assets any claims that were not properly paid from the SNT assets.

> **Critical Pointer:** In order to understand the proper priority among creditors of the SNT, the trustee must first determine whether the SNT is a third-party or first-party SNT. This issue is very important, because if the SNT is a first-party SNT, the trustee must give notice of the SNT termination to California's Medi-Cal agency, the Department of Health Care Services (DHCS). Also, if the beneficiary received Medicaid in other states, notice to those states must be performed. DHCS allows only a few things to be paid from SNT assets before DHCS' Medi-Cal bill must be paid. DHCS' Medi-Cal lien includes all the Medi-Cal used by the beneficiary during his or her lifetime. Paying the wrong claims before DHCS' lien is paid can cause the SNT trustee to be responsible for a breach of trust.

If the trust is subject to continuing court supervision, the trustee should prepare a court filing, called a petition, to settle the final account and to distribute the estate. The notice of report and account and petition for distribution will inform the beneficiaries that the trust has terminated. The trustee may also wish to send letters to the beneficiaries, informing them of termination. Preparation of the trustee's final accounting may take a substantial amount of time. The trustee may ask the beneficiaries to waive a final accounting if the beneficiaries have the necessary mental capacity.

For more information on trust termination, see chapter 10.

Chapter 1 Summary

✓ The SNT is a powerful tool that enhances the quality of life of persons with disabilities.

✓ There are two kinds of SNTs (the first-party and third-party SNT), which are treated differently in some circumstances during administration.

✓ Before serving as an SNT trustee, the SNT document should be reviewed by an SNT attorney to make sure it was set up correctly.

✓ Being an SNT trustee is both rewarding and difficult, and the SNT trustee should not underestimate the work that goes into being a trustee.

✓ The SNT trustee may always hire attorneys, CPAs, investment advisers, and other professionals to assist in the administration.

✓ There are many rules and responsibilities of being an SNT trustee that are set forth in many different places, including the SNT document, California law, Federal law, SSA POMS, DHCS Letters, and case law.

✓ The SNT trustee should know what kind of public benefits the SNT beneficiary receives or may be entitled to.

✓ The two types of public benefits the SNT trustee should understand are SSI and Medi-Cal, although he or she should also have some understanding of IHSS, Regional Centers, SSDI, Social Security, Medicare, Section 8, veteran benefits, and other benefits, if his or her beneficiary receives these benefits.

✓ SNT assets can be used in a very broad way to enhance the quality of life of a person with a disability.

✓ An SNT trustee has personal liability for his or her mistakes made while administering an SNT.

- ✓ An SNT has very specific requirements for record-keeping, accounting, investing, and tax reporting and payment.
- ✓ An SNT trustee must know what happens when an SNT terminates; what entity or person is paid first from remaining trust assets.

CHAPTER 2

Avoiding Common Mistakes in Administering SNT

Because the administration of a special needs trust is a difficult task, mistakes are often made. This chapter will go over some of the more common mistakes that arise during the administration of a special needs trust (SNT).

If an SNT trustee uses common sense during SNT administration, that trustee is destined to fail. The reason that common sense fails during the administration of these trusts is the disheartening uncertainty of the laws that govern these matters. For example, a trustee is required to understand both California trust law along with the federal regulations for SSI or the federal and state regulations for Medi-Cal when making a distribution from the trust. Sometimes, something that appears to be in the best interest of the person with a disability, which the trustee thinks he or she should have no problem paying, may actually cause the *loss* of public benefits. Frustratingly, even if in one year it is okay to spend money on something, that same item may be forbidden the next year by a change in law.

Below are the top mistakes an SNT trustee can make and advice on how to avoid being personally liable for making these mistakes.

MISTAKE NUMBER 1: NOT READING THE SNT DOCUMENT

All too often, the SNT trustee will invest assets, make disbursements, or perform other tasks when administering the SNT that are specifically forbidden by the trust document. Some of the advice in this book that would otherwise be acceptable for the trustee to perform is not acceptable if the SNT document states that the trustee cannot do it.

The SNT document is always the first place that the SNT trustee should look to determine if he or she is able to perform a certain task. If the SNT document is silent on the issue, then it may be best to see if there is any prohibition in California law or in the public benefits laws that might prevent such a distribution.

> **Example:** An SNT trustee wishes to purchase a home to be owned by the SNT for the use of the SNT beneficiary. Under California law and the public benefit laws, this is a perfectly acceptable way to spend the money in an SNT. However, this particular SNT document specifically forbids the SNT trustee from purchasing real estate. If the SNT trustee goes ahead and buys the property, he or she is in breach of trust and could be subject to removal as trustee, fines (called a surcharge), and pay for any damages incurred.

MISTAKE NUMBER 2: FAILING TO KEEP CURRENT ON SPECIAL NEEDS TRUST LAWS

An SNT trustee should have a system to alert him or herself of changes in the laws on SNT administration and public benefits eligibility. Chapter 11 lists some websites that will enable a trustee to keep current on these laws.

At a minimum, the SNT trustee should go to the website www.myersurbatsch. com and sign up for the Special Needs News. There we offer a monthly e-mail newsletter that identifies any significant changes in the laws and regulations concerning special needs administration. In addition, the website includes updates and revisions to this book.

The other website that should be regularly reviewed concerns California public benefits programs and is located at www.disability101.org. This website does an excellent job of providing simple explanations of the various California public benefits programs.

MISTAKE NUMBER 3: CONFUSING THE PUBLIC BENEFIT PROGRAMS

Public benefits recipients, their families, and even many attorneys often confuse the type of public benefits being received by an individual who is the beneficiary of a special needs trust. Confusion is quite common, for example, between Supplemental Security Income (SSI) and Social Security Disability Insurance (SSDI) benefits, because the monthly cash payments come from the Social Security Administration and often the payments are directly deposited.

For a more thorough discussion of the different types of public benefits, see chapter 4.

It is very important that the trustee know exactly what benefits the SNT beneficiary is receiving, because the trustee's job can drastically change depending on which public benefits program the beneficiary receives. If the only government benefits involved are entitlement programs, such as Social Security Disability Insurance (SSDI) and Medicare, which have no resource limits, SNT administration is much simpler. If, however, the person with a disability is receiving SSI and Medi-Cal, the SNT trustee must follow the rules of SSI. Yet if the person is on Medi-Cal only, the trustee must follow the rules of Medi-Cal, which are similar to SSI rules but have some surprising differences.

> **Hint:** One quick way to determine if the beneficiary is receiving SSI is to find out how much he or she is receiving from the government program. As of July 2011, the maximum amount of SSI an individual can receive is $830 per month. If he or she is receiving more than this amount, the beneficiary is not receiving SSI. To find the latest maximum monthly benefit for a person on SSI in California, see www.ssa.gov/pubs/11125.html or Google "SSI in California."

If the type of public benefit is still unclear, the SNT trustee should request a copy of the monthly check or bank statement if on direct deposit and inquire with the local Social Security office. It also may be apparent from when the checks arrive. SSI checks arrive on the first of each month, and SSDI checks arrive on the recipient's birthday, but no earlier than the tenth of the month. If SSDI has been received for a lengthy period, the checks arrive on the third of the month.

SSI and Medi-Cal Recipient: In most cases, the SNT beneficiary will be receiving SSI and Medi-Cal, because in California, if the SSI beneficiary receives any amount—even one dollar of SSI—he or she automatically receives Medi-Cal. Under this scenario, the trustee is responsible only for following the SSI rules and regulations, which are generally found in the Program Operation Manuel System (commonly called the POMS), the SSA's internal guidelines on how to administer the SSI program. The POMS rules can be found on their website and the website address is set forth in chapter 11.

> **Note:** This book will discuss the rules of SNT administration primarily as if the beneficiary receives SSI. So, unless otherwise stated, the rules set forth in this book mirror the SSI rules.

Medi-Cal-Only Recipient: In some cases, the SNT beneficiary does not receive SSI but still receives Medi-Cal under a different eligibility program. If this is the case, the trustee does not need to follow the SSI rules but must follow the Medi-Cal rules and regulations, which are found in the California Welfare and Institutions Code, California regulations, and All County Welfare Director's Letters. These rules can all be found on their respective websites, and the website addresses are set forth in chapter 11.

> **Note:** Generally, these rules are very similar to SSI's rules. However, there are some distinctions. In this book, we will make note if the Medi-Cal rules are different from those for SSI.

SSDI, Social Security, and Medicare Only: These public benefit programs are generally the easiest ones to manage by the SNT trustee. Eligibility for these programs do not depend on an individual's assets, thus making SNT disbursements will not have any effect on ongoing eligibility. Thus, the SNT trustee need only follow the terms of the trust document with respect to acceptable disbursements.

> **Warning:** The SNT trustee should make very sure that the beneficiary receives only these benefits and not SSI or Medi-Cal. It is possible for a beneficiary to have both SSI and SSDI or both Medi-Cal and Medicare. If this is the case, the SNT trustee must follow the rules of either SSI or Medi-Cal during administration.

Other Benefits, Such as Veteran Benefits, Section 8, Food Stamps, CalWorks: The SNT trustee should get a complete picture of the public benefits. An SNT trustee should understand how an SNT may affect these benefits if the SNT beneficiary is eligible. The difficulty with many of these benefits is that in some cases the rules are unclear and in other cases they are treated differently throughout California by the different agencies. We will do our best to highlight when these uncertainties arise and how different agencies may be treating different issues.

MISTAKE NUMBER 4: CONFUSING THE DIFFERENT TYPES OF SPECIAL NEEDS TRUSTS

It is critically important to determine, at the outset, what type of special needs trust is being administered. SNTs fall into two basic categories: (1) the third-party SNT; and (2) the first-party SNT. If it is a first-party SNT, the trustee must determine if it is a court-supervised SNT or not.

An SNT trustee has nearly identical duties in administering first-party SNT and third-party SNT. However, there are critical distinctions between the two that will cause the trustee problems if he or she does not understand the particular rules for each.

Here is how to determine whether the trust is a first-party SNT or a third-party SNT:

- A first-party SNT is funded with the person with a disability's money or assets. That's it. If the money being transferred to the trusts is the person with a disability's own assets, then the trust must be a first-party SNT to work. This type of SNT typically arises when the beneficiary with a disability has received a litigation recovery or the beneficiary receives an inheritance or gift in his or her own name and transfers the property to an SNT. However, if a person with a disability has existing assets and wishes to transfer them, he or she is allowed to do that as well.
- A third-party SNT is funded with money or assets that belong to a third person who is not the person with a disability. This is typically done through a parent's or grandparent's estate plan. However, anyone but the person with a disability can put money or assets into the trust.

Ownership of assets can be confusing. There may be legal issues, like community property issues or rights to an inheritance, that can be confusing to those not used to making these types of determinations. One question that often arises is whether the assets are the person with a disability. For example, if a person receives an inheritance in a living trust that is to go outright to the person with a disability, can the money instead be directed to a third-party SNT? The answer is no. If the person with a disability has legal ownership of those assets, they belong to him or her even if technically the assets were never in the name of the person with a disability. The only way to preserve eligibility for SSI and Medi-Cal in this example would be to place those assets in a first party SNT.

> **Example:** Peter, a person with a disability who is an SSI recipient, receives an inheritance of $50,000 as part of his Uncle Paul's will. Uncle Paul's estate is being probated in court, and his executor, Mary, wishes to give Peter his money but recognizes that by giving the money directly to him, he will lose his SSI and Medi-Cal.
> Mary suggests writing the check directly to Peter's third-party special needs trust, which had been previously set up and funded by Peter's parents. Mary believes that if Peter never touches the money, it was never his so it preserves his SSI eligibility.
> This is incorrect. Peter has a legal right to his inheritance even if he never actually receives it. Thus, the only way to preserve this money and keep SSI and Medi-Cal is to have the money transferred to a properly established first-party SNT. If Mary places Peter's inheritance into the third-party SNT, it would make the third-party SNT invalid for public benefit purposes and Peter would lose his eligibility for both SSI and Medi-Cal.

In order to understand the primary differences between the different types of special needs trusts, the SNT trustee should know the legal rules that must be followed in setting up the two types of trust.

The rules that make a *third-party SNT* legal are relatively easy to meet. For SSI purposes, the Social Security Administration ("SSA") defines a third-party trust as "a trust established by someone other than the beneficiary as grantor."[1] The SSA defines a grantor as "the individual who provides the trust principal (or corpus)."[2] The regulations impose basically two requirements for third-party SNTs:

(1) the beneficiary cannot have authority to revoke the trust; and
(2) the beneficiary cannot direct the use of trust assets for his or her support and maintenance under the terms of the trust.[3]

Generally, a third-party SNT is the best method for bequeathing or gifting assets to a person with a disability. This is the most common use of third-party SNTs. While the legal rules for setting up a third-party SNT are relatively easy to meet, this type of SNT also provides quite a bit of flexibility. As a result, these types of third-party SNTs may require more work to administer, because the trust document may require the SNT trustee to also provide lifetime care and advocacy for the person with a disability and may also include multiple beneficiaries.

The rules that make a *first-party SNT* legal are a bit more complicated. A first-party SNT is a federally authorized safe harbor trust that allows an individual with a disability to transfer his or her own assets into the trust without being penalized by needs-based public benefits programs. As long as the statutory requirements are met, an individual with a disability can transfer his or her assets into a first-party SNT without penalty. All other transfers to a non-first party SNT will trigger some type of penalty, usually a set term that the public benefits recipient is ineligible for benefits.

The type of first-party SNT that an individual trustee would be responsible for is often called a (d)(4)(A) SNT, Litigation SNT, or Payback SNT. The rules for this type of first-party SNT are as follows:

(1) Beneficiary must be disabled under Social Security Administration's rules;

---

[1]   POMS SI 01120.200(B)(17).

[2]   POMS SI 01120.200(B)(2).

[3]   42 U.S.C. §1382b(e)(3)(A), 20 C.F.R. §416.1201(a)(1); POMS SI 01120.200(D)(2).

(2) Person must be under age 65 when trust is established;

(3) Trust must be established by a parent, grandparent, legal guardian or the court;

(4) Trust must be for the "sole benefit" of the person with a disability; and

(5) Trust must include a provision that all Medi-Cal (or Medicaid from other States) will be paid back on the death of the beneficiary.[4]

The (d)(4)(A) SNT can be complicated to establish. If the SNT trustee is not sure that the SNT was set up correctly, the trustee should contact an experienced special needs planning attorney to make sure it was done properly. The above list will make the (d)(4)(A) SNT legal for Social Security purposes, but the State of California and the California regulations have some additional requirements.

If the (d)(4)(A) SNT is established by a court for a person with a disability who also lacks capacity to manage his or her own person affairs, then the (d)(4)(A) SNT must also have the following requirements:

(1) A "no contest" provision which is a provision that penalizes someone if they file a lawsuit against the trust is not allowed;

(2) Prohibit any changes to the SNT without court approval;

(3) Clearly identify the SNT trustee and any other person with authority to direct the trustee to make disbursements;

(4) Prohibit investments by the SNT trustee other than those permitted under the California laws of conservatorship;

(5) Require SNT trustees to post bond (at the expense of the trust) which is a type of insurance policy that the trustee will not steal the money in the trust;

(6) Require the SNT trustee to file court accounts and reports for court approval subject to very specific court rules one year after the trust is established and every two years thereafter;

(7) Require court approval of changes in SNT trustees and a court order appointing any successor trustee;

---

[4]   42 U.S.C. §1396p(d)(4)(A).

(8) Require compensation of the SNT trustee, the members of any advisory committee, or the attorney for the SNT trustee to be in just and reasonable amounts that must be fixed and allowed by the court.[5]

> **Warning:** A court-supervised (d)(4)(A) SNT is much more difficult and expensive to administer. It is strongly recommended that a special needs planning attorney be hired to assist in the administration. The rules are very tricky and many California probate courts are far too harsh on SNT trustees who make simple mistakes during administration.

If the SNT trustee is asked to administer the (d)(4)(A) SNT, he or she should ask for a copy of the court's order establishing the trust. The court's order may have additional requirements that the SNT trustee must follow.

> **Note:** A common misconception among many people including SSA eligibility workers is that every (d)(4)(A) SNT must be established by a court. This is wrong. There are many (d)(4)(A) SNTs that are established by a parent or grandparent for an adult person with a disability who has capacity. The SSA POMS refer to these trusts as "Seed Trusts."[6] A (d)(4)(A) SNT that is a "Seed Trust" does not need to follow the eight rules set forth above.

There are two other types of first-party SNTs that an individual SNT trustee in California will not be asked to administer. These two types of first-party SNTs are known as

(1) the Miller Trust. Not in use in California at all. The Miller Trust is a trust that is composed only of pension, Social Security, and other income in a state that does not allow an income "spend down."[7] It is named the Miller trust due to the Colorado case *Miller v Ibarra* (D Colo 1990) 746 F Supp 19; and

---

[5]   California Rules of Court 7.903(c).

[6]   POMS SI 01120.203(B)(1)(f).

[7]   42 U.S.C. §1396p(d)(4)(B).

(2) the Pooled SNT. An individual SNT trustee will not be the trustee of this type of SNT because it is administered by a nonprofit. The pooled SNT is a trust that contains the assets of an individual with a disability if (a) the trust is established and managed by a nonprofit corporation and uses separate accounts of pooled assets; (b) the accounts are established by a parent, a grandparent, a legal guardian, the individual beneficiary, or the court; and (c) the state will, on the beneficiary's death, receive all amounts remaining in the beneficiary's account (unless the account is retained in the trust) up to the amount of Medi-Cal benefits paid.[8]

MISTAKE NUMBER 5: SNT TRUSTEE FAILS TO ESTABLISH A SYSTEM TO REQUEST DISBURSEMENTS

The number one day-to-day complaint about an SNT trustee is his or her lack of communication concerning disbursements on behalf of the person with a disability. The easiest way to avoid this complaint is to set up a procedure on how to request disbursements and the procedure for approving or not approving disbursement requests.

The trustee should meet with the beneficiary, any legal guardians, and those friends and family willing to participate. A monthly budget should be established from this meeting so that monthly expenses may be paid without constant requests.

The disbursement procedure should determine whether disbursements can be made only during business hours, on weekdays, or after twenty-four hours from a written request. It is in the trustee's best interest to clearly communicate these policies to the beneficiary. This will go a long way in eliminating friction during the administration.

> **Helpful Hint:** In order to have a clear record of all disbursements, a good suggestion is for the SNT trustee to purchase a fax machine or document scanner for a beneficiary or his or her caregiver. In this way, disbursement requests can be faxed or scanned and e-mailed directly to the trustee's office and the trustee will have a written record of all requests.

---

[8]   42 U.S.C. §1396p(d)(4)(C).

See chapter 5 for a thorough discussion on how SNT distributions affect public benefits, and chapter 6 for a discussion on how to make distributions from an SNT.

MISTAKE NUMBER 6: SNT TRUSTEE MAKES DISTRIBUTIONS FOR PERSONS OTHER THAN PERSON WITH A DISABILITY

The SNT trustee's ability to make distributions to persons other than the beneficiary of an SNT will depend on the type of SNT that is being administered and whether the document authorizes it.

- **Third-Party SNT, May Be Authorized:** A third-party SNT trustee may make distributions to third parties but only if the trust terms allow gifts or distributions to others. Sometimes, a third-party SNT will allow disbursements for a spouse or child of the beneficiary with a disability. A third-party SNT may also authorize gifts to recognize the beneficiary's family and friends on their birthdays or during holidays. It is not improper to include such provisions and to make such payments in a third-party SNT when authorized. Also, a third-party SNT may be established so that there are multiple beneficiaries. This means that the person with a disability could be only one beneficiary under the trust.

- **First-Party SNT, Not Authorized.** A first-party SNT must only be used for the sole benefit" of the primary beneficiary during his or her lifetime. If there is a distribution that provides some benefit to the beneficiary, it will be considered for the beneficiary's sole benefit.[9] The disqualification for failing to meet this requirement will cost the beneficiary his or her SSI and linked Medi-Cal benefits. If the beneficiary is only receiving Medi-Cal, the SNT must still be solely for the beneficiary's benefit.[10] If a distribution is made as a gift to a third party or charity, it will not be for the sole benefit of the beneficiary. The harder question is paying for the minor children or spouse of the

---

[9]   42 U.S.C. §1382b(c)(1)(C)(ii)(IV).
[10]   42 U.S.C. §1396p(c)(2)(B)(iv).

person with a disability. See chapter 5 for a more complete discussion of "sole benefit."

Example: An SNT beneficiary would benefit from having a pool installed at his home. His doctor has said he requires exercise and a pool is the only safe place for this person to exercise. Public or other private pools will not let him attend because of liability concerns surrounding his disability. The family requests that the SNT trustee purchase a pool at the family home. This type of distribution would be authorized, even though other family members may enjoy the pool. The primary benefit and purpose of the pool is for the beneficiary. In this example, the SNT trustee may want to place a lien on the home or take a percentage ownership of the home for the purchase price of the pool to protect the beneficiary if the family decides to move later.

MISTAKE NUMBER 7: DISTRIBUTING MORE THAN TWENTY DOLLARS PER MONTH DIRECTLY TO SNT BENEFICIARY

The interplay of SNT distributions and continuing eligibility for public benefits programs, such as Supplemental Security Income (SSI), makes being an SNT trustee very complicated. In chapter 5, there is a thorough discussion of how different types of distributions will affect the person with a disability's public benefits.

One common mistake that many trustees make is giving money directly to the SNT beneficiary. Any money the trustee gives to the beneficiary directly will be considered by the Social Security Administration (SSA) as "unearned income" to the beneficiary under the SSI rules, and after a set-aside of the first $20 each month (general income exclusion), will reduce the SSI recipient's benefits on a dollar-for-dollar basis.[11] In other words, the trustee should never distribute cash directly to a beneficiary who is receiving SSI. The correct procedure is to pay vendors directly for goods and services in order to avoid the dollar-for-dollar reduction.

---

[11]   20 C.F.R. §416.1124(c)(12); POMS SI 00810.420, 01120.200(E)(1)(a).

Example: Kirby, an SNT beneficiary, is receiving $830 per month of SSI payments. Kirby asks for a $500 per month allowance from the SNT because the amount of SSI is insufficient to pay for his monthly expenses. The SNT trustee agrees and begins providing $500 per month to Kirby. The legal effect of this disbursement is that Kirby loses $480 from his monthly SSI check and nets only $20 from his SNT.

The better practice would be to take some of the monthly expenses that are being paid for with Kirby's SSI check and have the SNT pay them directly, this way Kirby has more available cash. Another solution is if Kirby qualifies for a credit card, he can use the credit card and send the bill to the SNT trustee to pay. See chapters 5 and 6 for a more thorough discussion.

Warning: The SNT trustee should be careful when there is a request to provide cash directly to an SSI recipient. Many SSI recipients have been receiving cash directly from other sources and still receive their full SSI check. The SNT beneficiary may insist that it is okay to provide the cash because he or she has received it for many years with no penalty. All that has happened is that the SSA has not yet caught up to this SSI recipient. Sometimes, the SSA will not find out for months (or even years). When it does find out (and the SSA is good at discovering these things), it will seek to have the money paid back. The SSA calls this an "overpayment." If the SSI recipient does not have the money, the SSA will reduce the monthly SSI check until the overpayment is repaid or may deny eligibility for SSI. Further, the SSA may (in extreme cases) allege fraud against the SSI recipient or those that provided those funds. It is simply not worth it to provide cash directly to an SSI recipient.

Another similar issue is where the SNT trustee reimburses the person with a disability for items he or she has purchased, even if the person with a disability purchased items that are exempt from being counted by public benefit agencies. This type of disbursement will also be treated as "unearned income" for SSI eligibility.

Example: Jody, an SNT beneficiary, uses her own money to pay for a $200 cell phone. She asks the SNT trustee to reimburse her for this payment. If the SNT trustee reimburses Jody for the phone, Jody will lose $180 per month of SSI (after the $20 set-aside amount). If, instead, the SNT trustee purchased the cell phone directly, there would be no reduction. Likewise, if Jody's friend purchased the cell phone and the SNT trustee reimbursed the friend, there would be no SSI reduction. See chapter 5 for a more thorough discussion.

SSI rules also provide that if the trustee distributes anything to the beneficiary that is equivalent to cash, it will be counted as SSI "unearned income."

Example: If an SNT trustee gives Richard an SNT beneficiary a gift card (or gift certificate) worth $500 that he can use to buy food or shelter directly, such as Wal-Mart, Target, restaurant, grocery store, or Visa gift card, it will be counted as SSI "unearned income" and will reduce Richard's SSI check by $480.[12] If the store does not sell food or shelter items, as in the case of Macy's, clothing stores (such as the Gap), bookstores, or electronics store, it will not be counted against the beneficiary. However, the gift card must also include a legally enforceable prohibition on selling the card for cash. If it fails to have this prohibition, it will still be considered as SSI "unearned income" in the month of receipt. See chapter 5 for a more thorough discussion.

Warning: A common misunderstanding is that a gift card that can pay for food or shelter will be treated as in-kind support and maintenance (ISM) (see chapter 4 for a full discussion of ISM) or only a $244.67 (in year 2011) reduction in SSI. This is wrong. It is treated as "unearned income," which results in a dollar-for-dollar reduction after the first $20. Thus, the SNT trustee should only use gift cards if they understand the legal

---

[12]   POMS SI 00830.522.

consequences of doing so. See chapter 6 for a discussion of these requirements.

MISTAKE NUMBER 8: A SNT TRUSTEE WHO REFUSES TO MAKE DISTRIBUTIONS FOR THE SNT BENEFICIARY

Too often, SNT trustees become overly concerned about the SSI and Medi-Cal rules and stop making distributions that could benefit the SNT beneficiary, even those that are perfectly acceptable. The primary purpose of any SNT is to improve the overall quality of life of the person with a disability. The trustee is asked to perform a balancing act between making distributions that do not violate the rules of the applicable benefit program (typically SSI and Medi-Cal) and providing the beneficiary with goods and services so that he or she does not have to live at the poverty level. The most difficult balancing task an SNT trustee is required to perform is deciding whether a distribution that will reduce (or even eliminate) a beneficiary's government benefits is in the beneficiary's best interest. See chapters 5 and 6 for a full discussion of acceptable distributions that will not interfere with public benefit eligibility at all.

In order to properly decide how and when to make payments from an SNT, the trustee must be familiar with the SSI rules on "income" and "resources." See chapter 4 for a more complete discussion of the public benefit rules. In general, the trustee should pay careful attention to the following issues when making distributions:

- **Resources.** An SSI and Medi-Cal recipient is entitled to only $2,000 in countable resources and an eligible couple, $3,000.[13] Thus, the trustee should not purchase items that are considered countable resources that will cause the beneficiary to exceed the applicable resource limitation. For example, the SNT trustee should not buy in the name of the SSI recipient a second automobile or vacation home.
- **Income.** A distribution of cash to a SSI benefits recipient by an SNT trustee will be counted as unearned income by the SSA. The trustee should not provide money directly to the beneficiary (or reimburse the beneficiary for money he or she has spent), because after the first $20

---

[13]   20 C.F.R. §416.1205(c).

(general income exclusion), each dollar so given will be considered to be "unearned income" and reduce the beneficiary's SSI payment dollar-for-dollar. See Mistake Number Seven above on the effect of providing cash directly to an SNT beneficiary.

- **In-kind support and maintenance.** A trustee should be extremely careful in providing "food" or "shelter" items to an SNT beneficiary. SSI benefits are intended to pay for a person's food and shelter. Hence, if the beneficiary receives food or shelter as a result of payments by the trustee, it is considered by the SSA as "in-kind support and maintenance" (ISM) and will result in a reduction (or possible elimination) of the beneficiary's SSI payments. However, the SNT trustee who understands this rule can provide a real benefit to the SNT beneficiary. See Mistake Number 9 for discussion of when making payments for food and shelter is acceptable.

MISTAKE NUMBER 9: FAILING TO DISTRIBUTE FOR BENEFICIARY'S FOOD OR SHELTER WHEN IT IS ACCEPTABLE

A common misunderstanding is that an SNT trustee can never make distributions for the beneficiary's food or shelter needs. This is incorrect. If the SNT beneficiary is an SSI recipient, then payment of food or shelter costs may cause a small reduction in the overall SSI check. This is usually okay, because the cost of food and shelter in California is so much higher than the highest SSI monthly payment.

As described below, even if the SNT beneficiary is a Medi-Cal-only recipient, then a substantial portion of the recipient's food and shelter costs can still be made from the SNT without any loss or reduction of Medi-Cal.

How SSI treats payments of food or shelter. An SSI recipient is expected to pay for all of his or her food and shelter costs out of the monthly SSI check.

> **Note:** Under SSI rules, "shelter" includes room, rent, mortgage payments, real property taxes, heating fuel, gas, electricity, water, sewerage, and garbage collection services.[14] Food does

---

14   20 C.F.R. §416.1130(b).

not include many things bought in a grocery store, such as paper products, soap, personal toiletries, and pet food.

An SSI recipient in California as of July 2011 is entitled to receive $830 per month. A portion of this is paid by the federal government in the amount of $674 and the balance of $156 is paid by the state of California.[15] The monthly SSI check is reduced if the SSI recipient receives income. As chapter 4 explains in detail, "income" is defined by the SSA and is not defined the same as how "income" is defined by the IRS for income tax purposes.

One type of SSA "income" is when someone else, including an SNT trustee, provides food or shelter to the SSI recipient. This type of SSI income is called "in-kind support and maintenance" (ISM).[16] If the SNT trustee provides ISM to the beneficiary, the beneficiary's SSI benefits will be reduced, but not on a dollar-for-dollar basis as with "unearned income." Instead, there are two different formulas that the Social Security Administration uses to reduce the SSI benefits for a person who receives ISM. Which formula is used depends on the household and living arrangements of the SSI recipient.

The two formulas that are used to place a value on ISM are the value of the one-third reduction rule (VTR) and the presumed maximum value rule (PMV). It is more common for an SNT trustee to be concerned with PMV because that is the rule where a third party (like an SNT) provides food or shelter to an SSI recipient.

- ○ **Value of One-Third Reduction Rule** (VTR): The VTR applies when the benefits recipient lives in another's house throughout a month, receives both food and shelter from inside the household, and does not meet his or her pro rata share of cost of the food and shelter expenses for the household. VTR reduces the SSI benefit by one third of the SSI federal benefit rate (FBR), or $224.67 (one third of $674 in 2011).[17] The VTR applies in full or not at all.[18]

---

[15]   This monthly amount can change each year. Check the Myers Urbatsch, PC website at www.MyersUrbatsch.com to learn if these amounts have changed.

[16]   20 C.F.R. §§416.1102, 1130; POMS SI 01120.200(E)(1)(b).

[17]   20 C.F.R. §§416.1131, 416.1133.

[18]   20 C.F.R. §416.1131(b).

Note: When an individual lives alone, the VTR will not apply, because there are no other household members from whom the individual can receive ISM. In this case, any ISM received from outside the household is counted using the PMV rule described below.

Example: Robert, an SSI recipient, lives in a home with three other people. His SSI benefit amount is $830 per month. Food and shelter expenses total $2,400 for the household. His pro rata share of the food and shelter expenses is $600. If the SSI recipient only pays $540 toward expenses, he is not meeting his pro rata share of costs. The SSA will reduce his SSI check by $224.67 (in the year 2011). If the VTR applies, even if the difference between what he paid and his pro rata share is only $60, Robert is still subject to the full one-third reduction.

o **Presumed Maximum Value Rule (PMV)**: The PMV applies whenever the VTR (see above) does not apply.[19] The PMV rule applies when an SNT trustee (or any third party) pays a SSI recipient's food or shelter costs.[20] The effect of these distributions are that the person's SSI benefits will be reduced by the lesser of one-third of the federal benefit rate plus the $20 general income exclusion or the actual value of what was received.[21] In 2011, the PMV is $244.67 (one third of the federal benefit rate is $224.67 plus the $20 general income exclusion).

Example: Beth, an SNT beneficiary and SSI recipient, lives with three roommates and has been able to afford her share of the rent from her SSI check. She wishes to live alone and asks the SNT trustee to pay rent at a new apartment. Her SSI benefit is $830 per month in 2011. The SNT trustee agrees to pay for a new apartment that costs $2,000/month. The effect of this payment is that Beth's SSI check will be reduced by $244.67 to $585.33 per month.

---

[19]   20 C.F.R. §416.1140.
[20]   POMS SI 01120.200(E)(1)(b).
[21]   20 C.F.R. §416.1140.

Warning: The loss of $244.67 from an SSI check is usually an acceptable loss if the SSI recipient will receive a nice, clean, and safe place to live. However, if the SSI recipient is receiving only $244 per month or less in SSI, paying for food or shelter will eliminate eligibility for SSI altogether. It is important that the SNT trustee knows exactly how much of the SNT beneficiary's monthly check comes from SSI. Further, the amount of the loss will change each year, so the SSI trustee should check to make sure he or she knows exactly what the amount of the PMV loss would be.

If the SNT beneficiary is a Medi-Cal-only recipient, the SNT trustee can make disbursements for food or shelter from the SNT but not for all of it.[22] The SNT trustee can come up with a percentage of the overall cost of food and shelter and pay that from the SNT, while the Medi-Cal recipient must pay the balance.

Example: Rhonda is an SNT beneficiary. She receives only Medi-Cal and not SSI, because she receives a monthly annuity payment of $1,000 per month. Rhonda's rent and utilities are $2,000 per month and her food cost is $500 per month. The SNT trustee could pay for a certain percentage of Rhonda's food and shelter costs without jeopardizing her benefits. Thus, the SNT trustee could pay 90 percent of the costs of $2,250 for food, shelter, and utilities, and Rhonda would pay the balance without any loss of her Medi-Cal.

MISTAKE NUMBER 10: FAILING TO MAINTAIN EXCELLENT RECORDS AND FAILING TO PROPERLY ACCOUNT FOR TRUSTEE ACTIONS

All SNT trustees must keep accurate records of their SNT transactions. It is very important to have complete records when the SNT trustee makes his or her annual report to the SNT beneficiary, makes a report to a court when

---

[22]   22 Cal Code Regs §50509.

required, files annual income tax returns with the IRS, and makes necessary reports to agencies providing public benefits.

It would be prudent for the SNT trustee to use a computer program, such as Quicken, to keep track of disbursements. The SNT trustee should keep receipts of all disbursements as well. This is one reason why requiring a beneficiary or his or her legal representatives to make a written request for disbursements is preferred as described in Mistake Number Five in this chapter.

> **Warning:** Recently, the Social Security Administration (SSA) (the agency that manages SSI) has been demanding that SNT trustees provide several years of records of SNT disbursement requests. In one case, it asked for over twenty-one years of records. If the SNT trustee is unable to provide these records, it will be presumed that the disbursements were made inappropriately and the SNT beneficiary will lose his or her eligibility for SSI or be charged with an SSI overpayment. For example, SNT trustees may distribute cash to themselves or to others, such as guardians, to use for the SNT beneficiary. There may be no problem with the use of the funds, but the inability to explain the expenditures can create future difficulties for both the beneficiary and trustee.

All SNTs have accounting requirements. If the SNT is not court supervised, the account must be done on a yearly basis and can be provided in a summary fashion. If the SNT is court supervised, the account is a very formal court filing in which it is strongly encouraged that you retain an attorney or a fiduciary experienced in court accountings to assist.

For further discussion of the requirement to maintain records and issue accounts, see chapters 3 and 7 of this book.

Mistake Number 11: Termination of First-Party (d)(4)(A) SNT-Making Inappropriate Disbursements Prior to Medi-Cal Recovery

When a first-party SNT terminates, a first-party SNT must pay back Medi-Cal (and Medicaid in other states if the SNT beneficiary received services in another state) before disbursements can be made to the SNT's remainder beneficiaries. Thus, the SNT trustee has to be very careful about how money in the SNT is spent prior to Medi-Cal being paid back.

The Medi-Cal agency in California (the Department of Health Care Services (DHCS) must be paid back from assets held in the first-party SNT. If an SNT trustee makes an inappropriate disbursement, he or she will be liable for breach of trust and may be required to reimburse Medi-Cal from his or her own assets.

In California, there is some discrepancy between what the Social Security Administration (SSA), the agency that runs SSI, says that the SNT trustee can pay and what the DHCS says that the SNT trustee can pay prior to the payback to DHCS. Oddly, even though there is no payback to SSA for SSI paid, the SSA has set some very strict rules (more strict than those of the DHCS) on what can be paid prior to the Medi-Cal recovery.

- **Priority under Medi-Cal Program.** Under DHCS' guidelines, the SNT may retain funds to pay the following expenses before paying the Medi-Cal reimbursement claims:

  - The cost of the individual's remaining investment fees and management fees, such as attorney's fees, trustee's fees;
  - Outstanding bills for the benefit of the disabled individual or spouse that fall within the terms of the trust; or
  - Burial/funeral expenses of the disabled individual or disabled spouse.[23]

- **Priority under SSI Program.** The Social Security Administration's rules on what can be paid before payment of Medi-Cal recovery claims are strict. Only the following administrative expenses may be paid before reimbursement of Medi-Cal payments:
  - State and federal taxes due from the trust because of the death of the beneficiary or termination of the trust and transfer of trust assets to the remainder beneficiaries
  - Reasonable fees for administration of the trust estate, such as an accounting of the trust to a court, completion and filing of

---

[23]   Medi-Cal Eligibility Procedures Manual Letter No. 192, p 9J-75.

documents, or other required actions associated with termination and wrapping up of the trust[24]

The following disbursements are expressly prohibited from being paid before reimbursement of Medi-Cal's payments:

- taxes due from the estate of the beneficiary other than those arising from inclusion of the trust in the estate;
- inheritance taxes due for residual beneficiaries;
- payment of debts owed to third parties;
- funeral expenses; and
  payments to residual beneficiaries.[25]

In California, the SSI rules expressly prohibit two kinds of expenditures expressly permitted by California's Medi-Cal rules: debts owed to third parties and funeral expenses. For practical purposes, when terminating a first-party SNT, the SSI rules must be followed if the beneficiary receives SSI (as is often the case), even if they were disregarded when drafting the SNT document.

Helpful Hint: Within days of the death of an SNT beneficiary, the beneficiary's family or friends may call the trustee to ask whether funeral expenses can be paid from the trust. As indicated above, the SSI rules allow the trustee to pay funeral expenses for the deceased beneficiary only after the Medi-Cal reimbursement is paid. If Medi-Cal's recovery claims exceed the remainder of trust assets, it is best to contact DHCS and seek approval for funeral payments before payment of the Medi-Cal claims. It is also prudent to confirm this agreement by a letter to the DHCS representative.

The best practice however is to prepay funeral and burial expenses before the death of the beneficiary. The trustee is authorized to make these distributions during the lifetime of the beneficiary.[26]

---

24   POMS SI 01120.203(B)(3)(a).
25   POMS SI 01120.203(B)(3)(b).
26   POMS SI 01120.203(B)(3)(c).

For more discussion of how Medi-Cal's recovery is handled after SNT termination, see chapter 10.

Chapter 2 Summary

The Top Mistakes Made by SNT Trustees

- ✓ Fails to read the trust document.
- ✓ Fails to keep current on changes in the laws for special needs trusts and public benefits.
- ✓ Confuses the different types of public benefits programs.
- ✓ Confuses the different types of special needs trusts.
- ✓ Fails to set up system to request disbursements.
- ✓ Wrongfully makes distributions to persons other than SNT beneficiary.
- ✓ Wrongfully gives cash directly to SNT beneficiary.
- ✓ Wrongfully refuses to make appropriate distributions to SNT beneficiary.
- ✓ Fails to make distributions of food and shelter when appropriate.
- ✓ Fails to maintain records and failing to properly account for trustee actions.
- ✓ Wrongfully makes distributions of first-party SNT assets on termination prior to Medi-Cal's recovery rights.

CHAPTER 3

Summarizing The Trustee's Legal Responsibilities

Serving as trustee is an important job. There are a host of rules that the trustee must follow. Some of these are obvious, like "don't steal trust assets." Others, however, are more subtle, like "don't get involved in a conflict of interest," meaning that a trustee cannot lend money to themselves even if they intend to pay it back with interest. Violating these rules can cause lots of problems for the trustee and the beneficiary of the trust. For example, the trustee has personal liability for any harm caused by him or her, meaning, the trustee can be fined, have to pay damages, be removed as trustee, or even in very extreme cases be jailed.

This chapter describes the rules that a trustee must follow, however, to keep it simple, a trustee should continue to repeat the mantra that this is "not my money" and can only be used as described in the trust document. If the trustee keeps this in mind, his or her job will be much easier. Attached as Appendices A, B, and D to this book are forms that can be reviewed and completed as you go through the following tasks. Appendix A includes the initial twelve steps an SNT trustee should consider when taking over a new trust; Appendix B is a chart of trustee's duties as spelled out in California law; and Appendix D is a form that is a one page summary of the type of trust that is being administered that will aid the trustee during administration.

> **Critical Pointer:** The trustee should have no doubts that he or she is correct when making trust decisions. It is strongly recommended that if there are any doubts, the trustee retain

an attorney experienced in assisting with SNT administration. The cost of the attorney will more often than not be much less expensive than trying to correct a mistake by a trustee. See chapter 11 on how to find a special needs planning attorney who specializes in SNT administration.

WHAT ARE THE SNT TRUSTEE'S INITIAL DUTIES?

The idea of taking on the trusteeship of an SNT may be overwhelming at first. However, if the trustee breaks up the trust duties into smaller parts, it will be much easier to manage. When an individual or entity begins to serve as an SNT trustee, certain tasks should be completed immediately. Initially, the trustee should

1. **Evaluate the beneficiary's living and personal care situation to determine whether any immediate action needs to be taken**. For example, a person with a disability may require drug therapy each month. If the parent administered the drugs to his or her child or took the child to a clinic for that treatment, a replacement needs to be located immediately who is willing to help and acceptable to the beneficiary. The beneficiary's living and personal care situation should be reevaluated at least yearly.

2. **Read the trust document**. Understand the terms of the trust. If there is any doubt, the trustee should consult an experienced SNT attorney to review the trust and receive advice on the trust term. The trustee, after reviewing the trust, should understand the distribution standard of the SNT. Does it authorize distributions that cause a loss or reduction in benefits? What are the requirements for bond or for accountings? Does the trust or order establishing the trust limit allowable investments? Does the trust require the trustee to report to Social Security for distributions that affect entitlement, or does it require the trustee to pursue all benefit programs for which the beneficiary may be entitled? Does it contain some improper terms—does it, for instance, authorize distributions for "support" of the beneficiary? The trustee should understand the limits of his or her authority when conducting trust business.

3. **Meet with the beneficiary, the trust advisory committee members, and the trust protector, if any**. The trustee

should meet with all parties named in the trust. A group meeting will help set appropriate standards and expectations from the start that may avoid disappointments and errors down the line. If the trustee is unclear as to how to manage the meeting, the trustee should consult with an attorney experienced in administering SNTs to either chair the meeting or to prepare an appropriate agenda. At the meeting, the trustee should develop a distribution plan for anticipated SNT expenditures that follows the distribution standard in the SNT and relevant public benefits rules, regulations, and administrative policy. During the meeting, the trustee should provide a system for the beneficiary (or advisory committee members) to contact the trustee to request distributions. Maybe the beneficiary will need a fax machine or a computer to have an efficient means to contact the trustee. The trustee should also set expectations as to how the trustee will be administering the trust.

4. **Determine which type of public benefits the beneficiary is receiving or may be eligible for**. It is important to know what benefits are being received because the type of benefits will determine how the SNT will be administered. The SNT should be asking a series of questions including what public benefits are the beneficiary receiving. What is the beneficiary's current payment level for any program for which the beneficiary receives a cash benefit? If the beneficiary is receiving Medi-Cal, is the Medi-Cal linked to SSI or is the beneficiary receiving Medi-Cal under the share of costs or no share of cost program? Is the beneficiary receiving subsidized housing? If so, under what program? Is the beneficiary receiving In-Home Supportive Services (IHSS)? If so, what are the terms of those services and who is providing them? Then, review the income and resource rules for those benefit programs. For a more complete discussion of these public benefits see chapter 4.

5. **Determine whether the trust in question is a first-party or a third-party SNT**. The administration of each type of SNT will be very similar, but there are significant differences. For example, a third-party SNT may have multiple beneficiaries whereas the first-party SNT must be drafted and administered to benefit only the primary beneficiary during his or her lifetime. Also, on the death of the beneficiary, remainder beneficiaries cannot be paid until after the Medi-Cal agency is paid.

6. **Determine whether the SNT is under court supervision.** Typically, a court supervised SNT is one that is a first-party SNT established by a court. Finding out whether the SNT is court supervised will let the trustee know the type of rules the trustee must follow. Generally, it is much easier to administer a trust that is not court supervised so it is important to know which type of trust is being administered.

7. **Prepare a budget for expected expenditures of SNT assets**. The trustee should work with a financial adviser to develop a realistic budget for the SNT beneficiary. The budget should be shared with the beneficiary and any key advisers. See chapter 6 for assistance in setting the budget.

8. **Determine who is responsible for the care and advocacy of the beneficiary.** Many times an SNT beneficiary lacks capacity to manage his or her own personal care or support. Sometimes, the SNT trustee will be the same person who has this legal responsibility. However, the SNT beneficiary may have others who have the legal duty to care for the beneficiary. The trustee will oftentimes be working with these individuals when making disbursements. A list of these people includes a conservator of person, SSA representative payee, or agent under a power of attorney. The extent and limits of the authority for each, and the scope of the trustee's responsibility in relation to the other individuals or entities involved as it concerns the beneficiary and administration of the trust is typically set up in the document or court order establishing the role. The trustee should seek copies of all documents giving them their authority to manage the beneficiary's care.

WHERE DOES AN SNT TRUSTEE FIND THE RULES ON HIS OR HER DUTIES?

The SNT trustee's legal responsibility is primarily set forth in the trust document. Although, there may be additional rules established by court order (if SNT established by court), trust law, public benefits laws, Program Operations Manuel Systems (commonly called POMS which is the Social Security Administration's book of rules), and sometimes State Medicaid (or in California called Medi-Cal) regulations. These are described in more detail here:

- **Trust document.** The trustee's authority comes first and foremost from the trust document, and his or her duties and powers as described there are the primary instructions. The trustee should read the trust document with care, and from time to time read it again. The trust document may contain specific provisions that take precedence over the general rules that apply to trusts—even the ones mentioned in this book. However, note that there are certain basic rules relating to trusts that will apply no matter what the trust document says. For example, a trust cannot allow or encourage illegal activity on the part of the trustee or the beneficiary.

- **Court Order.** If the trust was established by a court, then a written court order was issued establishing the SNT. Typically, the order will include specific trustee accounting requirements, bonding requirements, or specific distributions that are allowed or not allowed.

  Critical Pointer: A trustee should never administer a trust without a full copy of the trust document and if established by court order, a copy of the written order. This is the trustee's primary set of instructions.

While the above documents will generally provide all the authority a trustee will need, the trustee should also be aware that the trustee is subject to other rules that may not be spelled out in the trust document. These rules are set forth below:

- **Laws.** The California Probate Code ("Probate Code") provides most of the rules that an SNT trustee will need to know to do his or her job. Various provisions of the Probate Code cover things that are not specifically spelled out in the trust document. The Trustees Powers Act[27], the Uniform Prudent Investor Act[28], and California's Uniform Principal and Income Act (UPAIA)[29] hold particular relevance to all trustees. Other laws may be covered, including contract law, real

---

[27] Probate Code §§16200-16249.
[28] Probate Code §§16045-16054.
[29] Probate Code §§16320-16375.

estate law, and case law. An SNT trustee should always seek legal assistance whenever one of these laws is affected.

- **Case Law.** California court decisions relating to trusts are another source of legal authority for trustees. This is known as the "common law." The common law of California is found primarily in the opinions of California's Supreme Court and the Court of Appeals, but California courts may sometimes follow decisions from other jurisdictions as well.
- **Federal Law.** Certain federal laws, regulations, and case law are also important for the SNT trustee to know. Most public benefits programs the SNT beneficiary is receiving are a result of federal legislation. This includes SSI, SSDI, and the federal Medicaid and Medicare program. The beneficiary may also receive public housing, veteran benefits, or other federal benefits. The Code of Federal Regulations (CFR) are an important tool to know how these federal laws are to be administered.
- **POMS**[30] **and DHCS All County Letters.**[31] POMS is an acronym for Program Operation Manuel System and is the Social Security Administration's guide to its own employees on how the agency interprets SSI rules and regulations. The Department of Health Care Services (DHCS) All County Letters is DHCS' guide to its own employees on how the agency interprets Medi-Cal rules and regulations.

An SNT trustee needs to keep all sources of authority in mind as he or she carries out his or her trustee duties.

HOW SHOULD A TRUSTEE APPROACH HIS OR HER DUTIES?

- **Try to understand why the trust was created.** Understanding the intent behind the SNT will help the trustee fulfill his

---

[30] POMS can be found by Googling POMS or following the link at https://secure.ssa.gov/apps10/poms.nsf/chapterlist!openview&restricttocategory=05.

[31] The DHCS ACWDL can be found by googling All County Welfare Letters or following the link at http://www.dhcs.ca.gov/services/medi-cal/eligibility/Pages/ACWDLbyyear.aspx.

or her role as trustee. The main reason for creating a SNT is to enhance the quality of life of a person with a disability. This is generally done by preserving the beneficiary's right to public benefits and to provide the beneficiary a fund to pay for future needs. However, there may also be advocacy reasons, money management, and related reasons why such a trust is created.

- **Trustee should examine his or her motives.** Trustees should be extremely careful that everything they do or refrain from doing is motivated by the trustees' desire to execute their duties faithfully and to the best of their ability to the beneficiary. Trustees cannot allow themselves to be influenced by their personal feelings about an individual beneficiary or their own self-interest.

WHAT ARE A TRUSTEE'S LEGAL DUTIES?

Trustees are subject to a variety of duties. The penalty for breaching these duties can result in the trustee having to pay for any resulting damage to the trust out of his or her own pocket. Personal liability—even if the SNT trustee is not paid—is one of the things that go along with being a fiduciary.

> **Helpful Hint:** A shortened list of the following duties is set forth in Appendix B of this book.

1. Duty of Using General Good Sense
The law states that a trustee is required to administer the trust

> with reasonable care, skill, and caution under the circumstances then prevailing that a prudent person acting in a like capacity would use in the conduct of an enterprise of like character and with like aims to accomplish the purposes of the trust as determined from the trust document.[32]

A trustee is not allowed to manage the money as they might manage their own money. Instead, they must always do everything as a prudent person would given the same set of circumstances. This may sound simple but can

---

[32]   Probate Code §16040(a).

actually cause problems for someone not used to administering someone else's money. The question that should be asked every time the trustee is performing a trustee duty is "What would a prudent person do given these circumstances?"

2. Duty Is Greater If Trustees Are (or Hold Themselves Out as) Experts

If a trustee holds him or herself out as an expert in a certain trust duty, that trustee will be held to a higher standard of care than would any other trustee not making those claims. Thus, the standards for judging a trustee's job performance will take into account his or her special abilities (whether actual or claimed).[33] Accordingly, a trustee should be very careful when communicating to others about his or her background in serving as trustee. Generally, a trustee is not required to use any special skills or be held to the same standard as an expert when performing trustee duties. However, if the trustee has—or claims to have—special expertise in connection with any part of trust administration, such as investments, tax preparation, or legal background, the trustee will be held to the same standard of care as that expert.

> **Example:** A trustee claims that they are experts in tax preparation. The trustee then files a tax return that is inaccurate and costs the trust penalties from the IRS. The trustee will be held by a judge to a greater standard of care to that of an expert in tax preparation rather than to a layperson. Thus, proof of his or her breach of duty will be easier to meet than if a trustee without any special expertise in filing tax documents were to make the same mistake. Note, however, that the trustee who has held out an expertise in tax filings would not also be held to a higher standard under other trustee duties, such as investments.

---

[33] Probate Code §16014.

3. Duty to Carry Out the Terms of the Trust

Under California law, the trustee is under a duty to administer the trust according to its terms.[34] It will be difficult for anyone to find fault with the trustee's performance if everything is done in accordance with the terms of the trust document. If at any time a trustee has a reasonable doubt as to the correct interpretation of the trust document, the trustee should contact an attorney to assist, and if the attorney is unable to determine it as well, the trustee may petition a court for instructions.[35] The trustee should consult with chapter 11 of this book on finding an appropriate attorney and filing a petition for instructions with the court.

In many SNTs, the parents of the child with a disability may leave something called a memorandum of intent or letter of intent. This document will describe the parents' intent in how they wish to see the SNT assets used for the care of their child with a disability. While the trustee should always review the memorandum, the trustee should remember that this document is not legally binding on the trustee. Many times, the memorandum may recommend distributions that would violate public benefits rules or trust laws. The SNT trustee is free to disregard these suggestions. However, the trustee should also keep in mind that the parents have expressed their intent on how they would like to see the SNT assets used, so a properly serving trustee would take these wishes into account as much as possible.

The only time the trust document should not be followed is if the trust terms are contrary to public policy. The following list includes examples of when the trust terms should not be followed:

- If the trust terms are illegal or are against public policy.[36] An example would be if the trust terms authorized distributions for illegal narcotics or authorized distribution only if the beneficiary divorced his spouse.
- If the trust terms refused to let anyone remove the trustee on any grounds.[37] An example would be if the trustee stopped acting as

---

[34]   Probate Code §16000.
[35]   Probate Code §17200.
[36]   Probate Code §15203.
[37]   Probate Code §15642.

trustee but refused to resign. If the trust terms stated that the trustee cannot be removed for any reason, this provision will be ignored.

- If an attorney is serving as trustee, he or she cannot be paid as trustee and as attorney for trustee despite any trust terms that allowed this arrangement.[38]
- If the trust terms waive any right for beneficiaries to receive information. This provision must be ignored as invalid.[39]
- If the trust terms waive rights to notice of actions being performed by the trustee. This provision must be ignored as invalid.[40]
- If the trust terms waive (or limit) the trustee's duty to report and account to beneficiaries. These provisions must be ignored up to a certain extent. A trust can allow a beneficiary to waive an account and the trust may limit the time a person has to object to an account but cannot limit the account requirement entirely.[41]
- If the trust terms limit the trustee's liability.[42] A trustee's liability may be limited up to a certain point. However, a trustee will always be responsible for his or her breach of trust committed intentionally, with gross negligence, in bad faith, or with reckless indifference to the interest of the beneficiary, or for any profit that the trustee derives from a breach of trust.

4. Duty of Loyalty/Not to Self-Deal

A trustee cannot engage in any act that puts personal interests in conflict with those of any of the SNT beneficiary.[43] The prohibition against self-dealing applies regardless of the good faith of the trustee.[44] This means that even if the trustee has no intent to harm the trust or the beneficiary, if he or she engages in self-dealing he will be responsible for breach of trust.

---

[38] Probate Code §15687.
[39] Probate Code §16060.
[40] Probate Code §16061.7.
[41] Probate Code §16062.
[42] Probate Code §16461.
[43] Probate Code §16004(a).
[44] *People v Larkin* (ND Cal 1976) 413 F Supp 978.

A trustee must always act to further the interests of the trust and the beneficiary. The trustee is serving for the benefit of the beneficiary. If any situation should arise in which there is a conflict between the trustee's personal interests and the trust or between the trust and the interests of third parties, the trustee has an obligation to put the interests of the trust first.

A trustee should not buy trust property, because this creates the appearance that the trustee may have taken advantage of the trust. This is true even if the purchase was done at fair market value. A trustee who sells or leases personal assets to the trust likewise breaches his or her fiduciary duty against self-dealing.[45] Similarly, the trustee should never loan trust funds to him or herself or to family members The rules set forth in this paragraph are strictly applied not only to transactions in which the trustee deals directly with him or herself but also to transactions in which the trustee deals with entities (such as partnerships or corporations) in which the trustee is personally interested. These rules apply even though a particular transaction may be scrupulously fair, and even if it is advantageous to the trust.

A trustee will find very little sympathy with a judge or jury if he or she does something that looks like it may be improper, whether or not it really is. If someone questions the trustee's activities, the trustee may find themselves having the burden of proving that he or she acted properly. The trustee does not have the advantage of being presumed innocent until he or she is proven guilty. Most of the time, trustees will find the contrary presumption working against them.

5. Duty Not to Delegate

Once the trustee has accepted the position of trustee, he or she is responsible for the administration of the trust and should not turn over the administration of the trust to others.[46] This does not mean that the trustee must actually perform all of the administrative work. The trustee may employ agents to advise or assist the trustee in the performance of administrative duties, including accountants, attorneys, auditors, investment advisers, appraisers, or other agents.[47] However, the responsibility for the administration of the trust

---

[45] Probate Code §16004(a).
[46] Probate Code §16012.
[47] Probate Code §16247.

always remains with the trustee. While the trustee may hire agents to assist, he or she cannot blindly follow their advice. The trustee should seek advice when in doubt but make all final decisions after he or she has independently analyzed the matter. The trustee's reliance on the advice of a competent and qualified professional can be a defense to a claim that he or she breached his or her fiduciary duty to the plaintiff.

The duty not to delegate is not enforceable for the delegation of investment and management functions if prudent under the circumstances.[48] The trustee is required to exercise prudence in selecting an agent and in establishing the scope and terms of the delegation. The trustee is also required to exercise prudence by periodically reviewing the agent's overall performance and compliance with the terms of the delegation. See chapter 8 for a further discussion of the delegation of investment duties.

> **Example:** A trustee may hire an investment adviser to assist with the trust financial portfolio. However, a trustee should never delegate decisions on discretionary distributions to a third party, because courts assume that the person setting up the trust appointed that particular trustee because of his or her individual judgment concerning such matters.

If there is more than one trustee, each trustee cannot rely on the other trustees to administer the trust. Unless the trust agreement provides otherwise, all cotrustees must take an active role in administering the trust.[49] A cotrustee's failure to participate in trust administration could constitute unlawful delegation. However, ministerial acts (meaning those not requiring the exercise of personal judgment), can be delegated. In addition, investment and management functions may be delegated to one cotrustee, just as delegation may be made to an investment adviser.

To avoid unlawful delegation and provide for effective management of the trust, the cotrustees should agree in writing on a management method that will involve all cotrustees in active management and appropriately allocate ministerial duties. If one of the trustees acts improperly with respect to trust matters, the other trustee has an obligation to correct the situation. The trustee

---

[48] Probate Code §16052(a).
[49] Probate Code §15620.

has an obligation to be aware of what other trustees are doing on behalf of the trust. Each trustee is responsible to the beneficiary for the misconduct and breaches of duty of the other trustees.

6. Duty to Keep Records

The SNT trustee should keep excellent records. A sample of what should be included, in addition to the accountings, and the backup information upon which the accountings are based should include the following:

- **Notes from regular meeting with the beneficiary or his or her legal representatives.** For each meeting, keep a record of the date, the length of the meeting, and a summary of what was discussed. The trustee should also keep records of all other communications between the trustee and the beneficiary, including such things as copies of all correspondence.
- **Beneficiary's income tax returns.** If the trust document grants the trustee's discretion in making distributions to the beneficiary, the income tax returns can provide the trustee a great deal of helpful information. Those returns are signed under penalty for perjury. The beneficiary may be reluctant to share his or her income tax returns with a trustee, but the trustee's request for that kind of information is not unduly intrusive—no more so than a bank asking for the same documentation before deciding whether to loan money.
- **Beneficiary's annual budgets.** Because all SNT trustee's have complete discretionary authority with respect to distributions, the trustee should help prepare budgets for the beneficiary. This shows that the trustee has carefully considered the beneficiary's needs relative to discretionary distributions. For further discussion of how to set up a budget, see chapter 6.
- **Verification of out-of-pocket expenditures.** Since the trustee is entitled to reimbursement of all reasonable amounts the trustee advances on behalf of the trust, he or she should keep copies of proof of payment, such as canceled checks or receipts. For example, if the trustee is travelling with beneficiary and pays for all bills from a personal account, he or she can be reimbursed from the SNT and it is best practice to keep very careful track of these expenditures.

- **Communications with advisers.** Keep all copies of all correspondence between the trustee and his or her advisers, and always ask them to at least summarize any advice they give in writing.
- **Any and all information upon which any exercise of discretion is based.** These documents may include such things as beneficiary's bank statements, credit card statements, pay stubs, or other employment information, invoices, proposals, and any other information given to you to justify a request for a distribution.

For a further discussion of the record keeping responsibility, see chapter 7.

7. Duty to Account and Report to the Beneficiary

The trustee has a legal duty to account to the current beneficiary of the trust. The trustee is generally required to account, at least annually, at termination of the trust, and, on a change of trustee, to each beneficiary to whom distributions are being made.[50] The duty to account can be waived either by the trust document or the beneficiary. The type of account that must be provided will depend on whether the trust is court supervised or not court supervised. To determine whether the trust is court supervised or not, look at chapter 2.

The accounting typically includes information about

- how assets were invested;
- how trust assets were spent;
- what assets and liabilities the trust has;
- explain any unusual disbursements;
- the amount of money the trustee received for services; and
- the amount of money paid to advisers such as attorneys or accountants.

In order to simplify the accounting, it is best if the trustee keeps excellent records throughout the year. It is much easier to create an account with up-to-date records rather than digging through shoe boxes of receipts and trying to recreate what happened in the past year.

---

[50] Probate Code §16062.

For a complete discussion of the accounting requirements for both court supervised and non court supervised SNTs, see chapter 7.

8. Duty to Furnish Information to the Beneficiary

The trustee has a duty to keep the beneficiaries of a trust reasonably informed of the trust's administration.[51] Unlike the duty to account and the duty to furnish reports discussed above, this duty to inform cannot be waived. A beneficiary may make a reasonable request for information and the trustee must provide the beneficiary with a report of information about the assets, liabilities, receipts, and disbursements of the trust, the acts of the trustee, and the particulars relating to the trust that are relevant to the beneficiary's interest.[52]

A trustee who wishes to have a smoother administration should communicate on a regular basis with the beneficiary. The most common mistake of trust administration is lack of communication between the trustee and the beneficiary. If the trustee wishes to take an action that the beneficiary may have an issue with, it is typically better to notify that beneficiary and see if there will be a dispute later and try to fix it now.

9. Duty to Keep Trust Assets Separate

A trustee must keep the trust property separate and distinct from the beneficiary's other assets.[53] The beneficiary's SSI and other public benefits should be maintained in a separate bank account and never commingled with trust funds.

The trustee should obtain and use a separate tax identification number for the trust. A separate tax identification number can be obtained online.[54] The trustee should not use the beneficiary's social security number for any trust bank or brokerage account if owned and operated by the trust.

The trustee must also keep the trust property separate from his or her own property. In other words, the trustee should have a separate bank account

---

[51]   Probate Code §16060.

[52]   Probate Code §16061.

[53]   Probate Code §16009.

[54]   http://www.irs.gov/businesses/small/article/0, id=102767,00.html.

or accounts for the trust, and the trustee must not put either trust principal or income into his or her personal accounts.

10. Duty to Protect and Preserve Trust Assets

The trustee has a duty to protect and preserve the trust assets, and to insure them whenever practicable.[55] The trustee should be sure to consult a competent insurance agent regarding proper coverage for trust assets. Few things are worse than having a trust asset destroyed through no fault of the trustees and then discovering that the asset was not insured. In that case, the trustee's personal bank account may become the insurance company.

For a more complete discussion of the duty to protect and preserve assets, see chapter 8.

11. Duty to Enforce or Defend Claims

The trustee has a general duty to take reasonable steps to enforce claims of the trust.[56] This does not mean that the trustee must enforce every claim. The standard is whether a prudent trustee would take steps to enforce a claim in such circumstances. The trustee must evaluate such factors as whether there is a likely chance of success and whether a judgment would be collectible.[57] In one recent California case, a trustee was held responsible for breach of trust for prosecuting a claim that netted a much smaller recovery than it cost to obtain it.

The trustee also has a duty to take reasonable steps to defend actions that may result in a loss to the trust.[58] Depending on the circumstances, it may be reasonable to settle an action or suffer a default rather than to defend, but no matter how the case is resolved, a trustee who fails to exercise reasonable judgment faces liability.

---

[55]   Probate Code §16049.
[56]   Probate Code §16010.
[57]   Schwartz v Labow (2008) 164 Cal, App. 4th 417.
[58]   Probate Code §16011.

12. Duty to Invest Assets and Make Productive

The trustee ordinarily has a duty to invest trust property, preserve it, and make it productive.[59] The duty to invest, however, is not absolute. The trustee's investment powers are usually derived from the trust document. If not, these powers are set by California law and by the circumstances of the trust and its beneficiaries. All of these sources of investment powers are considered in determining whether an investment is proper.

In many SNTs, the trustee must comply with the Prudent Investment Standard.[60] This standard requires the trustee to invest the assets as a prudent person would, given the current and future circumstances of the beneficiary. However, if the SNT is court supervised, the trustee may have a very specific investment standard which must be followed. For a more complete discussion of the investment requirements, see chapter 8.

WHAT CAN HAPPEN IF AN SNT BREACHES A FIDUCIARY DUTY?

If an SNT trustee breaches a fiduciary duty, the court has broad power to fashion an appropriate remedy. A judge could require the SNT trustee to pay to the SNT any of the following:

- Any loss or depreciation in value of the SNT resulting from the breach of duty, with interest.[61]
- Any profit made by the SNT trustee through breach of duty, with interest.[62]
- Any profit that would have accrued to the SNT if the loss of profit is the result of the breach of duty.[63]

The court also has full discretion to excuse the SNT trustee from liability in whole or in part (including liability for interest) if the trustee acted reasonably

---

[59] Probate Code §§16006-16007.
[60] Probate Code §§16045-16054.
[61] Probate Code §16440(a)(1).
[62] Probate Code §16440(a)(2).
[63] Probate Code §16440(a)(3).

and in good faith under the circumstances as known to the trustee and if it would be equitable to do so.[64]

A judge has additional remedies he or she can award against an SNT trustee that has breached his or her duty. These remedies include

- **Reducing SNT Trustee's Compensation.** An SNT trustee's pay may be used to offset any damage suffered by the SNT, but even if the trustee's breach failed to cause any financial damage, the court may still take away the SNT trustee's pay.[65]
- **Surcharge the SNT Trustee.** If the SNT trustee's breach of duty resulted in financial harm to the SNT, the SNT trustee may have to repay the SNT from his or her own personal funds.[66]
- **Removal of SNT Trustee.** An SNT trustee may be removed, even if the trustee's breach never resulted in financial harm to the SNT. A judge has authority to do this to protect the SNT.[67]
- **Contempt.** If an SNT trustee disobeys a lawful court order, the fiduciary may be punished for contempt.[68]
- **Costs.** The court is allowed to award costs against an SNT trustee, "as justice may require."[69]

HOW DOES A TRUSTEE SIGN DOCUMENTS?

Whenever a trustee signs any document on behalf of the trust, he or she should always sign as *"[Your Name], Trustee of the John Smith Special Needs Trust."* It must be absolutely clear that the trustee, in his or her role as trustee is obligating the trust and not the trustee personally. If the trustee does this (assuming the trustee is acting within the scope of his or her authority as trustee), the trustee will not be personally liable for any obligation under that document.

---

[64] See Probate Code §§16440(b), 16441(b).

[65] Probate Code §16420(a)(7).

[66] Probate Code §16420(a)(3).

[67] Probate Code §17200. Probate Code §15642(a).

[68] Code of Civil Procedure §1209(a)(5).

[69] Probate Code §1002.

SHOULD A TRUSTEE HIRE SOMEONE TO DO AN EVALUATION OF THE SNT BENEFICIARY?

In most cases, this is not a legal duty of the SNT trustee. However, this is often done when the trustee is concerned that he or she does not have the personal relationship or experience to understand all the issues surrounding the beneficiary and his or her conditions and needs.

> **Helpful Hint:** The trustee should review the trust documents to see if a Memorandum of Intent was prepared. This may have valuable information on the beneficiary and his or her condition. A Memorandum of Intent is usually done when there is a third-party SNT as part of a parents' estate plan.

The trustee should generally do the evaluation in person. If he or she does not understand how the beneficiary's disability affects the beneficiary's life, then it is best to do an "in person" meeting which can eliminate many future communication problems. A disability can be difficult to describe in writing or over the phone and reviewing a medical diagnosis may not let the trustee understand how his or her beneficiary is being affected by the disability.

If the trustee does not feel comfortable doing the evaluation, he or she can hire a professional to do it. There are a host of different professionals who can do this, depending on what aspect of the beneficiary he wishes to further understand. For example, if it is disability related, a psychiatrist or neuropsychologist can assist. All of these evaluations can be paid for from the trust assets.

An evaluation of the beneficiary can include the following issues:

- Contact with family and whether continuing and facilitating such contact is part of the trustee's responsibility or to determine that contact might not be recommended.
- Disability, including an evaluation of the beneficiary's physical and mental condition.
- Rehabilitation and training programs in which he or she participates (or should be participating).
- Current living situation and whether it is still appropriate, including (when appropriate) an evaluation of the caregivers for the beneficiary.

- Financial condition, including available government benefits, to determine the beneficiary's needs and the effect of distributions from the SNT on the beneficiary's eligibility for public assistance.
- Exercise of his or her civil rights. For example, is the beneficiary receiving a fair wage for work performed or being denied his or her right to vote or marry?
- Current and future educational needs and programs.
- Recreational activities, leisure time, and social needs, and the appropriateness of existing program services.

After the initial evaluation, the evaluation should be repeated at least yearly, or when a major change occurs in the beneficiary's life, such as a move or marriage.

Chapter 3 Summary

- ✓ The SNT trustee has a great deal of power and responsibility when serving as a trustee for a person with a disability.
- ✓ The initial duties of the SNT trustee include knowing whether the SNT beneficiary requires immediate assistance; reading the trust document; meeting with the beneficiary, advisory committee, and trust protector; determining which type of public benefits the beneficiary is receiving; determining which type of SNT is being administered; determining if the SNT is court supervised; preparing a budget for the beneficiary; and finding out who is responsible for the care of the SNT beneficiary.
- ✓ The SNT trustee duties are found in a number of sources, primarily the trust document, a court order, California law, and federal law.
- ✓ Trustee should approach trustee duties by understanding intent of trust and understand his or her own motives in making decision on trust duties.
- ✓ The trustee has many legal duties, which must be followed. These duties include general prudence, carrying out terms of trust, no self-dealing, being loyal to SNT beneficiary, not delegating responsibility, asking for help if duties are more than trustee can manage, keeping records, providing information to SNT beneficiary, accounting and reporting to SNT beneficiary, protecting trust assets, keeping trust assets separate, making trust assets productive and investing trust assets.

- ✓ If an SNT trustee breaches a fiduciary of duty, the court may require the SNT trustee to repay (or surcharge) the SNT for any harm caused, disgorge profits, be removed, and pay costs, among other remedies.
- ✓ A court also has discretion to waive an SNT trustee's breach of fiduciary duty if the trustee acted in good faith and reasonably under the circumstances.
- ✓ Trustee should always sign name as trustee whenever conducting business as trustee.
- ✓ Trustee should consider doing an evaluation of the beneficiary.

CHAPTER 4

Understanding Public Benefits for Persons with Disabilities

One of the most important aspects of administering a SNT is to make sure that the trustee understands the eligibility rules of the public benefits programs that the person with a disability receives. It is important because the SNT trustee may disqualify the person with a disability from his or her public benefits if he or she improperly administers the SNT. This would result in the loss or reduction of payments for the beneficiary's health care and funds to help pay for the beneficiary's food and shelter.

Many SNT trustees believe that they can use good old-fashioned common sense when administering an SNT. Sadly, these SNT trustees will fail miserably, because the public benefit rules oftentimes make no sense whatsoever. For example, an SNT trustee cannot reimburse a Supplemental Security Income (SSI) recipient for the purchase of a television set, because the beneficiary will lose his or her eligibility for SSI. If however, the SNT trustee reimbursed the SSI recipient's best friend who bought the television, which would be perfectly fine. This is why it is important the SNT trustee have a good understanding of what public benefit rules will allow and not allow.

In this chapter, the basics of the public benefit rules are discussed. In chapters 5 and 6, you will find a more thorough discussion of how certain kinds of SNT disbursements will affect a person with a disability's public benefits. If the SNT trustee still feels that he or she is not comfortable making these types of decisions, he or she should go to chapter 11 to find assistance.

Public benefits can be broken up into three main categories which are described with more detail below:

- **Needs-based benefits** like SSI, Medi-Cal, and In-Home Supportive Services (IHSS)
- **Entitlement benefits** like Social Security, Social Security Disability Insurance (SSDI), Regional Center, and Medicare
- **Other benefits** like Section 8 and veteran benefits

Helpful Hint: An excellent starting point when learning about California public benefits programs is the website at www.disabilitybenefits101.org. This website provides an easy-to-understand format on all types of California's public benefits. There are lots of other websites that are also useful on specific public benefits programs that are found in chapter 11.

WHAT ARE NEEDS-BASED PUBLIC BENEFITS?

The following benefits are sometimes called "needs-based" or "means-tested" public benefits, because they have very strict income and resource requirements. These are the key public benefits that an SNT is designed to protect the following:

- Supplemental Security Income[70] (**"SSI"**). SSI provides a monthly cash payment for food and shelter to disabled, blind, or aged (age sixty-five or older) persons.
- **Medi-Cal**[71] (known as Medicaid outside the state of California). Medi-Cal pays for a broad array of medical treatments and is the only government program that pays for long-term nursing home care.
- In-Home Supportive Services **(IHSS),** which provides in-home care for persons with disabilities such as general housekeeping or shopping so the recipient can remain at home rather than having to live in an institution.

---

[70]   Title XVI; 42 U.S.C. §§1381-1383f.
[71]   Title XIX; 42 U.S.C. §§1396-1396v.

WHICH PUBLIC BENEFIT LAWS AND RULES DOES THE SNT TRUSTEE HAVE TO FOLLOW, MEDI-CAL'S OR SSI'S?

In most cases, the only rules the SNT trustee must follow are those for SSI eligibility. The reason is that in California, as long as the SNT beneficiary is eligible for at least $1 of SSI, he or she is automatically qualified for Medi-Cal.

In a minority of cases, the SNT beneficiary is eligible for Medi-Cal without being eligible for SSI. In these circumstances, the SNT trustee must follow Medi-Cal's rules and not SSI's. In most circumstances, the rules are very similar. However, there are differences. When these differences exist, an explanation is made in the book of how Medi-Cal will treat that situation.

WHAT DOES THE SSI PROGRAM PROVIDE?

The SSI program provides a monthly check to the person with a disability to pay for that person's food and shelter. The maximum amount of SSI an individual can receive in California in year 2011 is $830 per month, and $1,407.20 per month for a couple. These are the numbers most commonly used when administering an SNT. However, as seen in the chart below, the SSI amount can vary depending on the person with a disability's living situation, marital status, and whether the person's disability is blindness.

To determine the correct amount of SSI in California for years after 2011, see www.ssa.gov/pubs/11125.html or Google "SSI in California" and the link to the www.ssa.gov site should direct the trustee to the latest information.

Category	2011 total monthly payment	
Single people	**Disabled**	**Blind**
Independent living status	$830.00[1]	$908.00
Nonmedical board and care	$1,086.00	$1,086.00
Independent living status, no cooking facilities	$929.00	
Living in the household of someone else	$639.66	$718.32
Disabled minor child	$737.40	

Disabled minor child in household of another	$517.30	
Disabled couples		
Independent living status	$1,407.20	
Nonmedical board and care	$2,172.00	
Independent living status, no cooking facilities	$1,575.20	
Living in the household of someone else	$1,075.33	
Blind couples		
Independent living status	$1,554.20	
Living in the household of someone else	$1,222.33	
Blind person with a disabled spouse		
Independent living status	$1,498.20	
Living in the household of someone else	$1,166.33	

WHY DOES THE SNT TRUSTEE NEED TO KNOW THE SSI RULES ON RESOURCES AND INCOME?

If an SNT trustee does not understand these rules, it could cost the SNT beneficiary his or her eligibility for SSI and Medi-Cal. This is because the Social Security Administration (SSA) (the government agency that runs SSI) will count any distribution an SNT trustee makes to or for the beneficiary as some form of income, subject to the SSA's "income rules." Then, if the income is used to buy some kind of asset (or becomes an asset itself, such as money in a bank account), the asset will be subject to separate SSI "resource rules." Either can cause a loss or reduction of SSI, which can then result in loss of Medi-Cal.

In order to be sure that the trust distributions fall into the desired category, the trustee must maintain very accurate records of how the trust funds are invested and spent. These records will be needed if the SSA or other government agency wants verification of the expenditures the trustee has made. It is not unusual for the agencies to make a demand for verification, and the trustee should expect it.

In chapters 5 and 6, this book goes into great detail on the effect on SSI and Medi-Cal certain disbursements from an SNT will have on these public benefit programs.

WHAT ARE THE SSI RULES ON RESOURCES?

An otherwise eligible person is not entitled to SSI if the applicant's countable resources and those of the applicant's spouse exceed $3000. For an otherwise eligible single person, the resource limit is $2,000.

Countable Resources

Generally, a "countable resource" is any asset considered by SSI rules in determining eligibility (therefore a resource is sometimes called a "countable asset"). It could be tangible, like a second car, or it could be something like a savings or retirement account.

> **Example**: A single person with a disability has a checking account with $600, a savings account with $500, and an IRA account that is valued at $1,500. This person would not qualify for SSI, because his assets exceed $2,000. If he spent down his assets below the $2,000 before the first day of the next calendar month he would then qualify for SSI.

Excluded Resources

The beneficiary is allowed to have certain exempt assets, which are excluded from the $2,000 limit. These exempt assets are not counted in determining eligibility, and the beneficiary's ownership of them will not put the SSI benefits at risk. Therefore, the SNT trustee may freely purchase exempt assets for the beneficiary and give them to him or her with no loss in SSI or Medi-Cal.

The following assets are considered exempt resources by the SSA:

- A home of any value, including adjacent land, if the beneficiary lives in it or intends to return to it.
- One automobile of any value.

- Household goods (furniture, furnishings, household equipment, household supplies), personal effects (toiletries, items of personal care), education, clothing, and jewelry (however, giving the beneficiary food is "in-kind support," as explained below).
- Life insurance with a cash surrender value, if its face value is less than $1,500, and all-term life insurance.
- A burial plot, or other burial space, worth any amount.
- A revocable burial fund, worth up to $1,500.

All the assets above are specifically exempted by law. The trustee might note that a number of common and useful items are not specifically mentioned as exempt in the SSI regulations, but are not counted because they are included among "personal effects" or are services. These include recreational equipment, games and crafts, books and magazines, telephone, answering machine, television, radio, computer, Internet or satellite television service and cable service, musical instruments and stereo, travel and education, recreation and entertainment, and some home maintenance, such as gardening.

For a more complete list of exempt assets see chapter 5.

WHEN ARE SSI RESOURCES COUNTED?

Resources are counted on the first minute of the first day of each calendar month.[72] If resources exceed $2,000 at that moment, the person is ineligible for SSI for the whole month. Thus, it is possible for the SSI recipient to be over the resource limit during the calendar month but continue to receive the benefit if assets are spent down prior to the first minute of the first day of the calendar month.

> **Example**: An SSI recipient checking account balance is $1,300 and savings account balance is $500 on June 20. The next day, the recipient receives $2,200 from an inheritance. At this point, the SSI recipient's assets exceed the $2,000 limit. However, if the recipient spends his assets to below $2,000 before the end of the day on June 30, he or she will keep SSI eligibility in July.

---

[72]   20 C.F.R. §416.1207(a).

How Do the SSI Rules Define Income?

The SSA treats SNT distributions in one of four ways against the SNT beneficiary as either

1. Unearned income
2. Earned income
3. In-kind support and maintenance (ISM)
4. Not income

Each kind of income is discussed below in order.

> **Critical Pointer**: SSI income that is received during the calendar month is considered "income" throughout the month of receipt, even if it is deposited in a bank account. If, at the end of the month, it is still in the account, it becomes a "resource" in the next month and is then subject to "resource" rules that are discussed above.

> **Helpful Hint:** SSI defines the word "income" differently than what is commonly understood by that term. A common misunderstanding is that "income" for IRS purposes is the same as "income" for SSA purposes. It is not. So, it is important to understand how SSI income will be counted when administering the SNT.

1. Unearned Income

Any money received by the SSI recipient directly (not earned) will be considered "unearned income" and will reduce SSI benefits on a dollar-for-dollar basis. Examples of unearned income include the following:

- Gifts
- Annuities, pensions, and other periodic payments
- Alimony and support payments
- Dividends, interest, and royalties
- Rents
- Prizes and awards

As a result of the penalty, the SNT trustee should avoid making direct payments to the beneficiary, because there will be little advantage from doing so. If the SNT trustee's actions reduce the beneficiary's SSI benefits to zero, then both the beneficiary's SSI and Medi-Cal benefits will be put at risk. The SSA does allow the SNT beneficiary to receive $20 per month of any income with no reduction in benefits.

> **Example**: An SNT beneficiary asks the trustee to provide a monthly allowance of $500 per month to supplement the SSI check of $830 per month. If the SNT trustee chooses to authorize this monthly payment, the beneficiary will lose $480 per month of SSI. The net effect is that the beneficiary only receives $20 per month and loses $480 per month from his SNT.

> If instead, the SNT trustee gives the beneficiary cash directly from the SNT in any amount over $850 per month then the SSI recipient will lose his or her SSI for that month and will ultimately jeopardize his or her eligibility for Medi-Cal as well.

An SNT trustee may not reimburse the beneficiary for purchases he or she has made, even if the purchases are for exempt assets. The payment will simply be counted as direct income. In addition, SSI rules say that if the SNT trustee gives the beneficiary anything that is equivalent to cash, it will also be counted as direct income.

> **Example**: An SNT beneficiary pays $500 for an iPad. The SNT beneficiary asks the SNT trustee to reimburse him for the payment. If the SNT trustee agrees, then the beneficiary will lose $480 from his monthly SSI check. It is critical that payment of money is never made directly to the SNT beneficiary.

> If, instead, the SNT trustee had purchased the iPad directly for the beneficiary, then there would have been no loss of SSI benefit. Or, if the SNT trustee had reimbursed a friend of the beneficiary who had bought the iPad for the beneficiary, then that will also result in zero loss of SSI benefit.

2. Earned Income

An SSI recipient will lose eligibility for SSI payments based on earned income. Earned income may be paid in cash or in-kind. If it is in-kind and in exchange for labor, its full current market value is the amount used to determine countable income. Examples of earned income include

- Wages paid
- Net earnings from self-employment
- Payments for participating in a sheltered workshop or work activity center
- Royalties earned in connection with any publication of the individual's work
- Any honorariums received for services rendered

The SSI penalty on earned income is not as strict as it is for unearned income described above. Earned income only reduces a recipient's SSI monthly cash payment by 50 cents for each dollar earned, after taking an earned income exclusion of $65 (or, if the any-income exemption were unused, the total earned income exclusion would be $85).

> **Example:** An SSI recipient earns $900 per month from employment. He is receiving $830 per month in SSI. Due to the earned income, his benefits are reduced by $417 to $412. The reduction is calculated by taking the $65 per month earned income exclusion and then dividing the balance of remaining income by half. ($900-$65÷2 = $417).

3. In-Kind Support and Maintenance (ISM)

Another kind of income that SSA counts is the receipt of food or shelter by the SSI recipient. Oftentimes, an SNT trustee will pay for the beneficiary's food or shelter. This is called "in-kind support and maintenance" (ISM). In determining ISM, food and shelter is limited to the SSI's recipient's receipt of the following items:

- Food
- Mortgage payments (including property insurance required by the mortgage holder)

- Real property taxes (less any tax rebates or credits)
- Rent
- Heating fuel
- Gas
- Electricity
- Water
- Sewer
- Garbage removal

ISM causes a reduction in the beneficiary's SSI payment, *but not on a dollar-for-dollar basis*, as they are if the SNT trustee were to give the beneficiary cash directly. The theory behind the reduction or elimination is that SSI benefits are specifically intended to pay for a person's food and shelter, so if that person receives those things from another source, then less SSI benefits are needed. As a result, if the SNT trustee pays the beneficiary's grocery bill or rent, the SNT trustee is providing ISM to the beneficiary. In theory, the SSI recipient has less of a need for SSI benefits. Obviously, in reality, this amount of money in California is woefully short of providing even a minimum quality of life, which is why an SNT is so critically important to people with disabilities.

To determine the reduction of SSI, the SNT trustee should understand both the value of the one-third reduction rule (VTR) and the presumed maximum value (PMV). The difference between VTR and PSM isn't much.

A. Value of One-Third Reduction Rule (VTR)

VTR applies when the benefits recipient lives in another's house throughout a month, receives *both* food and shelter from a person inside the household, and does not meet his or her pro rata share of cost of the food and shelter expenses for the household.

The VTR reduces the SSI benefit by one-third of the portion of the monthly SSI check that the federal government pays for. This is called the federal benefit rate (FBR). In 2011, the reduction to SSI would be $224.67 (1/3 of $674 (FBR) in 2011).

> **Example**: Amir an SSI recipient who receives SSI of $830 per month moves in with an uncle who pays for all of Amir's food and shelter costs. Because Amir lives in the same house as his

uncle and receives free food and shelter, his SSI check will be reduced by $224.67. Thus, he will receive $605.33 per month.

B. Presumed Maximum Value (PMV)

The PMV rule applies when an SSI recipient receives either food or shelter from someone not living in the home or if food or shelter is paid while the SSI recipient lives in his or her own house. The reduction for PMV is valued at the lesser of its actual value or at its "presumed" value, which is one-third of the federal benefit portion, plus the $20 general income exclusion.

In 2011, the maximum PMV reduction amount is $244.67 (the 2011 FBR of $674, plus $20). Hence, if the *actual* value of the ISM that the beneficiary receives is below $244.67, the beneficiary's SSI payment will be reduced to reflect the actual value of the ISM received once the actual value of ISM is proven. Otherwise it is presumed that the value of ISM is $244.67. If the ISM received has a value greater than the PMV, the beneficiary's SSI benefit will only be reduced by $244.67.

> **Example:** The SNT trustee distributes $2,200 a month for the beneficiary's rent. This is ISM to the beneficiary each month. If the beneficiary is entitled to receive $830 in SSI, the payment of rent will cause a $244.67 reduction in monthly benefit.
>
> Thus, as a trustee you have provided a $2,200 apartment for the beneficiary's shelter; the beneficiary still receives $585.33 per month from SSI and the beneficiary is still eligible for Medi-Cal. This is generally a great trade-off—a much nicer apartment with only a modest reduction of SSI.
>
> **Helpful Hint:** The SNT trustee that has already maxed out the PMV because he or she has paid the SSI recipient's rent can also pay for all of the SSI recipient's food without any further reduction in the SSI check. There is no second PMV reduction for paying food as well as shelter.

4. Not SSI Income

Generally speaking, there is no SSI income triggered at all when an SNT trustee gives the beneficiary something other than money. In most cases, it is safe to provide such "income" to the beneficiary. This is because the value of any noncash item (other than food or shelter) is not counted as income if the item will become an exempt asset when it is retained into the following month.

For example, the SNT trustee can give the beneficiary music CDs, magazines, and a bed or other furniture, which are in-kind income but are not counted by SSI because they are exempt resources. The SNT trustee can also give the beneficiary something that will be used in the month it is received, such as cosmetics or razor blades. As a result, the SNT trustee may give the beneficiary any exempt resources. Further, the SNT trustee could pay for services that are not counted as income. This can include cable TV, Internet satellite television, cell phone, or any other type of similar service.

However, if the SNT trustee makes a disbursement for an item that will be counted in the next month as a resource, then the SNT beneficiary may lose his or her eligibility.

> **Example**: An SNT trustee purchases an automobile for $15,500 and the beneficiary takes title to the car. However, the SNT beneficiary already owns a motorcycle that is worth $10,000. Because an SSI recipient is only allowed to own one automobile (a motorcycle is counted as an automobile), then the second car will be counted as a resource against the SNT beneficiary and he loses eligibility for his SSI, because his recourses exceed the $2,000 resource limit.
>
> If, instead, the SNT trustee had purchased the automobile and kept title in the name of the SNT, the car would not be counted as an available asset. (See chapter 6 on how best to purchase an automobile by an SNT trustee.)

WHAT IS SSI "DEEMING," AND WHY DOES A MINOR OR SPOUSE NOT QUALIFY FOR SSI?

This is typically because the minor is still living with his or her parents and until age eighteen, the parents' assets and income are counted as the minor's for SSI resource purposes. Likewise for an SSI-eligible adult who is living with a spouse: the spouse's assets, and income are counted as part of the SSI-eligible persons for SSI eligibility purposes. This concept is called "deeming.[73]"

Generally, the resources of a minor child living with both parents (or a parent and step-parent) are deemed to include the parents' resources in excess of $3,000 (i.e., the resource allowance for a couple), or, if living with one parent, the parent's resources in excess of $2,000. The general resource exclusions apply to the parents' resources for deeming purposes plus the parents' pension funds are exempt.[74]

Generally, if an ineligible spouse and eligible spouse's nonexempt resources exceed $3,000, the SSI-eligible spouse will lose his or her benefits.[75] The SSA counts the value of all resources (money and property), minus certain exempt assets, when determining eligibility. In addition to the general exempt assets such as the home, automobile, and household goods and effects available to any individual, the ineligible spouse's pension funds (e.g., IRAs, 401k) are also exempt.[76]

It does not matter if money is actually provided to the minor or SSI eligible spouse for deeming to apply.[77]

When the minor turns age eighteen, the SSA will only count the minor's assets when determining SSI eligibility. If the SSI eligible spouse moves out, the other spouse's assets will not be counted.

> **Note:** Deeming only applies if the child is living with a parent. If the child is living in an institution or with a grandparent, deeming does not apply.

---

[73] 20 C.F.R. §416.1202(b)(1); POMS SI 01330.200.
[74] 20 C.F.R. §416.1202(b); POMS SI 01330.220.
[75] 20 C.F.R. §416.1205(c).
[76] 20 C.F.R. §416.1202(a).
[77] 20 C.F.R. §§416.1160(a), 416.1202.

How Does a Beneficiary Qualify for Medi-Cal?

There are many ways for a person to be eligible for Medi-Cal. The most common and described briefly below are listed below:

1. **Categorical Eligibility.** People who receive Supplemental Security Income (SSI) or California Work Opportunity and Responsibility to Kids (CalWorks) are categorically eligible to receive Medi-Cal. Thus, even if the SSI recipient receives even $1 of SSI, he or she is automatically receives Medi-Cal.

2. **Aged and Disability Federal Poverty Level ("A&D FPL").** This program provides free Medi-Cal services for persons with disabilities who meet the income and asset requirements of the A&D FPL program. It covers individuals and couples whose income is slightly higher than the SSI eligibility requirements.

3. **Aged, Blind, and Disabled** (sometimes called "**medically needy**" or "**share of cost Medi-Cal**"). This program provides full-scope Medi-Cal services to aged, blind, or disabled people with income above the eligibility levels of no-cost Medi-Cal programs (such as SSI and A&D FPL). The program usually requires that individuals incur a monthly "share of cost" (which is why it is sometimes referred to as "share-of-cost" Medi-Cal), which functions like a monthly copayment.

4. **250% California Working Disabled.** This program provides full-scope Medi-Cal to persons with disabilities who work and have income that is too high to qualify for other Medi-Cal categories. For this program, the recipient may have up to 250 percent of the federal poverty level in countable income and still receive Medi-Cal benefits. Enrollees pay a monthly, sliding-scale premium for this health coverage.

5. **Pickle Amendment.** The 1976 Pickle Amendment to the Social Security Act requires states to maintain SSI-linked Medi-Cal eligibility for SSI recipients who lose their SSI due to Social Security cost of living allowance. Eligibility extends to those who would have been eligible for SSI in the past, even if they never received it. Thus, the person would be eligible for Medi-Cal but not SSI.

6. **Medi-Cal Waivers.** A Medi-Cal waiver allows the Department of Health Care Services (DHCS) to waive certain Medi-Cal criteria for

persons who would not be able to receive Medi-Cal benefits because of too much income or resources. An example is the Home and Community Based Service (HCBS) waivers which allow community based Medi-Cal services for certain Medi-Cal beneficiaries to avoid hospitalization or nursing facility placement.

To obtain further information on these different Medi-Cal programs, see http://www.disabilitybenefits101.org/ca/programs/health_coverage/medi_cal/program2.htm.

WHAT IS IN-HOME SUPPORTIVE SERVICES (IHSS)?

In-Home Supportive Services (IHSS) provides people who have disabilities or are over the age of sixty-five with in-home and personal care services to help them live safely in their own home or maintain an independent living arrangement. It is important for the SNT trustee to maximize as much as possible the IHSS benefits received, because private paying for caregiving services can quickly deplete the assets in an SNT.

IHSS provides the following services:

- Domestic services, such as sweeping, vacuuming, taking out the garbage, wheelchair cleaning and battery recharging, and changing bed linens
- Related services such as meal preparation and clean-up, laundry, and shopping
- Personal care services, such as feeding, bathing, grooming, dressing, bowel and bladder care, and help with medications
- Transportation to medical appointments or alternative sources of services, such as day programs
- Removal and clean-up of yard hazards
- Heavy cleaning
- Protective supervision for cognitively or mentally impaired individuals to safeguard from self-injury or hazard
- Paramedical services, as ordered by a physician such as injections, range of motion exercises, catheter insertion, etc.

WHO IS ELIGIBLE FOR IHSS?

For an excellent summary of the three different types of IHSS eligibility, see the chart at http://www.disabilityrightsca.org/pubs/547001-App-J.pdf.

CAN AN SNT TRUSTEE JEOPARDIZE A BENEFICIARY'S IHSS ELIGIBILITY?

Yes. IHSS is available to any California resident, living in his or her own home, who is already eligible for Medi-Cal. As discussed above, the four eligibility categories people with disabilities most often use to get on Medi-Cal are as follows:

1. SSI-linked Medi-Cal called categorically eligible Medi-Cal
2. Aged and Disabled Federal Poverty Level Medi-Cal (A & D FPL)
3. California's 250% Working Disabled Program
4. Aged, Blind, and Disabled Medically Needy Medi-Cal (or sometimes called share-of-cost Medi-Cal)

The SNT trustee should make sure that distributions from the SNT do not reduce or eliminate eligibility for IHSS through these programs. For example, if the Medi-Cal is received because the SNT beneficiary has SSI, the loss of SSI would eliminate the recipient's Medi-Cal and linked IHSS service.

See chapters 5 and 6 on making appropriate disbursements to pay for additional services from a good IHSS worker.

WHAT ARE ENTITLEMENT PUBLIC BENEFITS AND DOES THE SNT TRUSTEE NEED TO WORRY ABOUT THEM?

The following benefits are generally called "entitlement benefits" because a person may still qualify for them and still have substantial wealth in his or her own name. These benefits were typically paid for with taxes while working. These include the following:

- **Social Security Retirement**.[78] This benefit provides a monthly check for eligible workers who are at least sixty-two years of age and sometimes will pay money for the worker's eligible spouse, ex-spouse, and in some instances the worker's children. To qualify for this benefit, a worker must have worked and paid taxes on wages for at least ten years of work, with the required amount of earnings.
- **Social Security Disability Insurance**[79] **(SSDI)**. To receive disability benefits, the worker must be so severely mentally or physically impaired as to be unable to perform any substantial gainful work, and the impairment must be expected to last (or has lasted) one year or to result in death. Generally, for disability benefits, a worker needs to have worked for several years.
- **Social Security Family Member and Survivor's Benefits**.[80] A parent's child with a disability may receive a percentage of the parents social security check if that child was disabled before age twenty-two. Payments to the child will begin when the parent is disabled, retires, or dies.
- **Medicare**.[81] Medicare provides health insurance for individuals who are age sixty-five or over, disabled, or have end-stage kidney disease or amyotrophic lateral sclerosis (ALS, also known as Lou Gehrig's disease). Medicare does not have an income or resource requirement. Typically, those eligible for SSDI or Social Security qualify for Medicare. Medicare does not provide complete coverage for all health-care needs. It only covers medically "reasonable and necessary" services. For example, it will not pay for many routine or preventive services, such as annual physical exams, eyeglasses, dental care, hearing aids, or long-term care at home or in a nursing home.

The good news for SNT trustees is that the administration of the SNT should not interfere with the beneficiary's eligibility for these benefits. Thus, if the only benefits that the SNT beneficiary receives are entitlement benefits and

---

[78] Title II; 42 U.S.C. §§401-418.

[79] Title II; 42 U.S.C. §§401-418.

[80] Title II; 42 U.S.C. §402(b)-(h).

[81] Title XVII; 42 U.S.C. §§1395-1395hhh.

he or she is not receiving any needs-based public benefits, the SNT trustee disbursements will not interfere with the beneficiary's public benefits.

> **Critical Pointer**: It can be very confusing to know which benefits an SNT beneficiary is receiving. Sometimes, even the SNT beneficiary and his or her legal representative will not know what benefits they have. This is because these public benefit programs are very similarly named and provide similar benefits, but each has significantly different eligibility rules. See chapter 2 for some suggestions on how to find out which benefits the beneficiary is receiving.

CAN AN SNT BENEFICIARY RECEIVE BOTH SSI AND SSDI?

Yes some SNT beneficiaries are eligible for both SSDI and SSI. This occurs when the claimant's SSDI payments and other benefits do not exceed SSI income and asset limitations.[82] The claimant may also then be eligible for health coverage such as Medicare, Medi-Cal, or private medical insurance coverage.

Many additional benefits programs may be available to an SSDI claimant, depending on his or her work history and the benefits his or her employer had provided. These may include the California State Disability Insurance (CSDI) program and privately sponsored short-term and long-term disability programs.

WHERE CAN THE TRUSTEE FIND A BENEFITS PLANNER?

Because public benefits laws are ever changing and very complex, it might be prudent for the trustee to obtain professional advice on obtaining and keeping public benefits. A list of benefit planners for different cities throughout California is found at http://www.disabilitybenefits101.org/ca/directories/planners.htm.

---

[82]   42 USC §402(k)(2)(B).

In addition to these individuals, there are private benefits counselors available who can assist. (One such is James Huyck whose contact information is provided in chapter 11.)

IF THE SNT BENEFICIARY ONLY RECEIVES MEDI-CAL AND NOT SSI, CAN SNT TRUSTEE PAY FOR FOOD, HOUSING, OR UTILITIES?

Yes. However, the SSI PMV rules do not apply to Medi-Cal or IHSS benefits. Instead, the SNT trustee may pay for some percentage of the beneficiary's food, clothing, shelter, and utilities without interfering with Medi-Cal eligibility. If the SNT trustee pays for the entire amount of these items, the Medi-Cal recipient will have income that may increase the beneficiary's Medi-Cal share-of-cost or even loss of Medi-Cal. [83]

Practitioners differ in their advice on how much of an item of need should be paid for, *for example* whether the trustee should pay 75 percent of the cost up to 99.99 percent of the cost. In the author's opinion, it is probably safer to pay something more significant than 1 percent of the item of need.

> **Example:** SNT beneficiary is on Medi-Cal (but not SSI) and wants the SNT trustee to pay for his food and rent. The cost of the food is $500 per month and the rent $2,000 per month. If the SNT trustee were to pay the entire $2,500 amount, then the beneficiary would have an additional $2,500 in countable income for Medi-Cal eligibility. Instead, if the SNT trustee paid only $400 per month for food and $2,400 per month for rent and the SNT beneficiary paid the remaining $200 per month for the balance of the food and shelter, then the beneficiary would continue to receive all Medi-Cal.

SHOULD AN SNT TRUSTEE ALWAYS PAY FOR AN SSI RECIPIENTS FOOD OR SHELTER?

Not necessarily. There are generally two circumstances when an SNT trustee should not or cannot pay for an SSI recipient's food or shelter.

---

[83]   22 C.C.R. §50509.

1. **The SSI recipient is not receiving a big enough SSI check.** There are times when an SNT beneficiary receives only a few hundred dollars of SSI because the SSI recipient may have other sources of income. If the SSI recipient receives less than $244.67 per month in SSI (in 2011) and the SNT trustee makes a payment for food and shelter as ISM, the SSI recipient will lose his or her SSI payment and categorical eligibility for Medi-Cal if the ISM amount is greater than the SSI recipient's SSI check.

   Example: An SNT beneficiary who is receiving SSI of $200 is also receiving retirement benefits of $650 per month. The SNT beneficiary wants the trustee to pay for his rent and utilities that total $900 per month. The effect of the SNT trustee making this payment is that the beneficiary will lose up to $244.67 of his SSI check. Because the beneficiary is only receiving $200, the entire amount of the SSI check is lost. This will eliminate the beneficiary's categorical eligibility for Medi-Cal. The loss of SSI is usually not a big issue, but the loss of Medi-Cal can be devastating.

   Note: In the prior example, even if the SNT beneficiary will lose his categorical eligibility for Medi-Cal because he lost his SSI check, the SNT trustee should determine if the beneficiary can otherwise qualify for Medi-Cal. There are other ways for an SNT beneficiary to qualify for Medi-Cal. The SNT trustee should know whether the beneficiary can qualify for Medi-Cal under the medically needy Medi-Cal, share-of-cost Medi-Cal or under a waiver program. A further description of the other types of Medi-Cal programs is discussed later in this chapter.

   If the SNT trustee is uncertain of the beneficiary's ability to qualify for Medi-Cal, he or she should hire a public benefits consultant. To find a public benefits consultant, see chapter 11. It is possible to hire a special needs planning attorney to assist, but it is usually not cost effective to have an attorney provide these types of services at their hourly rate versus the typically lower rate of the public benefits expert.

2. **The SNT document does not authorize such disbursements**. In every trust document the trustee of the trust is given instructions on what he or she can and cannot spend money on. This trust provision is often called the "distribution standard." In general, there are two kinds of distribution standards, a purely supplemental standard or a fully discretionary standard as described below:

• **The Purely *Supplemental* Distribution Standard:** Some SNTs specifically prohibit the trustee from making any distributions that will reduce or eliminate eligibility for SSI for any reason. As described above, payments for food or shelter will reduce or even eliminate SSI eligibility. Thus, the SNT trustee is prohibited from making any disbursements that will reduce the SSI check. This kind of SNT may be easier for a trustee to manage, as distributions or payments for "food" or "shelter" are prohibited and therefore do not require the trustee to determine the impact of these distributions on the beneficiary's public benefits. However, this type of standard also seriously hampers the ability of the SNT trustee to improve the beneficiary's life by paying rent on a nicer apartment or paying for the beneficiary's food. It is possible for the SNT trustee to modify the distribution standard by modifying the trust document. This will require a petition to a probate court as described in chapter 11.

    Example: A supplemental distribution standard will often look like this sample: "The trustee shall not make any distribution that will reduce or eliminate eligibility for public benefits."

• **The *Discretionary* Distribution Standard**: Some SNTs will allow distributions that can be made even if they reduce the amount of benefit or even eliminate public benefit eligibility. This type of distribution pattern is known as a "discretionary distribution standard." This requires that the trustee carefully examine how the rules regarding SSI "in-kind support and maintenance" will be applied. The beneficiary's SSI benefits will be reduced or eliminated if he or she receives ISM. The trade-off, however, is that the well-being and standard of living of the beneficiary may be enhanced, even after the SSI reduction is imposed. This is generally the more acceptable distribution standard for maximizing the quality of life of the person with a disability.

Example: A discretionary distribution standard will often look similar to this sample: "The trustee may distribute to or apply for the benefit of Beneficiary such amounts from the principal and income, up to the whole thereof, as the trustee, in the trustee's discretion, considers necessary or advisable to meet Beneficiary's special needs for the remainder of his life."

Note: The author of this book always prefers the fully discretionary distribution standard. It provides the most flexibility to the SNT trustee to enhance the quality of life of the beneficiary with a disability by allowing the trustee to decide to forego all or a portion of public benefits if it is in the beneficiary's best interests to do so.

HOW CAN THE TRUSTEE RECEIVE SSA AND DHCS NOTIFICATIONS AND OTHERWISE KEEP INFORMED OF BENEFICIARY'S SSI AND MEDI-CAL ELIGIBILITY?

In order to receive notifications and keep informed, the trustee must make sure that the appropriate Social Security Administration (SSA) agency and Department of Health Care Services (DHCS) agency has the trustee's address and the beneficiary's address. Further, the SNT should request that he or she receive copies of all communications affecting the beneficiary's benefits.

The trustee should also instruct the beneficiary to be sure to let the beneficiary know promptly of receipt of any SSA notices.

The SNT trustee might find it helpful to be named an authorized representative for SSI and Medi-Cal purposes. If the trustee chooses to do this, he or she is then taking on the legal responsibility of maintaining the beneficiary's eligibility for public benefits. This is a duty the SNT trustee typically does not have unless there is specific wording in the SNT document requiring the trustee to keep the beneficiary eligible.

- To become an authorized representative for an SSI recipient, the trustee must sign and submit to SSA a written statement appointing him or her to represent the SNT beneficiary in their dealings with SSA.

The trustee will need to complete Form SSA-1696 (Appointment of Representative) for this purpose. The form can be found here: http://www.ssa.gov/online/ssa-1696.pdf.

- To become an authorized representative for Medi-Cal, the trustee should complete and sign a MC 306 Appointment of Representative, which can be found at http://www.dhcs.ca.gov/formsandpubs/forms/Pages/MCEBbyNumber.aspx.

Note: Please keep in mind that an authorized representative for an SSI recipient is not the same thing as a SSI representative payee. An authorized representative is allowed to communicate with SSI and represent the beneficiary before the Social Security Administration. A representative payee is appointed by the SSA to receive monthly checks which are then spent on the recipient's behalf.

DOES THE SNT TRUSTEE HAVE TO REGULARLY REPORT TO THE SOCIAL SECURITY ADMINISTRATION (SSA)?

Generally, no. If the SNT document does not require the trustee to maintain the beneficiary's eligibility for benefits, there is no legal requirement that the trustee provide ongoing reports to the SSA. In that case, it is up to the SNT beneficiary or his or her legal representative to make the reports to the SSA.

However, in some SNT trust documents, the trustee may be required to make all necessary reports to appropriate public benefit agencies or may be required to maintain the beneficiary's eligibility for all public benefits. If the trust document includes such a term then the trustee is responsible for making a report to the SSA. To see what is required in an SSA report, see next question and answer.

However, even if the SNT document does not require the SNT trustee to maintain benefits, the SSA has the right to audit SNT records. In that case, the SNT trustee would need to comply with SSA's reasonable requests.

Note: Regardless of whether the SNT trustee is required to maintain benefits, the SNT trustee may want to send the reports anyway if he or she does not believe the beneficiary is providing the reports. The SNT trustee will eventually have to deal with the potential loss of future public benefits so it may just be easier to send the reports now so there is not a later SSA overpayment request and loss of benefits.

WHAT TYPES OF THINGS MUST BE REPORTED TO SSA?

The SSI program requires periodic reports from all SSI recipients.[84] If the SSI recipient has a representative payee, the payee is obligated to make the report. These reports must be completed for eligibility to continue. Reports are required if the following changes occur in the life of the SSI recipient:
Moves or changes of address (COA)

- Persons moving in or out of the household
- Death of a household member
- Changes in income and resources for recipients and individuals involved in deeming cases. These individuals are:

  - ineligible spouses and ineligible children living with recipients,
  - parents living with eligible children,
  - essential persons,
  - sponsors of aliens and living-with spouses of sponsors, and
  - eligible aliens with the same sponsor.

- Changes in help with living expenses
- Entering or leaving an institution
- Marriage, separation, or divorce
- Leaving the United States for more than thirty days in a row
- Changes in school attendance (if under age twenty-two)
- Death of the recipient or individuals involved in deeming cases
- Fugitive felons status (fleeing prosecution, unsatisfied warrants, probation and parole violation)

---

[84]   POMS SI 02301.005.

The report is due within ten days after the end of the month in which the event took place. Thus, if the SSI recipient moved in July, the report would be due by August 10.

The report may be brief, but it should be in writing to the SSA and it should include the beneficiary's name and Social Security number, a description of the event that triggered the report, and the date of the event. The SNT trustee should keep a copy of all reports sent to the SSA.

> **Critical Pointer:** All communications to the SSA should be done by certified mail. The SSA is notorious for losing correspondence and claiming they never received notice.

The effect of failing to make a required report on time, the SSI program is entitled to reimbursement for all SSI benefits incorrectly paid to the beneficiary and SSI can assess a penalty of up to $100, depending on the lateness of the report.[85]

HOW DOES A TRUSTEE FIND THE BENEFICIARY'S LOCAL SSA OFFICE?

If the SNT trustee is not sure which office the report should be sent to, the trustee should go to http://www.socialsecurity.gov/locator/ and use the beneficiary's zip code to find the local office.

WHAT NEEDS TO BE REPORTED TO DHCS IF THE BENEFICIARY RECEIVES ONLY MEDI-CAL?

When a person accepts a Medi-Cal card, that person (or his or her representative) must report all changes in either income or resources that could affect his or her eligibility. These changes should be reported to the Medi-Cal regional office that serves his or her home county. These changes may be made by calling, writing, or visiting the Medi-Cal regional office. All changes *must* be reported within ten days after the change happens (or within ten days after the

---

[85]   POMS SI 02301.100.

beneficiary realizes the change has taken place.)[86] Failure to report a change may result in the beneficiary receiving the wrong Medicaid benefits.

Changes to report include the following:

- **Living Arrangements or Change of Address.** Any change in where a beneficiary or his or her spouse lives and/or gets mail must be reported. (This includes if the beneficiary moves in or out of someone's household, enters a hospital or nursing home, leaves a hospital or nursing home, or moves from one medical facility to another.)
- **Income Changes.** Any increase or decrease in the amount of money or change in the source of money that a beneficiary or his or her spouse receives must be reported. (Income includes all earned or unearned income, gifts, or any type of money that belongs to the beneficiary.) If a beneficiary applies and is approved for benefits for which he or she is entitled, he or she must report this change within ten days.
- **Resource Changes.** Any change in what a person owns must be reported. this means that the beneficiary buys, sells, gives away, or receives any asset (thing of value) or any part of an asset, he or she must report the change to the Medi-Cal regional office. (Resources or assets include any property the recipient owns or has interest in; money in banks, credit unions, etc.; stocks; bonds; life insurance policies and any other items of value.)
- **Family Size.** Any change in the family size must be reported. (This includes the death of a beneficiary, the death of a spouse, the moving of a beneficiary's child under the age of eighteen out of the beneficiary's household.)
- **Change in Health Care Coverage.** Any change in a beneficiary's health-care coverage.

---

[86]   Cal.C.C. §50185(a)(4).

IF SSA NOTICE IS RECEIVED DENYING OR REDUCING BENEFICIARY'S SSI, WHAT SHOULD TRUSTEE/ BENEFICIARY DO?

Unless the SNT document requires it or if the trustee is also the SSA representative payee for the beneficiary, the trustee does not have the legal responsibility to do anything. However, it is generally better practice for a trustee to assist the beneficiary if the beneficiary is unable or unwilling to appeal to preserve SSI eligibility. In order to make sure that the SNT trustee obtains all relevant SSA communications, see question and answer above on how to become an SSA authorized representative.

If the SSA sends notice that it intends to reduce or eliminate the beneficiary's SSI, an appeal should be filed immediately. SSI recipients generally have sixty days from the time they receive notice from the SSA to file appeals.[87] The letter from SSA will typically set forth the sixty-day right. The SSA presumes that an individual receives the notice five days after the date of the letter unless the individual can show that he or she received it later.[88]

> **Critical Pointer:** It is the better practice to appeal within ten days of receipt of the notice. If the appeal is filed within ten days, any SSI payments currently being made will continue until a decision is made, often called "aid paid pending."[89] If made after the ten days, SSI payments will be discontinued pending the appeal. If the recipient loses the appeal, benefits received may have to be paid back. Typically, the SSA will not inform the SSI recipient of this right.

Unless it is an obvious mistake that can easily be corrected, the SNT trustee should contact an attorney to assist with the appeal. To locate an SSA appeals attorney, see chapter 11.

---

[87]　See, 20 C.F.R. §§416.1409, 416.1433.

[88]　20 C.F.R. §1401.

[89]　20 CFR §416.1336(b).

SHOULD THE TRUSTEE ALSO BE THE BENEFICIARY'S SSI REPRESENTATIVE PAYEE?

Not necessarily. It might make sense if the beneficiary does not have the ability to manage his or her own SSI check and has no trustworthy family or friends able to assist. A representative payee is an individual or organization appointed by SSA to receive Social Security or SSI benefits for someone who cannot manage or direct someone else to manage his or her money.

The main responsibilities of a payee are to use the benefits to pay for the current and foreseeable needs of the beneficiary and properly save any benefits not needed to meet current needs. A payee must also keep records of expenses. When SSA requests a report, a payee must provide an accounting to SSA of how benefits were used or saved.

> **Note:** The monthly SSI checks should always be kept separate from the SNT accounts.

To become an SSI representative payee, the trustee should contact the SSA office nearest to the beneficiary to apply to be a payee. The trustee then submits an application, SSA Form SSA-11 (Request to be selected as payee) and documents to prove the trustee's identity. To locate a copy of the form with instructions on completing the form, see https://secure.ssa.gov/poms.nsf/lnx/0200502115.[90]

The trustee will need to provide his or her social security number or, if the trustee represents an organization, the organization's employer identification number. SSA requires the trustee to complete the payee application in a face-to-face interview (with certain exceptions).[91]

CAN AN SNT BENEFICIARY WORK AND STILL KEEP SSI AND MEDI-CAL?

Yes. There are several SSI and Medi-Cal programs that allow a person to work and remain eligible for public benefits. It is important to remember that each

---

[90] POMS GN 00502.115.

[91] POMS GN 00502.113.

program requires the SNT beneficiary to apply for them. Otherwise, public benefits can still be lost.

The public benefit work programs and incentives include

1. Impairment-Related Work Expense (IRWE)
2. Ticket to Work Program
3. Section 1619(a) and (b) Program
4. Plan for Achieving Self-Support (PASS)
5. 250% California Working Disabled Program (Medi-Cal Only)

A brief description of each program is set forth below

> **Note:** An excellent resource for work programs for persons with disabilities can be found in the SSA's Red Book, at www. ssa.gov/redbook and www.disabilitybenefits101.org.

1. Impairment-Related Work Expense (IRWE)

An IRWE is a good tool for the SNT beneficiary who is working and trying to reduce the effect on his SSI or SSDI.[92] The SNT beneficiary can deduct the cost of the IRWE from his or her income, thus reducing (or eliminating) any impact on the SSI benefit.

IRWE's are expenses for services or items related to the person with a disability's impairment that he or she pays in order to support work activities. A payment for a service or item is excludable as an IRWE when

*   the individual

    o   is disabled (but not blind); and
    o   is under age 65; or
    o   received SSI as a person with a disability (or received disability payments under a former State plan) for the month before attaining age 65; and

*   the severity of the impairment requires the individual to purchase or rent items and services in order to work; and

---

[92]   20 C.F.R. §416.976; POMS SI 00820.540(B)(3).

- the expense is reasonable; and
- the cost is paid in cash by the individual and is not reimbursable from another source (e.g., Medicare, private insurance); and
- the payment is made in a month the individual receives earned income for a month in which he or she both worked and received the services or used the item; or the individual is working but makes a payment before the earned income is received.

Note: The SNT trustee cannot pay directly for IRWEs to receive the deduction; the IRWE's payments must be made by the beneficiary directly.

Example: George an SNT beneficiary receives $830 per month of SSI begins working and earns $600 per month from employment. If there are no other deductions, George will lose $257.50 from his SSI check ($600 earned income—$65 earned income exclusion—$20 general exclusion—½ of remaining earned income).

If however, George is only able to work at all because he paid for transportation by wheelchair van of $100 per month and a one-time fee of $300 for corrective eyewear. In this case, given the same facts as above George would only lose $57.50 from his SSI check for that month ($600 earned income—$65 earned income exclusion—$20 general exclusion—$400 IRWE—½ of remaining earned income). This is a savings of $200.

EXAMPLES OF DEDUCTIBLE AND NONDEDUCTIBLE IRWE[93]

TYPE OF EXPENSE	IRWE DEDUCTIBLE	NOT DEDUCTIBLE
Transportation Costs	The cost of structural or operational modifications to your vehicle that you need in order to travel to work, even if you also use the vehicle for nonwork purposes. The cost of driver assistance or taxicabs that is required because of your disability rather than the lack of public transportation. Mileage expenses at a rate determined by us for an approved vehicle and limited to travel to and from employment.	The cost of your vehicle whether modified or not. The costs of modifications to your vehicle that are not directly related to your impairment or critical to the operation of your vehicle, for example, paint or pin striping. Your travel expenses related to obtaining medical items or services.

---

[93]   From SSA's Red Book, see http://www.ssa.gov/redbook/2011/ssdi-and-ssi-employments-supports.htm#4.

Attendant Care Services	Services performed in the work setting. Services performed to help you prepare for work, the trip to and from work, and after work; for example, bathing, dressing, cooking, and eating. Services that incidentally also benefit your family, for example, meals shared by you and your family. Services performed by your family member for a cash fee where he/she suffers an economic loss by reducing or ending his/her work in order to help you. This includes your spouse reducing work hours to help you get ready for work.	Services performed on nonworkdays or help with shopping or general housekeeping, for example, cleaning and laundry. Services performed for someone else in your family, for example, babysitting. Services performed by your family member for payment "in-kind", for example, room and board. Services performed by your family member for a cash fee where he/she suffers no economic loss. This includes services provided by your nonworking spouse.
Medical Devices	Deductible devices include wheelchairs, dialysis equipment, pacemakers, respirators, traction equipment, and braces.	Any device you do not use for a medical purpose.
Prosthesis	Artificial hip, artificial replacement of an arm, leg, or other parts of the body.	Any prosthetic device that is primarily for cosmetic purpose.

Residential Modifications	*If you are employed outside of home,* modifications to the exterior of your house that permit access to the street or to transportation; for example: • Exterior ramps • Railings • Pathways *If you are self-employed at home,* modifications made inside your home in order to create a workspace to accommodate your impairment. This includes enlarging a doorway into an office or workroom and/or modifying office space to accommodate your dexterity challenges	*If you are employed outside of home,* modifications to the interior of your house. *If you are self-employed at home, you cannot deduct any modification-related expenses that will be deducted as a business expense when determining SGA.*
Routine Drugs & Routine Medical Services	Regularly prescribed medical treatment or therapy that is necessary to control your disabling condition, even if control is not achieved. This includes: • Anti-convulsant drugs • Blood level monitoring • Radiation treatment • Chemotherapy	Drugs and/or medical services used for your minor physical or mental health problems, for example: • Routine physical examinations • Allergy treatments • Dental examinations • Optician services

	• Corrective surgery for spinal disorders • Anti-depressant medication • Your physician's fee relating to these services.	
Diagnostic Procedures	Procedures related to the control, treatment, or evaluation of your disabling condition; for example, brain scans, and electroencephalograms.	Procedures not related to your disabling condition, for example, allergy testing.
Nonmedical Appliances & Devices	In unusual circumstances, devices or appliances that are essential for the control of your disabling condition either at home or at work; for example, an electric air cleaner if you have severe respiratory disease. Your physician must verify this need.	Devices you use at home or at the office that are not ordinarily for medical purposes and for which your doctor has not verified a medical work-related need. These include: • Portable room heaters • Air conditioners • Dehumidifiers • Humidifiers
Other Items & Services	Expendable medical supplies; for example, incontinence pads, elastic stockings, and catheters. The cost of a service animal including food, licenses, and veterinary services.	An exercise bicycle or other device you use for physical fitness, unless verified as necessary by your physician. Health insurance premiums.

2. Ticket to Work Program

Ticket to Work is a federal program designed to help SSI or SSDI recipients, aged eighteen to sixty-four, to obtain, retain, or maintain employment and, eventually, reduce their dependence on cash benefit programs.[94] The recipients will receive a "ticket" that they may use to obtain supportive services, such as vocational rehabilitation, training, referrals, job coaching, and counseling from an approved Employment Network (EN) or State Vocational Rehabilitation agency (VR agency) of their choice.

The program is completely voluntary; there is no penalty if a recipient decides not to participate. If the SSI recipient is making sufficient progress toward his or her employment goal while enrolled in the program, the SSA will suspend medical continuing disability reviews. This is a significant benefit. Under normal circumstances, if the SSA conducts a medical review and determines that the SSI recipient is no longer "disabled" (i.e., working sufficiently to reach SGA, he or she would lose all of his or her benefits. For more information, see http://www.yourtickettowork.com/index.

3. Section 1619(a) and (b) Program

These programs allow a disabled or blind SSI recipient to qualify for continued SSI recipient status or to receive Medi-Cal even when working and receiving more than the amount normally allowed from employment.[95] Under §1619(a) of the Social Security Act, an individual may continue to qualify for SSI cash payments even though his or her gross earnings are at or above the work limit allowed (called "Substantial Gainful Activity" by the SSI and SSDI programs) provided all other nondisability requirements (e.g., residency, income, resources) are met.

To be eligible for continued Medi-Cal coverage under §1619(b), an individual cannot have earnings that would be sufficient to replace SSI cash benefits, Medi-Cal benefits, and publicly funded personal or attendant care. The SSA annually determines a threshold amount to measure whether an individual has sufficient earnings to replace these benefits for each state (also

---

[94] 20 C.F.R. §411.125. See 42 U.S.C. §1320b-19; 20 C.F.R. §§411.100-411.250; POMS DI 55001.001.

[95] 42 U.S.C. §1382h(a)-(b); 42 C.F.R. 416.260-416.269; POMS SI 02302.000.

called the "chartered threshold"). In 2011, the threshold amount for California was $34,324.[96]

If an individual's earnings exceed the threshold amount, the SSA may still make an individual threshold determination to incorporate specific needs the individual may have. In addition to the applicable threshold requirement, to qualify under §1619(b), a recipient must

- have used SSI in the previous month;
- continue to meet medical disability requirements;
- continue to meet nondisability requirements (except for earnings), such as resources, unearned income, and residency;
- and need Medi-Cal health coverage to continue to work.

4. Plan for Achieving Self-Support (PASS)

The PASS program allows certain people with disabilities to set aside earned or unearned income.[97] Social Security will exempt this income when it is placed into an approved PASS plan and used toward a vocational goal, such as college or a training school. PASS is a SSI program. The beneficiary must meet SSI financial rules to use the program. A detailed application is required. PASS can be a valuable tool for competitive employment. Several factors make PASS an effective tool for someone wanting to work under the SSI program[98]:

- PASS reflects individual choice. Individuals choose their own work goal.
- PASS is self-financed. Individuals use their own funds to pursue the plan. The receipt of, or an increase in, SSI benefits up to the amount of the Federal Benefit Rate (FBR), and any applicable state supplement, replaces some or all of the funds that the individual uses for PASS.
- PASS is largely self-directed. Individuals decide what goods and services are needed to reach the work goal.

---

[96] POMS SI 02302.200.
[97] 42 U.S.C. §§1382a(B)(4)(A)-(B), 1382b(a)(4); 20 C.F.R. §§416.1180-416.1182; POMS SI 00870.001.
[98] POMS SI 00870.001.

5. California's 250% Working Disabled Program

If the SNT beneficiary is working, disabled, and his or her income is too high to qualify for Medi-Cal, the California 250% Working Disabled Program may allow the SNT beneficiary to receive Medi-Cal by paying a small monthly premium.[99]

To qualify, the SNT beneficiary must

- meet the medical requirements of Social Security's definition of disability;
- be working and earning income;
- have assets worth less than $2,000 for an individual ($3,000 for a couple); the same asset exclusions apply for this program as the ones mentioned above;
- have countable income less than 250% of the Federal Poverty Level; Disability income does not count for this program; this means that SSDI, Worker's Compensation, California State Disability Insurance, and any federal, state, or private disability benefits are not considered as income for this program; and
- have countable unearned income less than the appropriate SSI benefit rate.

The SNT beneficiary is allowed when qualifying for this program to earn a fair amount of money and still qualify for public benefits.

WHAT OTHER PUBLIC BENEFITS MUST AN SNT TRUSTEE KNOW ABOUT?

There are other public benefits that a person with a disability may have that an SNT trustee should be familiar with:

- **Section 8 Housing** (known as "Housing Choice Voucher Program"). Under Section 8, beneficiaries receive a "voucher" or "subsidy" that they can apply to the rental of the housing unit of their choice—as long as the unit meets the Section 8 program requirements.

---

[99]   Welf & I C §14007.9; ACWD Letter No. 00-16 (Mar. 16, 2000).

A local Public Housing Agency (PHA) then delivers the subsidy to the landlord under a contract with the US Department of Housing and Urban Development (HUD). The beneficiary pays rent from 30 to 40 percent of their adjusted monthly income, and the PHA subsidy pays the remainder. The program allows very low-income individuals and families to choose where to live (see below for further discussion).

- **Veteran Benefits**. There are many persons with disabilities who became disabled as a result of military service or who previously served in the military. It is important to determine if these individuals can receive additional benefits from the US Department of Veterans Affairs. VA benefits can include compensation (for service-connected disabilities), pensions (for nonservice-connected disabilities), and medical and other benefits. Depending on the type of benefit, it may be available to veterans of military service, their dependents, and their survivors (see below for further discussion).

WHAT ARE SECTION 8 HOUSING PUBLIC BENEFITS?

The federal Section 8 program began in 1975 as a way to assist people with disabilities, the elderly, and low-income individuals to rent decent, safe, and affordable housing in the community.[100] Section 8 housing assistance programs fall into two general categories: tenant-based assistance (vouchers) and project-based assistance.

- Tenant-based assistance is rental assistance that is not attached to a structure or particular rental unit. It is administered by a local public housing authority (PHA). Under a tenant-based assistance program, tenants are given rental assistance vouchers and then find landlords willing to accept them. The vouchers are "portable" and tenants may move to different rental units owned by landlords willing to accept the vouchers.

---

[100] In 1975, when this housing assistance program was established, it was referred to as the "Section 8 " program. In many communities, it is still referred to by this name. However, a federal housing law passed in 1998 gave the program a new name the Housing Choice Voucher Program (HCVP). Because it is more familiar, this book uses the term "Section 8" to refer to the new HCVP.

- Project-based assistance is linked to a specific federally subsidized apartment. The assistance does not travel with a tenant and, if a tenant moves, it is lost.

HOW MUCH RENT DOES A DISABLED TENANT PAY UNDER SECTION 8?

The amount of rent the Section 8 recipient must pay is typically 30 to 40 percent of his or her monthly-adjusted income, with a minimum of $25 per month. Typically, the Section 8 recipient will pay 30 percent of their monthly-adjusted income for his or her share of the rent. To determine the monthly-adjusted income amount, the PHAs conduct a thorough examination of the household's income, including any assets, and calculate an annual adjusted income for that household. The adjustments to the income derive from HUD program regulations, which specify the types and amounts of income and deductions to be included in the calculation of annual and adjusted income. The Section 8 household's share of the rent is called the "total tenant payment."

Section 8 has its own rules on how assets are treated and what counts as income, which differ from other governmental agencies like Social Security or the Internal Revenue Service. The pertinent rules come from HUD and are contained in a Guidebook No. 7420.10G, entitled the "Voucher Program Guidebook, Housing Choice," available on the HUD website (herein the "Guidebook").[101]

Annual income is defined as all earnings, and includes employment wages, public benefits, and disbursements from any investments or pension plans.[102] Annual income includes income earned from assets during the twelve-month period and to which any family member has access.[103] The adjusted annual income is computed by reducing the family's gross annual income by any applicable standard deductions for seniors, persons with disabilities, and dependent children.[104]

---

[101] http://www.hud.gov/offices/adm/hudclips/guidebooks/7420.10G/7420g05GUID. pdf.

[102] 42 USC §1437a(b)(4), 24 CFR §5.609.

[103] 24 CFR §5.609.

[104] 24 CFR §5.611(a); Voucher Guidebook 7520.10, §5.5.

Some examples of noncountable income are lump-sum additions to assets (e.g., if the SNT beneficiary receives an inheritance or litigation recovery); any amounts received specifically for, or as reimbursements of, medical expenses; amounts received by an SSI recipient that are disregarded as income by SSI because they are set aside for a PASS; and income received of a live-in aide, such as a personal care attendant, who provides necessary support services for a tenant with disabilities.[105]

DO THE ASSETS OF AN SNT BENEFICIARY COUNT AGAINST SECTION 8 ELIGIBILITY?

Unlike SSI and Medi-Cal, the Section 8 program does not have resource limits. However, resources indirectly affect eligibility because income generated by resources is counted. A portion of an individual's assets will count toward the "annual income" determination. Income from assets is treated differently, depending on the amount of assets on hand.

Assets less than $5,000. If an individual with a disability's net assets are worth less than $5,000, all income derived from the assets is counted toward "annual income."[106]

> **EXAMPLE:** Kirby Rouser holds a Section 8 voucher and pays $150 each month in rent. Last year, his mother passed away and bequeathed him $3,500 in stocks. From these stocks, he earned a $360 end-of-year dividend (equal to $30 per month). Kirby will now have to pay approximately an additional $10 per month toward rent.

Assets greater than $5,000. If an individual with a disability's net assets are worth more than $5,000, the family must count toward annual income the greater of either (1) all income derived from the assets or (2) a percentage of the total value of the assets based on the passbook savings rate, as determined by HUD each year.[107] This is called the imputed income. The PHA will never count the full cash value of the asset toward annual income.

---

[105]   24 CFR §§5.609(c), 982.316.
[106]   Voucher Guidebook 7520.10, §5.4, Determining Income from Assets.
[107]   Voucher Guidebook §5.4, Determining Income from Assets.

Example: A husband and wife establish a $20,000 trust. Each year, the couple receives a $1,000 disbursement from the trust. The HUD passbook savings rate is 2 percent. The couple's annual income of $1,000 from the trust exceeds $400, which is 2 percent of the total value of the trust. Therefore, the PHA will count $1,000 toward annual income.

HOW WOULD AN SNT BENEFICIARY OBTAIN SECTION 8 HOUSING?

An individual applies for a Section 8 voucher with his or her local public housing agency (PHA). Section 8 is not an entitlement benefit, meaning that just because one is eligible to receive it does not mean that he or she will receive it. Because the demand for housing assistance almost always exceeds the number of Section 8 vouchers available, PHAs are usually unable to assist a Section 8 applicant immediately.

Unfortunately, most areas in California have long and growing waiting lists for vouchers; many PHAs have even stopped accepting new applications because of the size of the backlog. Generally, waiting times can vary between several months and several years.

For people with disabilities, there may be special set aside vouchers available. PHAs have several types of available vouchers. The most common would be the "Mainstream Housing Opportunities for Persons with Disabilities" voucher, which allows nonelderly persons with disabilities, who often face difficulties in locating suitable and accessible housing on the private market, to lease affordable private housing of their choice. Recipients of this assistance are selected from the regular waiting list.

Federal fair housing laws require that HUD and PHAs make reasonable accommodations in their policies, procedures, and programs to ensure active participation by people with disabilities. Thus, a person with a disability may request a reasonable accommodation in the PHA's policies for accepting Section 8 applications. Some examples of changes to the application process that can be requested as a reasonable accommodation include the following:

- allowing additional time to submit an application;
- allowing applications to be dropped off at the PHA by a friend, family member, advocate, service provider, etc.; and
- conducting home visits in order to allow an applicant.

PHAs must allow Section 8 vouchers to be used in "special housing types"—including group homes, congregate housing, and shared housing—as a reasonable accommodation for a person with a disability.

CAN THE SPECIAL NEEDS TRUST BE A SECTION 8 LANDLORD?

Yes. If the SNT owns real estate, the trustee can apply to accept Section 8. This is generally a good result, because the SNT is able to generate some income from the home that it would not otherwise be able to receive.

All housing leased through the Section 8 program must meet HUD's housing quality standards and must be physically inspected by the PHA. Further, the SNT trustee must enter into a lease that meets the PHA/HUD requirements. Finally, the housing unit must have rent that is reasonable when compared to similar units in the community. This rule is referred to as "rent reasonableness."

DOES AN SNT PROTECT ELIGIBILITY FOR THE SECTION 8 BENEFICIARY?

Not specifically. This means that there is no statute that specifically allows an SNT to preserve Section 8 eligibility. However, under existing Section 8 rules, an SNT can be used in conjunction with a Section 8 recipient to preserve eligibility for Section 8. The issue is that Section 8 is an income-based program, and resources do not play much of a role in the program. Thus, when an SNT owns assets, the assets themselves are not counted against the Section 8 recipient. However, any income earned from the assets will typically increase the Section 8 recipient's rent payment.

One way that an SNT may be harmful to a Section 8 recipient's eligibility is when income or principal is regularly distributed from an SNT. Some California public housing agencies (PHAs) will count that distribution as Section 8 income, unless a specific exclusion applies.[108] If there is no income distributed from the trust (i.e., it is reinvested in trust assets), then nothing is counted as income.

---

[108]   Voucher Guidebook 7520.10, §5, Ex. 5-2.

Note: Some California PHAs are not counting any distributions from the SNT as income for a Section 8 recipient. Thus, there is no effect on Section 8 eligibility from any SNT distributions. However, it is difficult to name the counties that do not do this versus those that do. Counties change their position often. In order to find out if the county where the SNT beneficiary resides is one that does not count these disbursements, contact a local attorney who specializes in special needs planning. To find such an attorney, see chapter 11.

The PHAs that count disbursements as income state that a regular recurring distribution from an SNT is included in income.[109] There are numerous categories of distributions that are specifically excluded from being treated as Section 8 income.[110] A few of them include the following:

- Temporary, nonrecurring, or sporadic income (including gifts)
- Lump-sum additions to family assets, such as inheritances, insurance payments (including payments under health and accident insurance and worker's compensation), capital gains, and settlement for personal or property losses
- Amounts received by the family that are specifically for, or in reimbursement of, the cost of medical expenses for any family member
- Income of a live-in aide
- Amounts received by a person with disabilities that are disregarded for a limited time for purposes of Supplemental Security Income eligibility and benefits because they are set aside for use under a Plan to Attain Self-Sufficiency (PASS)
- Amounts received by a participant in other publicly assisted programs which are specifically for or in reimbursement of out-of-pocket expenses incurred (special equipment, clothing, transportation, child care, etc.) and which are made solely to allow participation in a specific program[111]

---

[109]   Voucher Guidebook 7520.10 §5, Ex. 5-2, Income Inclusions, (7).
[110]   Voucher Guidebook 7520.10 §5, Ex. 5-2, Income Exclusions.
[111]   Voucher Guidebook 7520.10 §5, Ex. 5-2, Income Exclusions.

Warning: Some California PHAs have taken the position that each and every distribution from an SNT is income to the Section 8 recipient. These PHAs are even counting SNT disbursements that include payments for medical expenses or nonrecurring gifts as income. This practice should be fought. It is not consistent with the law and regulations. In order to find an attorney who can help fights these PHAs, see chapter 11.

Example: Mark Schwartz is a Section 8 recipient beneficiary of an SNT. Mark's SNT trustee makes a one-time payment for a Las Vegas vacation for Mark and is paying Mark's monthly electric bill of $100. There are no other distributions currently being made from the SNT.

The existence of the SNT itself will not render Mark ineligible for Section 8 benefits, nor will it cause any reduction of his Section 8 voucher. The payment of the trip to Las Vegas will not be counted against Mark, because it is a gift. However, the $100 a month will be added to Mark's monthly income and will increase the amount of money he will have to pay for his monthly rent as it is a regularly recurring payment from the trust. In practical terms, Mark will have to pay around $30 a month for his share of the rent, since his monthly adjusted income has increased by $100 and he is required to pay 30 percent of his adjusted monthly income toward rent. The HUD formulas are a little more complicated than this, but these figures are close approximations.

WHERE CAN AN SNT TRUSTEE FIND MORE INFORMATION ABOUT SECTION 8?

The Technical Assistance Collaborative (TAC) is a national nonprofit organization that advances proven solutions to the housing and community support needs of vulnerable low-income people with significant and long-term disabilities. They issue an excellent publication called *Section 8 Made Simple* and *Priced Out in 2008* among many other publications. Its website is http://www.tacinc. org. You will find plenty of great information there.

WHAT IF THE SNT BENEFICIARY IS A VETERAN?

There are many persons with disabilities who became disabled as a result of military service or who previously served in the military. It is important to determine if these individuals can receive additional benefits from the US Department of Veterans Affairs (VA). For more information on federal benefits, see www.va.gov. For additional California's veteran benefits, see http://www.cdva.ca.gov/newhome.aspx.

VA benefits are available to veterans of military service, their dependents, and their survivors but the availability of these benefits depends on the background of the veteran. For an online guide of available federal benefits, see http://www1.va.gov/OPA/publications/benefits_book.asp.

WHICH VETERANS ARE ELIGIBLE FOR BENEFITS?

Eligibility for most VA benefits is based upon discharge from active military service by other than dishonorable conditions.

Active service means full-time service, other than active duty for training, as a member of the Army, Navy, Air Force, Marine Corps, or Coast Guard, or as a commissioned officer of the Public Health Service, Environmental Science Services Administration or National Oceanic and Atmospheric Administration, or its predecessor, the Coast and Geodetic Survey. Generally, men and women veterans with similar service may be entitled to the same VA benefits.

DOES A SPECIAL NEEDS TRUST PROTECT A VETERAN'S ASSETS WHEN REQUESTING BENEFITS?

There are no rules in the United States Code, the Code of Federal Regulations, or the VA's policy manual regarding VA treatment of trust assets and income or transfers of assets to SNTs. There have been two opinion letters from a VA Office of General Counsel opinion and a Board of Veterans Appeals decision on point.

An opinion by the Portland (Oregon) Regional Counsel of the VA held that assets placed in a SNT were includible in the claimant's net worth for purposes of determining eligibility for a pension.[112] The trust in question was a first party

---

[112]   1997 VAOPGCPREC Lexis 656 (Aug. 29, 1997).

special needs trust prepared on behalf of the surviving spouse of a veteran, with a child serving as trustee.

At present, it appears that an SNT will not preserve eligibility for needs-based VA benefits. Although there are other strategies that can assist a veteran receive services. An SNT trustee should consult with a local veteran organization or seek the services of an attorney who is authorized to practice before the VA.

Chapter 4 Summary

- ✓ Understanding public benefits rules is one of the most important things a SNT trustee will need to understand when administering trust.
- ✓ Using common sense alone without understanding the rules will cause loss of eligibility and other problems for the SNT trustee and the SNT beneficiary.
- ✓ SSI and Medi-Cal are the two types of benefits a SNT trustee will need to understand very well.
- ✓ If SNT beneficiary receives Medi-Cal and not SSI then Medi-Cal rules must be followed and not Social Security Rules.
- ✓ SNT trustee should know if SNT beneficiary is receiving SSI and SSDI and Medi-Cal or Medicare.
- ✓ SSI and Medi-Cal are needs based benefits meaning that the SNT beneficiary can only have $2,000 in assets and very limited income.
- ✓ Not all of a SSI recipient's assets are counted, some are exempt, like a home of any value or car of any value, plus other assets.
- ✓ Disbursements from SNT by trustee can be counted as income for SSI eligibility.
- ✓ Cash given directly to SNT beneficiary will be counted as unearned income and reduce SSI benefit dollar for dollar after first $20.
- ✓ An SNT trustee paying for food or shelter is counted as in-kind support and maintenance income and will reduce SSI by a modest reduction of either $244.67 or $224.67 in 2011.
- ✓ There are a variety of ways to obtain eligibility for Medi-Cal, but the primary way for most persons with disabilities is eligibility for SSI.
- ✓ IHSS is a Medi-Cal paid for program that pays for in home care for persons with disabilities.
- ✓ Not all SNTs authorize payments for food or shelter depending on the terms of the document.

✓ The SSA has reporting requirements when the SSI recipient has a change of assets or income which must be done ten days into the next month after the change occurred.

✓ The SNT trustee may have a requirement to do reporting only if the SNT document requires it or the trustee is the beneficiary's representative payee.

✓ DHCS has reporting requirements when the Medi-Cal only recipient has a change of assets, income, address, or health-care coverage within ten days of the event.

✓ SNT beneficiary may also receive Social Security, SSDI, or Medicare but these benefits are entitlement benefits, meaning the SNT trustee cannot screw them up.

✓ SSI recipient may work and continue to receive benefits through different programs.

✓ Section 8 benefits may be affected if the SNT trustee makes regular recurring disbursements from the SNT.

✓ Not all Public Housing Agencies (PHAs) will count these disbursements.

✓ SNT trustee should assist SNT beneficiary who may be eligible for VA benefits to apply for pension, aid and assistance, and health care.

CHAPTER 5

Knowing How SNT Distributions Affect Public Benefits

A common question from SNT trustees to the author is, "Can I pay for [name any item or service under the sun] for my SNT beneficiary?" This chapter is designed to assist the trustee in making these decisions. Prior to making an actual disbursement, the trustee should also consult chapter 6 which describes the best way a disbursement can be made to reduce the impact on the beneficiary's public benefit eligibility.

> **Critical Pointer:** A common misconception of SNTs is that they are not useful, because they can only pay for a small number of items and services for the person with a disability. This is untrue. The SNT is designed to enhance the quality of life of the person with a disability. Thus, it can pay for any item or service that will do so. This includes everything on the planet that humans have come up with to make our lives easier or better. Given the large number of items and services out there, the SNT is really a wonderful tool that greatly improves the overall quality of life of a person with disabilities.

The universe of available SNT distributions is extraordinarily large and this chapter will not be able to cover every possible scenario, (although we try). In order to assist the trustee, there are a host of questions/answers in this chapter on the effect of different types of disbursements will have on beneficiary's public benefits. Attached as Appendix G is a decision-making tree that will provide a step-by-step analysis to determine whether a disbursement is acceptable or not. Attached as Appendix M, is a list of SNT permissible distributions of items and services that will not interfere with SSI or Medi-Cal—the so-called No-Brainer List.

Do Distributions from SNT Affect a Beneficiary's Eligibility for Public Benefits?

Yes. Disbursements from the SNT will affect eligibility in a variety of ways depending on the type of public benefits the beneficiary receives, what is purchased, and how it is purchased. Typically, disbursements that will reduce or eliminate beneficiary's public benefits will be treated by the Social Security Administration (SSA) as unearned income, in-kind support or maintenance (ISM), or as an available resource. Thus, the SNT trustee should be familiar with the SSI rules on assets and income, described in chapter 4. Once a trustee understands how disbursement may affect (or not affect) the beneficiary's eligibility for public benefits, disbursements can be made that will enhance the beneficiary's quality of life.

Even If an SNT Trustee Makes a Disbursement That Will Not Interfere with Public Benefits, Should the Distribution Be Made?

Not always. Just because a distribution will not interfere with public benefits, does not mean that it should automatically be made. The SNT trustee still has a fiduciary duty to maintain the trust for the benefit of the beneficiary. The trustee must consider whether the payment for this item or service meets with the overall budget for the beneficiary and is in the beneficiary's best interest.

> **Example:** The SNT trustee has $150,000 in trust. The beneficiary needs to have transportation and requests the purchase of a car. He has found his dream car, the Porsche 911 Turbo, with a price tag of $122,000. While the purchase of the car would not interfere with the beneficiary's public benefits (because it is an exempt resource), it may not be prudent to make such a disbursement, especially if the beneficiary has numerous other needed expenditures. Although, under the terms of the SNT and the public benefit eligibility requirements,

Kevin Urbatsch

technically, the SNT trustee would be in his legal rights to make this distribution without breaching his fiduciary duty. The trustee's decision may be different if the beneficiary has only months to live and has always dreamed of owning this type of Porsche.

WHERE CAN AN SNT TRUSTEE FIND HELP ON DISBURSEMENT REQUESTS?

If after reading this chapter, the SNT trustee is still confused on a specific distribution, chapter 11 provides different ways the trustee can find help typically by hiring a special needs planning attorney or benefits consultant to assist.

IS THERE A SYSTEMATIC WAY TO DECIDE IF AN SNT DISTRIBUTION WILL INTERFERE WITH SSI OR MEDI-CAL ELIGIBILITY?

In order to help the trustee determine what is an acceptable SNT distribution, we have provided a checklist in Appendix G to assist in making a decision on whether to make a distribution.

> **Note:** Built into the checklist is the presumption that the SNT trustee understands what SSI considers unearned income, in-kind support and maintenance (ISM), available resource, food, shelter, "sole benefit," and other important public benefit considerations. Thus, it is important that the SNT trustee use this checklist with a firm understanding of these various terms, which are discussed in chapter 4.

WHAT ARE THE SNT TRUSTEE'S LEGAL RIGHTS IN MAKING DECISIONS ABOUT DISTRIBUTIONS?

The SNT trustee will nearly always be given absolute discretion to make distributions on behalf of the beneficiary. This means the SNT trustee has the right to say yes or no to any distribution request. However, under California law, even when a trust instrument confers "absolute," "sole," or "uncontrolled" discretion, the trustee still must conform to fiduciary principles, which means that the trustee may not act in bad faith, and may not disregard the purposes of the trust.[113]

The SNT trustee should protect him or herself by keeping a log of all disbursement requests and indicate on the request his or her reasoning in accepting or rejecting each request.

> **Examples:** An SNT beneficiary makes a request to purchase cable service. The SNT trustee has full discretion on all distributions. The trustee denies the request because he believes the beneficiary watches too much television. The SNT trustee would be protected from being second guessed by the beneficiary or even a court, even if he is being unreasonable because he is not acting in bad faith or against the purpose of the trust. While the purchase of cable television will not interfere with public benefits and is otherwise an acceptable distribution, the SNT trustee still has discretion to make the decision on whether to buy it or not.
>
> However, assume that the SNT trustee refused to make any distributions at all from the SNT because he does not believe that people with disabilities should be provided any additional items or services not already provided by the government. The SNT trustee would be breaching his fiduciary duty and would be abusing his or her discretion. Because the SNT was established to provide items and services to enhance the quality of life of the beneficiary with a disability, the trustee refusing to make any distributions at all would be violating the whole intent and purpose of the terms of the trust and his or her failure to make any distributions would be considered bad faith.

---

[113] Probate Code §16081(a).

What Items or Services Cannot Be Purchased by an SNT Trustee?

In general, an SNT trustee cannot pay for items that are illegal or against public policy.[114] SNT disbursements may further be limited by the terms of the SNT document.

The SNT document may preclude the trustee from making certain specific types of disbursements. Some common examples include liquor, pornography, and cigarettes. As discussed in the next question and answer, if the SNT document precludes this type of disbursement, then the SNT trustee cannot make it.

A common misunderstanding is that an SNT cannot pay for food, clothing, or shelter. This is not true unless the SNT document forbids the disbursement. While the payment for these items may affect the amount of SSI or Medi-Cal a beneficiary may receive, a trustee may still pay for it. In fact, with a properly drafted SNT, these items are a common distribution from an SNT. For further discussion, see specific question/answer on paying for food and shelter in this chapter and in chapter 6.

An example of the broad authority an SNT trustee has in deciding on making disbursements is illustrated by describing how some SNT trustees have participated in authorizing services that are legal in one state and not another. One SNT trustee authorized a distribution for a beneficiary to travel to Nevada, where prostitution and gambling are legal, and was willing to pay for the trip and the services. Others have authorized distributions for marijuana when the beneficiary had a California medical marijuana card. While this is legal under California law, the federal government has not agreed that medical marijuana is legal. In both circumstances, the trustee made a decision as to whether the requested activity was legal or not. If a trustee is going to make this type of distribution, it would be prudent to have an attorney familiar with criminal law determine if the requested action is a violation of the criminal code. If a SNT trustee refused to make these types of distributions, he or she would not be abusing her discretion.

> **Critical Pointer:** Just because an SNT trustee may make certain types of disbursements does not necessarily mean he

---

[114] Probate Code §15203.

or she should. Many SNTs do not preclude an SNT trustee from distributing cash directly to a beneficiary. But an SNT trustee should query whether he or she should make that disbursement. The effect of doing so would be a loss of SSI and Medi-Cal with little benefit received for the beneficiary. For example, if the SNT trustee makes a $500 per month allowance to the beneficiary, the beneficiary would lose $480 from his or her SSI check. This only allows the beneficiary a modest amount of money ($20 per month) with an accompanying loss of SSI and the inability to invest the SNT assets distributed. This would be a terrible disbursement to make, even though there is no legal prohibition against it.

HOW OFTEN SHOULD THE SNT TRUSTEE REVIEW THE SNT TERMS BEFORE MAKING A DISTRIBUTION?

The SNT trustee should consider reviewing the SNT document every time a new disbursement request is made. An SNT trustee is obligated to administer the trust strictly by the documents terms.[115]

There are certain SNT provisions the trustee should know whether the SNT includes (or not):

(1) The SNT trustee must know if the SNT has a discretionary or supplemental distribution standard. For a discussion of these distribution standards, see chapter 2. If a supplemental distribution standard, the SNT trustee cannot pay for anything that will reduce SSI payments, like food or shelter items. If a discretionary distribution standard, the trustee is authorized to make such payments if doing so is in the best interests of the beneficiary.

(2) Most SNTs include a list a specific list of items and services that are generally acceptable to purchase. If the item is on that list, the trustee can be comfortable knowing that it is an authorized disbursement. Even when an item is not on the list, the trustee is not prevented from making that distribution if the document does not exclude it and it is in best interests of beneficiary.

---

[115] Probate Code §§16000, 16040(b), 16200.

> **Critical Pointer:** Even though an SNT may authorize a specific distribution, the SNT trustee is not required to make the distribution if, in his or her discretion, the purchase of the item or service is not acceptable for some reason. For example, if the SNT beneficiary wants a home but is requesting a mansion, the SNT trustee can deny this request even though the purchase of principal place of residence would not interfere with public benefit.

Finally, the SNT trustee should review the SNT's terms for items or services specifically not authorized. For example, some parents set up third-party SNTs for children that do not allow disbursements for cigarettes and alcohol, or they limit distributions to times when the beneficiary is drug free. The SNT trustee should be aware of any of these specific limitations in the trust document and must honor them.

WHAT DOES "SOLE BENEFIT" MEAN FOR FIRST-PARTY SNT DISTRIBUTIONS?

A requirement for a qualifying first party SNT is that it must be for the "sole benefit" of the beneficiary.[116] Generally, distributions for "sole benefit" mean that distributions have to provide a direct benefit to the beneficiary. For nearly all distributions, this will not be an issue, because the beneficiary is receiving the full benefit of the distribution.

> **Note:** This rule does not typically apply to third-party SNTs. However, some third-party SNTs may also include this limitation, either by design or by ignorance. If a third-party SNT includes a "sole benefit" limitation, the SNT trustee must honor it. To determine the distinction between first and third party SNTs, see chapter 2.

The tougher decision on whether a disbursement is for beneficiary's "sole benefit" is when a distribution may possibly benefit persons other than the beneficiary. This may happen when a distribution is made for an item that other

---

[116] POMS SI 01120.203(B)(1)(e).

people can use, like an automobile or television. Thus far in California, as long as the distribution provides some benefit to the beneficiary, it is acceptable, even if others may derive some benefit from the distribution.

> **Example:** An SNT makes a distribution for the purchase of a salt water spa for a beneficiary who has cerebral palsy. The beneficiary lives with his parents. While the spa may benefit the parents, who may use it in the future, it is of primary benefit for the beneficiary and would meet California's definition of sole benefit.

> **Note:** In other states, the "sole benefit" rule is strictly interpreted. In those states, no disbursements can be made if someone else derives any benefit from the disbursement. It is important to keep up on any developments in this area in California. One way to do so is to join the author's Special Needs News monthly e-newsletter which can be done by going to the author's website, at www.MyersUrbatsch.com.

CAN SNT TRUSTEE MAKE GIFTS TO BENEFICIARY'S FRIENDS OR FAMILY OR DONATIONS TO CHURCH OR CHARITIES?

The answer depends on which type of SNT is being administered.

- For first-party SNTs the answer is always no. Gifts to friends or families and donations to charities are strictly prohibited, because these distributions are not made for the "sole benefit" of the beneficiary. If the first-party SNT authorizes these disbursements, it would not be a valid SNT.[117]
- For third-party SNTs, the answer is maybe. It will depend on the terms of the trust document. If the SNT's terms allow gifts or donations to be made, then these distributions can be made without interfering with public benefits eligibility.

---

[117] 42 U.S.C. §1382b(c)(1)(C)(ii)(IV); POMS SI 01120.203(B)(1)(e).

> **Note:** To determine the distinction between first and third party SNTs, see chapter 2.

WHAT IS THE EFFECT ON A BENEFICIARY'S SECTION 8 ELIGIBILITY WHEN MAKING SNT DISBURSEMENTS?

It depends on which county the beneficiary resides in and the type of disbursement.

SNTs and Section 8 are not fully compatible. Under Section 8, recipients receive a "voucher" or "subsidy" that they can apply to the rental of the housing unit of their choice—as long as the unit meets the Section 8 program requirements. A local Public Housing Agency (PHA) then delivers the subsidy to the landlord under a contract with the US Department of Housing and Urban Development (HUD). The recipient pays a portion of the monthly rent, based on the recipient's adjusted income, and the PHA subsidy pays the remainder.

The existence of the SNT itself has no impact on eligibility for Section 8. However, several California PHAs are now using the HUD regulations to increase a recipient's total tenant payment or eliminate Section 8 altogether. These PHA's have interpreted HUD regulations to mean that any SNT distribution will be counted as Section 8 income to a recipient, unless the distribution meets one of HUD's definitions of exempt income.[118] The most useful types of Section 8—exempt income (with the most helpful of all in bold typeface) for SNT beneficiaries are as follows:

- Medical Expense Reimbursements: Amounts received by the family that are specifically for, or in reimbursement of, the cost of medical expenses for any family member.
- PASS Amounts: Amounts received by a person with a disability that are disregarded for a limited time for purposes of Supplemental Security Income eligibility and benefits because they are set aside for use under a plan for achieving self-support (PASS).
- Reimbursements: Amounts received by a participant in other publicly assisted programs that are specifically for or in reimbursement of out-of-pocket expenses incurred (special equipment, clothing,

---

[118] HUD Voucher Guidebook §5.2, Exhibit 5-2, Income Inclusions (7), (9), and Exhibit 5-3, Assets Included (11).

transportation, child care, etc.) and which are made solely to allow participation in a specific program.

- **Temporary, nonrecurring or sporadic income (including gifts).**
- Deferred SSI or SSDI: Deferred periodic amounts from supplemental security income and social security benefits that are received in a lump sum amount or in prospective monthly amounts.
- DD Assistance: Amounts paid by a state agency to a family with a member who has a developmental disability and is living at home to offset the cost of services and equipment needed to keep the developmentally disabled family member at home.

If a trustee learns that a PHA in the beneficiary's county is taking this position, it might be a good idea to see if the PHA will provide a reasonable accommodation for a person with a disability by not counting the SNT disbursements as income. Federal fair housing laws require that HUD and PHAs make reasonable accommodations in their policies, procedures, and programs to ensure active participation by people with disabilities. For further discussion of Section 8 housing, see chapter 4.

If a trustee has a Section 8 recipient and is concerned that the PHA in the beneficiary's county is enforcing these rules, he or she should review chapter 6 to learn how best to distribute SNT assets on behalf of a Section 8 recipient.

> **Example**: Mitsie O'Brien is a person with a disability and recipient of Section 8 housing who is beneficiary of a first party SNT. If the trustee distributes $250 a month from the SNT to pay Ms. O'Brien's transportation costs and $1,000 for a television set, the $250 will be counted as annual income, because it does not meet one of the income exclusions for Section 8. The result is an increase in Ms. O'Brien share of payment of Section 8 housing of around $75 per month (roughly $250 recurring payment of which 30 percent is used to pay her share of rent). The $1,000 payment for the television set is not counted, because it would meet the definition for exempt income of a temporary or nonrecurring distribution from the SNT.

> **Critical Pointer**: Many public housing agencies (PHAs) are unfamiliar with these rules and have not (and in many cases

are still not) enforcing them. For many years, special needs attorneys reported little to no interference with Section 8 when establishing and administering SNTs. Recently, however, a few county PHAs throughout California are taking the position that every distribution from a first-party SNT will be counted as a Section 8 recipient's income. A SNT trustee should check with local special needs attorneys to see if the county where the beneficiary resides is enforcing these rules and, if so, should review chapter 6 to learn how best to distribute SNT assets on behalf of a Section 8 recipient and chapter 11 to find a local special needs planning attorney.

Note: A recent California case may be used to avoid the result above. In *Finley v. City of Santa Monica* (Cal. Sup. Ct. County of Los Angeles, No. BS 127077, May 25, 2011), a California trial court determined that distributions of principal from a special needs trust are not countable income for purposes of calculating a Section 8 recipient's rent because the principal of the trust would not be a countable asset if held directly by the Section 8 recipient. This is great news for SNT beneficiaries who also receive Section 8. Check the author's website for further discussions on this topic.

WHAT IS THE EFFECT OF A TRUSTEE BUYING EXEMPT ASSETS, GOODS, OR RESOURCES FOR BENEFICIARY?

There is no effect on public benefits when an SNT purchases an exempt asset for a beneficiary. The beneficiary is allowed to have certain exempt resources, which are excluded from the SSI and Medi-Cal resource limits of $2000 for an individual and $3,000 for an eligible couple.[119] These exempt assets are not counted in determining eligibility, and the beneficiary's ownership of them will not jeopardize his or her SSI benefits. Therefore, the trustee may purchase exempt assets for the beneficiary and they can own these items in their own name without interfering with benefits.

The following assets are exempt by law:

---

[119] 20 C.F.R. §416.1205(c).

- A home, including the land on which the home stands and other buildings on that land, if the beneficiary lives in it or intends to return to it.[120] If the beneficiary does not receive SSI but does receive Medi-Cal, the home's assessed value may be limited to $750,000.
- Household goods (which include, but are not limited to, furniture, appliances, electronic equipment such as personal computers and television sets, carpets, cooking and eating utensils, and dishes) and personal effects (which include, but are not limited to, personal jewelry including wedding and engagement rings, personal care items, prosthetic devices, wheelchairs, and educational or recreational items such as books and musical instruments) regardless of value.[121] The rules now defines household goods as items of personal property, found in or near a home, that are used on a regular basis, or items needed by the homeowner for maintenance, use, and occupancy of the home and defines personal items as items of personal property that ordinarily are worn or carried by the individual, or are things that otherwise have an intimate relation to the individual.
- One automobile (or other vehicle) of unlimited value if used for transportation for the individual or a member of the individual's household.[122]
- Life insurance with a cash surrender value, if its face value is less than $1500, and all term life insurance.[123]
- A burial plot, or other burial space, of any value.[124]
- A revocable burial fund, worth up to $1500.[125]

---

[120] 20 C.F.R. §416.1212.

[121] POMS SI 01130.430; 20 C.F.R. §416.1216. Old rules limited the dollar value of these items but regulations effective March 9, 2005 eliminated the dollar value limit for household goods and personal effects. See 70 Fed Reg 6344; 20 C.F.R. §416.1102.

[122] 20 C.F.R. §416.1218. Regulations effective March 9, 2005 eliminated the dollar value limit of an automobile. See 70 Fed Reg 6344; 20 C.F.R. §416.1102. It had previously been limited in value to $4500.

[123] 20 C.F.R. §416.1230.

[124] 20 C.F.R. §416.1231.

[125] 20 C.F.R. §416.1231(b).

WHAT IS THE EFFECT OF A TRUSTEE PAYING FOR ASSETS, GOODS, OR RESOURCES NOT IDENTIFIED AS EXEMPT ASSETS?

It depends. If the trustee buys the item and distributes it to the beneficiary who owns it, he or she may lose eligibility for SSI or Medi-Cal depending on value of item. If instead, the trustee purchase this type of item and owns it in the SNT's name, it will not affect eligibility for public benefits.

> **Example**: SNT trustee is asked to purchase a car for the beneficiary, who is receiving SSI and Medi-Cal. The beneficiary already owns one car in his name. The SNT trustee may still purchase a second car for the beneficiary, but the title must be in the name of the SNT. The beneficiary is only allowed to own one car in his name without interfering with his SSI and Medi-Cal. A second car owned by the SNT will not count as the beneficiary's resource or asset for public benefit eligibility purposes.

WHAT IS THE EFFECT OF PAYING FOR SERVICES FOR THE BENEFICIARY?

It depends. If the trustee pays the service vendors directly for services (that are not considered food or shelter), the distribution will have no impact on public benefit eligibility.[126] Some examples of these services include telephone, cable, Internet access, recreation, vehicle costs (maintenance, insurance, and registration if SNT includes an automobile), hair care, pet care, and many others.

> **Example**: SNT trustee is asked to pay for the beneficiary's cable, phone, Internet, house cleaning, and lawn care. The SNT trustee may purchase all of these services by paying the vendors directly. None of these items will have any effect on the beneficiary's eligibility for SSI or Medi-Cal, because they cannot

---

[126] POMS SI 00815.400.

be used to offset his or her need for food or shelter and are not medical care costs covered by Medi-Cal.

Note: See Appendix M for a more complete list of available items and services that may be purchased without interfering with beneficiary's public benefits—the "No-Brainer" list.

Warning: A SNT trustee should not reimburse beneficiary for services the beneficiary paid for, even if those services would have been considered exempt if paid by the SNT trustee. If the SNT trustee reimburses the SSI recipient/beneficiary, the amount of SSI will be reduced as "unearned income."

What Is the Effect of Paying for a Beneficiary's Medical Needs?

It depends. The trustee is authorized to pay for beneficiary's medical needs that are not already being paid for by Medi-Cal or other public benefit programs. This disbursement will always be exempt from consideration as income under the SSI program and most other public programs.[127]

As a result, the purchase of any good or medical service for the SNT beneficiary not already available through Medi-Cal or another public benefit program that can be justified by a medical authority's order will not cause a reduction in SSI benefit levels. The term "medical authority" is broadly interpreted and includes, in addition to medical doctors, many other health-care providers, such as podiatrists, chiropractors, physical therapists, and psychologists. Other common distributions that can be made include dental work, acupuncture, and massage expenses.

> **Example**: SNT trustee is asked to pay for the beneficiary's monthly massage. The SNT trustee may purchase this service by paying the vendor directly. This item items will have no effect on the beneficiary's eligibility for SSI or Medi-Cal, because Medi-Cal does not pay for this service.

---

[127]   See 20 C.F.R. §416.1103(b).

Example: A first-party SNT trustee is asked by beneficiary's mother to purchase a treadmill for her son, the beneficiary. Her son used a wheelchair for mobility and was unable to walk. Mother said her son was like Christopher Reeves and that it was part of his therapy. The SNT trustee asked for a prescription from a medical professional that authorized this treatment. The mother could not provide the prescription, so the SNT trustee refused, because such a distribution would violate the "sole benefit" terms of the SNT.

WHAT IS EFFECT OF DISBURSING CASH TO AN SNT BENEFICIARY WHO RECEIVES SSI OR MEDI-CAL?

The disbursement of cash to an SNT beneficiary will reduce the amount of the monthly check from SSI or create (or increase) a share-of-cost for Medi-Cal, depending on whether the SNT beneficiary receives SSI or only Medi-Cal.

For the SNT beneficiary who is receiving SSI, providing cash of over $20 per month to a SSI beneficiary is nearly always a bad idea. If the beneficiary is on SSI, any cash provided to the beneficiary will be treated as SSI unearned income and reduce the SSI check dollar-for-dollar after the first $20 given.[128]

For the beneficiary who does not receive SSI, but still receives Medi-Cal, distributing cash directly to the beneficiary will increase the beneficiary's Medi-Cal share-of-cost.[129]

Example: The SNT beneficiary is receiving $830 per month from SSI. The SNT trustee decides to give the beneficiary $500 per month as an allowance to supplement the SSI. The effect of the monthly cash disbursement is a loss of SSI of $480. Thus, the beneficiary only receives an extra $20 per month of spending cash but has lost $480 per month from his SNT that could have been used to pay for acceptable items and services.

Example: The SNT beneficiary is receiving Medi-Cal as a medically needy person, but not SSI. The SNT trustee decides

---

[128] POMS SI 00810.420, 01120.200(E)(1)(a).
[129] 22 Cal Code Regs §§50503, 50507.

to give the beneficiary $500 per month as an allowance. The effect of the monthly cash disbursement is that the $500 per month will be counted as Medi-Cal income and will be calculated as part of the beneficiary's share-of-cost requirement. Thus, the beneficiary (depending on his other income) may have to pay an additional $500 per month toward his medical care before Medi-Cal will cover his or her medical costs.

WHAT IS THE EFFECT OF PAYING FOR A BENEFICIARY'S FOOD, SHELTER, AND UTILITIES IF RECEIVING SSI OR MEDI-CAL?

It depends. If the beneficiary is an SSI recipient, his or her monthly SSI benefit will be reduced (or possibly eliminated) by the application of SSI in-kind support and maintenance (ISM) income and the presumed maximum value (PMV) calculation. See chapter 4 for a more thorough description of ISM and PMV.

If the beneficiary is a Medi-Cal only recipient (meaning eligible for Medi-Cal without also receiving SSI) then, if done correctly, the payment of food, clothing, and shelter will have no impact on public benefits. If done incorrectly, it could create an increase in the share-of-cost paid to Medi-Cal. See chapter 4 for a more thorough description of share-of-cost Medi-Cal.

Beneficiary Receives SSI:

SSI counts as ISM both payments from an SNT of the beneficiary's food and shelter. SSI shelter is defined as mortgage payments (including property insurance required by the mortgage holder); real property taxes (less any tax rebates or credits); rent; heating fuel; gas; electricity; water; sewer; and garbage removal.

> **Example:** A beneficiary is receiving $830 of SSI per month and has been paying for all of his food or shelter from his SSI check. He wants to move to a safer neighborhood but to do so his rent will increase to $1,200 per month. It is obvious he cannot afford to pay it from his SSI check and asks the SNT trustee to pay the rent. The payment of rent by the SNT will be counted as ISM. ISM reduces the beneficiary's SSI check by the PMV rule. This rule would reduce the beneficiary's SSI check

by a maximum of $244.67 per month in year 2011 (1/3 of the federal portion of the SSI check + $20 any income exclusion). Meaning, the beneficiary will continue to receive $585.33 per month from SSI, pay no rent, and live in a safe apartment in a nice neighborhood. This is a good result.

However, if the beneficiary had been receiving SSI in the amount of $220 per month before receiving payment of food and shelter from the SNT, then the trustee's payment of rent would completely eliminate the beneficiary's SSI eligibility under the PMV rules. This is because the deduction of $244.67 for PMV applies in full and would reduce the SSI check to zero. This means that the loss of SSI will also cause a loss of SSI eligible Medi-Cal[130] and that paying food or shelter may not be in the beneficiary's best interest in this scenario.

Beneficiary Receives Medi-Cal (but not SSI):

If the beneficiary is receiving Medi-Cal (but not SSI), then it is still possible for the SNT trustee to pay for a certain percentage of the beneficiary's food, clothing, shelter, and utilities without interfering with Medi-Cal eligibility. If the SNT trustee pays the entire amount of need for these items, DHCS will count that as Medi-Cal in-kind income which would create an increase in the share-of-cost owed by beneficiary.[131] Share of cost is like a co-pay for private health insurance.

> **Example:** SNT beneficiary is receiving Medi-Cal (but not SSI) and wants the SNT trustee to pay for his food, utilities, clothing, and rent, which total $2,500 per month. If the SNT trustee pays the entire $2,500, it would be counted as in-kind income by Medi-Cal and increase the beneficiary's share-of-cost by $2,500. This would result in the beneficiary having to pay $2,500 for his medical care covered by Medi-Cal before it would begin to pay covered medical services—generally not a good

---

[130] It is possible that the beneficiary could receive another type of Medi-Cal, so even paying food or shelter here may be appropriate. It is best to review these types of situations with a special needs planning attorney or benefits counselor.

[131] 22 C.C.R. §50509.

result. If however, the SNT trustee pays for some (but not all) of the beneficiary's food, clothing, utilities, or rent, then there is no effect on the beneficiary's Medi-Cal.

Practitioners differ in their advice on how much the trustee should pay. Technically, it is possible to pay up to 99.99 percent of the cost. However, it may be more prudent to pay something around 75 percent—not for any legal reason, but just because it looks better.

The ability to pay for a beneficiary's food or shelter will depend on the type of distribution standard the SNT has. If the distribution standard is discretionary, meaning distributions can be made that may reduce or even eliminate public benefits, and the beneficiary is on SSI, then it is possible for the trustee to make a distribution for food or shelter. If the distribution standard is supplemental, meaning a distribution cannot reduce or eliminate public benefit eligibility and the beneficiary is on SSI, then the trustee cannot make such a distribution. See chapter 2 to determine which type of distribution standard the SNT has.

> **Example:** A beneficiary is receiving $830 of SSI per month and has been paying for all his food or shelter from his SSI check. He wants to move to a safer neighborhood, but to do so will increase his rent $1,200 per month. It is obvious he cannot afford to pay it from his SSI check and asks the SNT trustee to pay the rent. The SNT trustee reviews the SNT distribution standard and determines it is a supplemental standard, meaning that the trustee is prevented from making any distributions that would reduce or eliminate public benefit eligibility. Because the payment of rent would reduce or eliminate SSI, the trustee is prohibited from making this distribution. If living in a safer neighborhood is of great importance, the SNT trustee may wish to petition a court to modify the distribution standard to allow a discretionary distribution standard. A description of this procedure is described in chapter 11.

What Is the Effect of Paying for a Beneficiary's Clothes If the Beneficiary Is Receiving Either SSI or Medi-Cal?

Paying for the beneficiary's clothing has no effect on SSI eligibility. This is a change from prior law. Before 2005, paying for clothing was considered the same as paying for food or shelter and treated as "in-kind support and maintenance" (ISM) income, but these rules changed and clothing was taken off the list.[132] Thus, the trustee can purchase all the clothing the beneficiary could need without interfering with SSI eligibility.

However, if the SNT beneficiary receives Medi-Cal only (and not SSI) then the purchase of beneficiary's clothes may result in an increase in the share-of-cost to receive Medi-Cal.[133] However, as long as the SNT trustee did not pay for *all* of the beneficiary's clothing, the purchase of clothes would not impact Medi-Cal eligibility at all.

What Is the Effect of Paying a Beneficiary's Credit Card Bill?

If a trustee pays a credit card bill for a beneficiary who is eligible for SSI, the effect on public benefits will depend on whether the credit card bill includes items that are considered SSI food or shelter. If the trustee pays for food or shelter items on the bill, the beneficiary will be charged with SSI in-kind support and maintenance (ISM) up to the presumed maximum value (PMV), meaning that the beneficiary will lose $244.67 of SSI payment for the month of payment. ISM and PMV are discussed in detail in chapter 4.

> **Note**: SSI counts as ISM, food, or shelter. Shelter is defined as (mortgage payments [including property insurance required by the mortgage holder], real property taxes [less any tax rebates or credits], rent, heating fuel, gas, electricity, water, sewer, and garbage removal).

---

[132] Regulations effective March 9, 2005, eliminated "clothing" from the definition of income and from the definition of in-kind support and maintenance. See 20 C.F.R. §416.1102.

[133] 22 C.C.R. §50509.

If the credit card bill includes nonfood, nonshelter items, the beneficiary's public benefits are not affected by the payment. The only exception would be if the item purchased would be a countable resource in the following month, like a second car in the name of the beneficiary.

> **Example**: SNT trustee is asked to pay for beneficiary's credit card bill. The bill includes food purchases of $250 and clothing purchase of $300. The SNT trustee can either just pay the $300 for the clothing and have no impact on the beneficiary's public benefits or pay for the entire amount and have the $250 food purchase counted as ISM income.

WHAT IS THE EFFECT ON A BENEFICIARY'S SSI OF PURCHASING GIFT CARDS OR GIFT CERTIFICATES?

The effect on SSI will depend on the type of gift card or gift certificate. A gift card or gift certificate will have no effect on public benefits if the card or certificate

1. cannot be used to purchase food or shelter (like a Macy's or Best Buy); and
2. cannot be resold.[134]

Absent evidence to the contrary, the SSA will presume a gift card or gift certificate can be resold. For example, evidence to the contrary may include a legally enforceable prohibition on resale or transfer of the card imposed by the card issuer or merchant printed on the card. Obtaining a gift card or gift certificate that complies with the rules are difficult (if not impossible) to obtain.

Further, if the gift card or certificate is held until the first day of the next calendar month, it will be counted as a resource. This means the unspent value of the card or certificate will be counted against the $2,000 resource limit for an individual or $3,000 for a couple.

> **Warning:** If a gift card or certificate can be used to buy food or shelter (e.g., restaurant, grocery store, or Visa gift card) or does not have a legal prohibition against resale, it is *not* treated

---

[134]   POMS SI 00830.522.

as ISM but rather as unearned income in the month of receipt. Thus, if a gift card is given to a beneficiary with a value of $500, which can be used to pay for food (e.g., at Wal-Mart, because it includes a grocery store), the beneficiary would lose $480 per month from her SSI check under the unearned income rules.

Example: Trustee distributes a Best Buy gift card worth $2,500 to the beneficiary. There is a restriction on the resale of the gift card. In the month of distribution, there is no effect on beneficiary's public benefits. Best Buy does not sell food or shelter items, so it will not be treated as unearned income. However, if the value of the card is not spent down so that all the beneficiary's resources are below $2,000 by the first day of the next calendar month, he or she would lose SSI in the next calendar month and for each month thereafter until done so.

Example: Trustee distributes a Wal-Mart gift card worth $2,500 to the beneficiary, who receives SSI in the amount of $830 per month. There is a restriction on the resale of the gift card. However, Wal-Mart stores sell groceries. SSA will treat the gift card at its face value as unearned income in the month it is received, meaning that the beneficiary's SSI will be lost in the month of distribution (after first $20 reduction of dollar for dollar on benefits).

If the beneficiary only spends $500 in the month of receipt, then the $2,000 balance will be counted as a resource on the first day of the next calendar month. Any remaining value on the card is a resource beginning the month following the month the gift card was received, meaning that if the card is not spent down so that all the beneficiary's resources are below $2,000, he or she would lose SSI in the next calendar month and the following months until done so.

WHAT IS THE EFFECT ON SSI OF PURCHASING A HOME OUTRIGHT WITH TRUST ASSETS?

There is a modest impact on beneficiary's SSI payment if a home is purchased outright for the beneficiary as his or her principal residence when using an SNT's assets. The home purchase would be considered SSI income in the form of in-kind support and maintenance (ISM) in the month of purchase only. This means that the beneficiary would lose SSI of $244.67 (in 2011) for only the month of purchase. This is true even if title to the home was held in the name of the beneficiary or in the name of the SNT. Subsequently, the beneficiary's SSI would *not* be reduced by ISM for as long as he or she lived in the home as his or her principal residence.

If the home is purchased outright in the name of the beneficiary, after the first month of ISM, the home will have no effect on the beneficiary's public benefits as long as it remains the beneficiary's principal residence. This is because a principal place of residence is an exempt asset for SSI and Medi-Cal eligibility purposes.[135]

> **Example**: The SNT trustee pays $600,000 for a home on August 2011 and title is held in the name of the beneficiary. The beneficiary would lose $244.67 (the 2011 PMV amount) of SSI in August 2011 as ISM. Going forward, the SNT beneficiary may live in the home without any further reduction of SSI.

If the home is purchased outright in the name of the SNT, the SSA considers the SNT beneficiary to have an "equitable ownership under a trust."[136] This means that the home purchase would be considered ISM income in the month of purchase only; or a one-month SSI reduction of $244.67 (in 2011). After the initial month, the SNT beneficiary may live in the home rent free without it being considered ISM.[137]

> **Example**: If the SNT trustee purchases a home for $500,000, the SNT beneficiary would lose $244.67 (the 2011 PMV amount)

---

[135]   20 C.F.R. §§416.1210(a), 416.1212.

[136]   POMS SI 01120.200(F)(1).

[137]   POMS SI 01120.200(F)(2).

of SSI in the month of purchase as ISM. Going forward, the SNT beneficiary may live in the home rent free without any further reduction of SSI.

Pointer: See chapter 6 for a description on how best to purchase a home and hold title.

WHAT IS THE EFFECT ON SSI OF PURCHASING A HOME WITH A MORTGAGE?

If the home is purchased with a mortgage and title is held in the name of the SNT, the payment of the mortgage will be treated as in-kind support and maintenance (ISM) in the form of shelter in the month of the purchase.[138] The subsequent monthly mortgage payments will also result in the receipt of income in the form of ISM, each valued at no more than the presumed maximum value (PMV).[139]

Example: If the SNT trustee purchases a home for $500,000 with a down payment and a mortgage with monthly payments of $1,800 for twenty years, the SNT beneficiary would lose $244.67 (the 2011 PMV amount) of SSI in the month of purchase as ISM. Going forward, each and every month the mortgage is paid, the SNT beneficiary would also lose $244.67 a month as ISM (or that year's current PMV rate).

Warning: It is nearly impossible to find a lender who will provide a mortgage to a trust. The only available lenders are generally private money lenders, who will charge a very high rate of interest, which makes it uneconomical to purchase a home from an SNT with a mortgage.

See chapter 6 for a description on how best to purchase a home and hold title.

---

[138] POMS SI 01120.200(F)(3)(b).
[139] POMS SI 01120.200(F)(3)(b).

WHAT IS THE EFFECT ON SSI OF SELLING A BENEFICIARY'S HOME?

If the principal residence of the beneficiary is sold and title is held by the SNT (either first party or third party), then there is no effect on SSI. The assets will still be held in the exempt SNT and not affect the beneficiary's SSI eligibility.[140]

However, if the beneficiary sells the principal residence when title is held in his or her name, the proceeds of the home sale will be an available resource if not spent within three month on a new primary residence.[141] If there are remaining assets from the purchase of a new primary residence, the beneficiary can then either fund the assets to a first party SNT or spend down these asset to below $2,000 for an individual or $3,000 for a couple.

> **Example:** Beneficiary has been residing in home owned in beneficiary's name as her primary residence. She decides to sell the home to buy a smaller one. She nets $500,000 from the sale. She buys a new home within two months for $200,000. The $300,000 will be counted as an available resource for SSI purposes unless otherwise spent down or transferred to a first party SNT.
>
> If it took more than three months to buy a new home, the entire $500,000 would be counted as an available resource of beneficiary and she would lose her SSI.
>
> If the SNT had owned the home and made the sale, the entire $500,000 would remain exempt at all times for SSI eligibility purposes.

WHAT IS THE EFFECT OF RENTING OUT ROOMS IN THE BENEFICIARY'S PRINCIPAL RESIDENCE?

The effect of renting out rooms in the beneficiary's principal residence depends on who owns the property.

---

[140] POMS SI 01120.200(F)(1). POMS SI 01120.201(I)(1)(b) (first party SNT), SI 01120.200(F) (third party SNT).

[141] POMS SI 01130.110.

1. If the SNT owns the primary residence, then rental income will have no effect on the beneficiary's public benefits. The SNT is an exempt asset—and that includes any income earned from trust assets.
2. If the beneficiary owns his or her own residence, the rental income will count as unearned income.[142] This means that for every dollar of rent received (after the first $20) will reduce the SSI check dollar for dollar.

If the home is owned by the beneficiary, the beneficiary may deduct certain expenses (up to the pro-rata share of home rented) to reduce the effect the rent will have on the beneficiary's SSI for the following:

*   interest and escrow portions of a mortgage payment (at the point the payment is made to the mortgage holder);
*   real estate insurance
*   repairs (i.e., minor correction to an existing structure);
*   property taxes;
*   lawn care;
*   snow removal; advertising for tenants; and
*   utilities.[143]

There are also certain nondeductible expenses:

*   principle portion of a mortgage payment; and
*   capital expenditures (i.e., an expense for an addition or increase in the value of property which is subject to depreciation for income tax purposes).[144]

> **Example:** The SNT beneficiary owns a primary residence with six rooms. He rents to his cousin one room for $1,000 per month. The total allowable expense deduction for the rental is $300 per month. However, because the renter only rents 1/6 of the home, the deduction is reduced to 1/6 of the expense

---

[142]   POMS SI 00830.505(A)(4).

[143]   POMS SI 00830.505(A)(11).

[144]   POMS SI 00830.505(A)(12).

deduction, or $50. Thus, the SNT beneficiary will lose $930 from his or her SSI each month during the rental. The calculation is $1,000 rent—$50 allowable deduction—$20 one time exclusion = $930. Because in year 2011, the maximum SSI authorized for an individual is $830 per month, this SNT beneficiary would lose his or her SSI and will then lose his or her categorical eligibility for Medi-Cal.

If the beneficiary is a Medi-Cal-only recipient and the home is owned in the name of the beneficiary, the beneficiary who has income from real property may deduct certain expenses from gross rents. These deductions include property taxes and assessments, mortgage interest payments, insurance, utilities, and upkeep and repairs.[145] The principal on a mortgage is not deductible.[146]

WHAT IS THE EFFECT OF MAKING HOME MODIFICATIONS OWNED BY A BENEFICIARY OR SNT?

Making modifications to the beneficiary's principal place of residence will have no impact on a beneficiary's public benefits. When SNT pays for improvements or renovations to the beneficiary's principal place of residence, the beneficiary does not receive income, even if the home is in the name of the beneficiary. Disbursements from the trust for improvements increase the value of the home and, unlike other household operating expenses, do not provide in-kind support and maintenance (ISM).[147]

Moreover, making home modifications to a home owned by the SNT will have no impact on public benefits. It merely increases the value of an asset owned in a qualifying SNT.

> **Example:** SNT trustee pays $45,000 for renovations to the beneficiary's bathroom to make it handicap accessible, to install a wheelchair ramp for accessibility, and to fix the roof. There is no effect on the beneficiary's SSI benefits. The home

---

[145]   22 Cal Code Regs §50508.

[146]   22 Cal Code Regs §50508(a)(1)(B).

[147]   POMS SI 01120.200(F)(3)(c).

modifications are not considered income or ISM and as a result will not reduce the beneficiary's SSI check at all.

What Is the Effect of Making Home Modifications to a Home Owned by Someone Else?

There should be no effect on SSI or Medi-Cal when modifying a home owned by someone other than beneficiary or the SNT. However, there may be an issue if the disbursement is made from a first-party SNT and the disbursement could be considered not for the "sole benefit" of the beneficiary. As discussed in chapter 4, a first-party SNT's assets must be used for the "sole benefit" of the beneficiary. The distinctions between acceptable purchases and those that may trigger a penalty can be quite narrow, and different facts will have different results. It is strongly recommended that the trustee consult an experienced special needs practitioner in making this type of determination.

In order to make a first party SNT disbursement acceptable, the trustee should make sure there are protections in place to preserve beneficiary's rights. Some possible issues that could arise include the homeowner selling the property or the homeowner dying and heirs evicting the person with a beneficiary. Other possible issues include unforeseen creditor issues of the homeowner or even foreclosures. In order to protect against these issues, a trustee could require a life estate in the property or an occupancy agreement binding on heirs and owners that legally allows the beneficiary to reside in the home for life. The trustee could obtain co-ownership in the home or characterize the distribution as a loan on the property and take a secured interest in the home.

> **Example:** First-party SNT trustee is asked to pay for a new roof to the beneficiary's parents' home, where the beneficiary lives. The modification, while likely required for the beneficiary's safety, is not truly for the beneficiary's "sole benefit," because a roof repair is typically for the benefit of the property's owners. In this case, it is likely the distribution would not be treated as for the sole benefit of beneficiary. However, if the trustee agreed to make disbursement in exchange for a percentage ownership in home equal to the disbursement amount in relation to overall value of property, then it should qualify as an acceptable disbursement as an investment of the SNT.

Example: First-party SNT trustee is asked to pay for modifications to a bathroom in a home where the beneficiary is renting an apartment. The modifications are required for the beneficiary's safety. In this case, the distribution would be for the "sole benefit" of beneficiary as its primary purpose is to provide a direct benefit to the beneficiary.

See chapter 6 for suggestions on making this type of distribution while at the same time providing some protections for the beneficiary.

WHAT IS THE EFFECT OF BUYING A CAR, SECOND CAR, RECREATIONAL VEHICLE, OR BOAT?

The purchase of an automobile (and even distribution of title to the automobile to the SNT beneficiary) will not affect public benefits eligibility as long as it is the beneficiary's *only* automobile, because one automobile of any value is an exempt resource.[148]

See chapter 6 for a description on how best to purchase an automobile and hold title.

There is a broad definition of the term "automobile." The SSA defines it to mean any registered or unregistered vehicle used for transportation. Vehicles used for transportation include but are not limited to cars, trucks, motorcycles, boats, snowmobiles, animal-drawn vehicles, and even animals.[149] However, the primary purpose of the "automobile" must be for transportation and not pleasure. The following vehicles do not meet the definition of an automobile:

- A vehicle that has been junked
- A vehicle that is used only as a recreational vehicle (e.g., a boat used on weekends for pleasure)[150]

Thus, if the beneficiary does not own a vehicle, the trustee could purchase one and distribute it to the beneficiary, who could own it in his or her name.

---

[148] 20 C.F.R. §§416.1210(c), 416.1218; 22 Cal Code Regs §50461(a).

[149] POMS SI 01130.200(B)(1).

[150] POMS SI 01130.200(C)(3).

If the SNT trustee wants to purchase a boat to be used for pleasure or purchase a second automobile, motorcycle, truck, snowmobile, etc., the trustee can do so even if the beneficiary already owns another vehicle by holding title in the name of the SNT. The SNT trustee cannot purchase these items and distribute them to beneficiary, because they would be counted as resources. Because the individual beneficiary is limited to $2,000 in resources and $3,000 for a couple, the purchase of these items would disqualify him or her from SSI.

> **Example:** SNT trustee has already purchased a modified van for beneficiary. The beneficiary owns the van in his name. There is no effect on SSI of having distributed the modified van to the beneficiary. Now the beneficiary would like to purchase a boat to be used for fishing on the weekends. The trustee can purchase the boat but must hold title in the name of the SNT. A distribution of the boat to the beneficiary in his name would be counted as an available resource.

WHAT IS THE EFFECT OF PAYING FOR THE BENEFICIARY'S CAREGIVERS?

A common request to the SNT trustee is to use assets to pay for a caregiver to assist the beneficiary. This type of care will have no effect on the beneficiary's public benefits, except in one circumstance: when the request is to supplement the pay of the beneficiary's In-Home Supportive Services (IHSS) worker. See next question for the effect this distribution will have.

See chapter 6 for a thorough discussion of hiring caregivers

WHAT IS THE EFFECT OF HIRING AND IHSS WORKER AS A CAREGIVER?

The In-Home Supportive Services (IHSS) program provides in-home and nonmedical personal care services to persons with disabilities to enable them to remain in their homes. The services available through the IHSS program include routine house cleaning, shopping, meal preparation and clean-up, and laundry. Nonmedical personal care services include bathing, grooming, and other personal hygiene care. Persons can receive transportation, yard abatement, heavy cleaning, protective supervision, and certain paramedical services. For a further discussion of IHSS program see chapter 4.

Because IHSS caregivers have no job security and usually receive minimal wages, it is difficult to attract and retain individuals to this type of employment. When a good IHSS caregiver is working for the beneficiary, the beneficiary may ask the SNT trustee to supplement this low pay to retain the services of the IHSS worker. Or, the SNT trustee may be asked to hire the IHSS caregiver to provide additional services because the caregiver already understands beneficiary's needs and may be less expensive than hiring agency caregivers.

For most persons receiving IHSS, the IHSS caregiver's salary from the state cannot be supplemented.[151] For example, if IHSS will pay a caregiver for 10 hours a month at $10 an hour, a trustee cannot augment the worker's salary by paying an additional $5 hour on top of the $10. However, the trustee can hire the IHSS caregiver for additional hours and pay a premium wage for those hours.

Further, the IHSS worker cannot be hired to supplement services already contracted for through the IHSS program. For example, if the IHSS worker is contracted to do laundry for five hours a month, the SNT trustee cannot pay the IHSS worker to perform an additional five hours of laundry.

> **Example**: An IHSS worker is being paid $10 an hour for ten hours of work, which is divided up for four hours for shopping and six hours for cleaning. The SNT trustee can pay $20 an hour for an additional ten hours of work, which is set up for five hours of transportation and five hours for yard work, which brings the IHSS's worker pay up to $15 an hour for all the work provided and does not interfere with the benefits provided.

See chapter 6 for the appropriate way to hire an IHSS worker

WHAT IS THE EFFECT OF PREPAYING FOR THE BENEFICIARY'S FUNERAL?

This will depend on how the pre-paid funeral is owned.

---

[151] 42 C.F.R. §447.1; MPP Regs §30-767.4.

- If SNT trustee prepays for a funeral and attendant costs and distributes the ownership of the prepaid funeral to the beneficiary, the entire value of the prepaid funeral is exempt, except for revocable set asides money, which can add up to only $1,500. Anything over that amount will be counted as an available resource for SSI and Medi-Cal eligibility purposes.[152]
- If the SNT trustee prepays for funeral and attendant costs and the SNT owns all the contracts and burial plots and insurance, the entire amount is exempt and will have no effect on the beneficiary's public benefits.

> **Critical Pointer:** An SNT trustee of a first-party SNT will want to consider prepaying for a beneficiary's funeral. As described in chapter 10, on termination of a first-party SNT, under SSI rules, the trustee cannot use funds in the SNT to pay for the beneficiary's funeral before paying the government the amount it paid in Medi-Cal on behalf of the beneficiary. This means that if the government's recovery right is greater than the amount remaining in trust, there may be no available funds to pay for the beneficiary's funeral. This means that other friends or family members must pay for the burial, which can easily cost over $10,000 or. If they are unable to do so (or nonexistent), a cremation is paid for by the county. It would be an ignoble end to a meaningful life. Currently, DHCS will allow a trustee to pay for the funeral, but special permission should be requested. See chapter 10 for discussion on paying for a funeral.

WHAT IS THE EFFECT OF AN SNT INVESTING IN A BUSINESS?

The SNT trustee may be asked to invest in a business. It can either be as a simple investment or it may be part of a strategy to have the business hire the beneficiary to work to provide private health insurance benefits through

---

[152] 20 C.F.R. §416.1230(b)(8); 20 C.F.R. §416.1230. 20 C.F.R. §416.1231(b); 20 C.F.R. §416.1231(a) (SSI) and 22 Cal Code Regs §50477; ACWD Letter No. 93-71 (Oct. 4, 1993); Welf & I C §11158; 22 Cal Code Regs §50479 (Medi-Cal).

employment, rather than relying solely on Medi-Cal. If the business is owned by the SNT, it would have no effect on the beneficiary's public benefits.

> **Warning:** In a first-party SNT that is under court jurisdiction, the investment in a business must be approved through a court.[153]

There are however numerous considerations that must be made when doing this type of investment. Any investment in a business must comply with the investment standard of the trust. If the SNT is under the Uniform Prudent Investment Act (as described in chapter 8), investment in the business must comply with that rule. Moreover, the management of the business may greatly increase the number of hours and overall commitment of the trustee. A trustee should carefully evaluate if he or she is interested in owning and operating a business. If the SNT trustee is attempting to do this, he or she should seek assistance from an experienced special needs planner.

WHAT IS THE EFFECT OF BUYING A BUSINESS AND DISTRIBUTING IT TO THE BENEFICIARY?

The SNT trustee may be asked to invest in a business in the name of the beneficiary. While certain resources of a business may be distributed to the beneficiary in his or her name without interfering with public benefits because they are otherwise exempt, there is not an unlimited exemption for property used in a trade or business under both SSI and Medi-Cal.[154] The business exemption can apply to real property, motor vehicles, and cash (on hand or in checking accounts, but not savings accounts), as well as equipment, inventory, licenses, and materials.[155] For example, all the limousines in a limousine service can be excluded from the applicant's countable assets. Property used in a trade or business is excluded from resources regardless of the value or rate of return as long as it is in current use or, if not in use for reasons beyond

---

[153]   Cal Rules of Court 7.903(c)(4); Probate Code §2574.

[154]   42 U.S.C. §1382b(a)(3); POMS SI 01130.500-01130.504; ACWD Letter Nos. 91-28 (Mar. 22, 1991), 95-22 (Apr. 3, 1995).

[155]   20 C.F.R. §416.1220; 22 Cal Code Regs §50485.

the individual's control, as long as there is a reasonable expectation that the use will resume.[156]

A separate issue will be the income earned from the business. It will still be counted against a beneficiary for public benefits eligibility purposes. If beneficiary receives SSI, the income will be counted as earned income (or possibly unearned income) and reduce or eliminate SSI eligibility, and if the beneficiary receives only Medi-Cal (and not SSI), the income may add or increase a "share of cost" in obtaining Medi-Cal.

> **Critical Pointer:** The SNT trustee should understand the effect a business's property and income will have on the beneficiary's public benefits. Purchasing and managing a business is fraught with technical details; if the SNT trustee is attempting to do this, he or she should seek assistance from an experienced special needs planner.

WHAT IS THE EFFECT OF MAKING PAYMENTS ON BEHALF OF THE BENEFICIARY'S MINOR CHILD OR SPOUSE?

The answer will depend on the type of SNT that is being administered. If it is a third-party SNT, it is up to the trust document to determine if assets can be used to make payments for the child or spouse of a beneficiary. There is no effect on SSI or Medi-Cal if such distributions are made pursuant to terms of document. Further, if the beneficiary is divorced and there is a valid child support order, the trustee can be compelled to pay child support even if it violates the terms of the trust.[157]

There is no easy answer for the first-party SNT. The best advice is to petition the court and ask for direction from a court on whether such disbursements can be made. (See chapter 11 on how to petition court to make request.) The discussion is difficult because a disbursement may violate the "sole benefit" requirement of a first party SNT and there are no laws or regulations that let us know if such a disbursement would violate this rule.

---

[156] See POMS SI 01130.501; ACWD Letter No. 91-28 (Mar. 22, 1991).
[157] *Ventura County Dep't of Child Support Servs. v Brown* (2004) 117 Cal.App.4th 144.

Experienced Florida special needs attorney David Lillesand makes a compelling argument that paying these expenses would not violate the "sole benefit" rule because there is no federal regulation or even a POMS provision that addresses the use of first-party SNT funds to pay for a person with a disability's spouse or children. Public policy and state nonsupport criminal statutes, however, indicate that withholding support for spouses or children would violate the law. The SSA has indicated that payment of taxes, administration costs of the trust, and attorney's fees do not violate the sole-benefit rule. Because first-party SNTs are self-settled trusts not safe from the claims of legitimate creditors, it would seem not only right, but proper, that trust funds be used to support the beneficiary's legal dependents. However, there is no definitive guidance on this issue.

The easier situation would be if there were an existing spousal or child support order already in place against the beneficiary. In this case the trustee is certainly authorized to pay for the valid debts and judgments against the beneficiary. Moreover, there are criminal consequences in not paying child support. Thus, keeping a beneficiary out of jail would certainly be in the "sole benefit" of the beneficiary.

> **Example:** The first-party SNT trustee is asked to pay for the beneficiary's minor child's food and shelter. If the SNT trustee pays for the minor child's support, the beneficiary's first-party SNT could be subject to attack from the SSA or DHCS, because it may no longer be counted as for the "sole benefit" of the beneficiary. The SNT trustee could argue that paying the legal support obligations of the beneficiary is for the beneficiary's "sole benefit." At this time, there is no definitive guidance if this distribution would be authorized.

WHAT IS THE EFFECT OF PAYING FOR A RESTAURANT MEAL?

A common request from an SNT beneficiary is for purchase of a restaurant meal. It appears that the Social Security Administration (SSA) will count the entire meal as "food." This is questionable. While the food that forms the part of the meal is certainly food, the payment for the tip, service, and part of the bill that constitutes the restaurant's overhead is certainly not food. Thus, an SNT trustee should be able to pay for nearly the entire meal and characterize these payments as waiter and food preparation service. The balance could be paid by the beneficiary directly or the trustee could distribute $20 per month to the beneficiary for his or her share of the meal.

The balance of the payment of the restaurant meal would be treated as in-kind support and maintenance (ISM) and valued at no more than the presumed maximum value (PMV), meaning that the SSI check would only be reduced by $244.67 per month in 2011 or the value of the meal whichever is less. In one example in the POMS, the SSA states that the entire restaurant meal would be counted as ISM. However, it appears that this did not set SSA policy but was used without consideration of the factors identified above.[158]

> **Critical Pointer:** A restaurant meal paid for while the beneficiary is on vacation is not counted as ISM. See next question on paying for vacations.

WHAT IS THE EFFECT OF PAYING FOR VACATION COSTS, INCLUDING HOTEL AND RESTAURANT MEALS?

An SNT beneficiary may take a vacation and maintain his or her benefits. When an SNT beneficiary is temporarily absent from a permanent living arrangement, in-kind support and maintenance (ISM) continues to be valued based on the beneficiary's permanent living arrangement.[159] The SSA does not count ISM the beneficiary receives during his or her temporary absence. This is true even if the SNT pays for food (e.g., restaurant meals) or shelter (e.g., hotels) during the absence.

An SNT trustee should be aware that SSI benefits will be terminated if a benefits recipient is out of the country for more than thirty days.[160] There are exceptions for certain blind or disabled children of military parents stationed overseas and students who are temporarily abroad for study purposes.[161]

---

[158] POMS SI 01120.201(l)(1)(d).

[159] POMS SI 00835.040.

[160] See POMS SI 00501.410.

[161] See instructions in POMS SI 00501.415 for blind or disabled children of military parents stationed overseas and POMS SI 00501.411 for students temporarily abroad.

Example: The SNT beneficiary wishes to visit his family in New Orleans. The trustee is asked to pay for the beneficiary's hotel bills, restaurant meals, and other travel costs for the trip. The SNT trustee is authorized to pay for all of these items without any reduction of the beneficiary's eligibility for public benefits.

An issue may come up where the beneficiary wants to pay for a friend or family member to come with him or her. In order to pay for a companion, see the next question.

What Is the Effect of Paying for Travel Companions for the SNT Beneficiary?

Oftentimes, an SNT beneficiary is unable to attend events or go on vacations without assistance. In these situations, the SNT trustee may be asked to pay for someone (or several people) to assist the beneficiary in enjoying these activities.

These disbursements will generally not interfere with public benefits from either a first-party or third-party SNT. The only issue would be in a first-party SNT if the distribution would be considered for the "sole benefit" of the beneficiary. The easiest way to solve this issue is to have a medical professional require that the beneficiary use a companion if traveling or going out in the community.

Example: A first-party SNT beneficiary who has cerebral palsy would like to go on a cruise. The beneficiary is able to do some things for herself but requires assistance with bathing, dressing, eating, and transportation. Her doctor has made a written recommendation that she not go on a cruise without assistance. The SNT trustee is asked to pay for an assistant to help the beneficiary while on the cruise. The SNT trustee can pay for the attendant's full costs during the cruise and pay reasonable salary for her services. There is no effect on public benefits in paying for the companion.

Example: A first-party SNT beneficiary has schizophrenia but with medication is able to manage all of his personal care. The beneficiary asks the trustee to pay for his friend to assist him on his trip to Hawaii. The beneficiary is unable to get a doctor to agree that he requires any assistance with his any of his needs. The SNT trustee should refuse this distribution because it would not be for the "sole benefit" of the beneficiary.

WHAT IS THE EFFECT OF PAYING FOR ALCOHOL, COFFEE, AND CIGARETTES?

Some SNT beneficiaries will make requests for the purchase of alcohol, coffee, or cigarettes. The author's advice is that distributions for these items are acceptable.

Cigarettes will be okay because in no way can a cigarette be considered food. Alcohol and coffee, however, could be considered food by an overzealous SSA eligibility worker. This is an issue that is really debatable, as alcohol and coffee offer little to no nutritional value. Sadly, the SSA instructions do not give us a strict definition of what is "food." Is it only items that are eaten that offer some nutritional value, or is it anything that is consumed?

However, even if alcohol or coffee were considered food, paying for them would be treated as SSI in-kind support and maintenance (ISM) and valued at no more than the presumed maximum value (PMV), meaning that the SSI check would only be reduced by $244.67 per month in 2011 or the value of the purchase, whichever is less. Thus, in general, if the beneficiary seeks payment for these items, it should not be a problem.

> **Critical Pointer:** A trustee should carefully review the trust document. Some people who set up SNTs for people with disabilities will have prohibited distributions for the purchase of alcohol or cigarettes.

WHAT IS THE EFFECT OF PAYING FOR DATING OR ROMANCE?

Many SNT trustees seem to have a hard time handling requests that will aid in the love life of persons with disabilities. The effect of nearly all these services will have no effect on the beneficiary's public benefits and hopefully will greatly enhance his or her quality of life.

Common requests to an SNT trustee that will not interfere with public benefits include online dating services, birth control (not paid for by Medi-Cal), the beneficiary's share of a movie or other type of date (except dinner), sex toys and aids, the beneficiary's wedding ring, the beneficiary's share of wedding costs, and the beneficiary's share of honeymoon costs, including hotel and restaurant meals.

Common requests to a third-party SNT trustee that generally will not interfere with public benefits if authorized by the document include gifts, flowers, shows, engagement rings, and wedding rings. It is important to remember that these disbursements would not be for the "sole benefit" of the beneficiary and could not be distributed from a first-party SNT or a third-party SNT that limited disbursements to "sole benefit."

Common requests that will impact public benefits include restaurant meals. As discussed elsewhere in this chapter, a certain portion of the meal would be counted as food and calculated under the ISM rules.

WHAT IS THE EFFECT OF PAYING FOR PORNOGRAPHY?

Many SNT trustees have a difficult time agreeing to pay for the beneficiary's review of legal pornography (whether online, in movies, or in print) for an SNT beneficiary. The issue is generally not with public benefits eligibility (as there is no effect on beneficiary's public benefits in making such distributions) but rather the salacious content of the materials.

There is no right or wrong answer to this issue, but the SNT trustee is there to make SNT distributions that will enhance the quality of life of the beneficiary, not to sit in judgment of other people's lifestyles. If the SNT trustee agrees to the distribution, it is probably best to set boundaries early and let the beneficiary know exactly what types of disbursements will be acceptable to the SNT trustee.

WHAT IS THE EFFECT OF PAYING FOR THE BENEFICIARY'S PETS?

The distribution for a beneficiary's pet will have no effect on a beneficiary's SSI or Medi-Cal. Payment for pet supplies is not counted as in-kind support or maintenance. It also is counted as for the "sole benefit" of the beneficiary if he or she is beneficiary of a first party SNT. Common requests that are authorized include pet supplies, veterinarian services, pet food, pet toys, grooming, dog walker, pet sitter, and anything else related to the care of pets.

WHAT IS THE EFFECT OF THE SNT TRUSTEE LENDING MONEY TO THE BENEFICIARY?

A beneficiary may receive cash as a loan from the SNT trustee, if it is bona fide and made in good faith. The receipt of the cash will not be treated as income.[162] However, if, on the first day of the next calendar month from the receipt of the loan, the loan proceeds have not been spent, the cash will be counted as an SSI resource.[163] If the loan is over $2,000, the individual beneficiary will lose eligibility for SSI.

The loan must be a bona fide loan. To see how to make a qualifying loan, see discussion in chapter 6.

WHAT IS THE EFFECT OF MAKING A DISTRIBUTION THAT EXHAUSTS TRUST ASSETS?

Unless the trust document states otherwise, a distribution that takes all the money in the SNT will not interfere with public benefits. Whether the complete exhaustion of SNT assets is intentional or unintentional, the result is the termination of the trust, because there can be no trust without a corpus.[164] If the SNT is a first-party SNT, notice of the termination must be provided to the SSA and DHCS. This may also trigger a request from the SSA or DHCS for an accounting of how assets in the trust were spent.

See chapter 10 for more information on terminating an SNT.

> **Helpful Hint:** A first-party SNT trustee may want to consider the possibility of retaining a nominal amount of assets to avoid termination. This might be prudent if the beneficiary remains disabled and continues to receive public benefits, because there is always the possibility that he or she may receive additional

---

[162]   POMS SI 00815.350.
[163]   POMS SI 01120.220(D)(3)(a).
[164]   Probate Code §15202.

assets in the future—whether from an unplanned inheritance, a personal injury settlement, or some other source. The existing first-party SNT could remain in existence indefinitely to serve as a potential repository for those assets, thus avoiding the delay and expense of establishing a new SNT.

Chapter 5 Summary

✓ Making distributions to enhance the quality of life of the beneficiary is one of the primary purposes of any special needs trust.

✓ A major consideration on distributions is whether it will interfere with the beneficiary's eligibility for public benefits.

✓ A decision tree checklist that a trustee should use each time he or she makes a distribution is included in Appendix G.

✓ An SNT beneficiary who is receiving Section 8 benefits may have special requirements from SNT distributions that will not interfere with benefits.

✓ Specific distributions discussed and analyzed in this chapter include paying for exempt goods, services, medical costs, food and shelter, home purchase and sale, home or rental modifications, cash or monthly allowance, pet supplies, vacations, paid companion, business, rental income, pornography, romance and dating, alcohol, cigarettes, and coffee, expenses of minor child or spouse, restaurant meal, caregivers, funeral, clothing, and automobiles.

✓ Unless trust document says otherwise, it is okay to make distributions that spend all the money in the trust during beneficiary's lifetime.

✓ In Appendices the end of the chapter is a nonexhaustive list of distributions that the distribution of will not interfere with the beneficiary's public benefits

CHAPTER 6

Setting the Budget and Making SNT Distributions

An SNT trustee should be proactive in deciding how best to make distributions that will enhance the quality of life of a beneficiary with a disability. The best way to do this is to set up a budget of items and services that will be paid from the SNT on a monthly basis. Next, the SNT trustee should make sure that distributions that are made will not interfere with the beneficiary's public benefits; or, if the disbursement will interfere with public benefits, that the SNT trustee knows to what extent. As discussed in chapter 5, different types of SNT distributions will have different effects on a beneficiary's public benefit eligibility.

This chapter will guide the trustee in making distributions the right way by first going over general methods for distribution, then going into specific types of distributions for homes, cars, caregivers, and other items.

WHY SHOULD A TRUSTEE SET UP A BUDGET?

A trustee has many important duties that he or she must keep in mind while serving as trustee. These include following the terms of the trust, acting in the best interests of the beneficiary, properly investing trust assets, keeping great records, paying taxes, and providing accounts when requested. All of this is made easier by setting up a budget.

How Does a Trustee Set a Budget for an SNT Beneficiary?

The easiest way to set a budget is to do it in four steps:

- list monthly income;
- identify and list all expenses;
- compare income and expenses; and
- be ready to make appropriate changes.

Setting up a budget should be done by having discussions with the beneficiary (and his or her advocates, friends, and family) on how the SNT assets should be used to enhance the beneficiary's quality of life.

> **Helpful Hint:** Use the list in Appendix M and go over it with the beneficiary (and with those who know the beneficiary well) to see what kinds of items and services he or she expects the trust to pay for on a monthly basis and those items he or she may desire. Some trustees have reported that with certain beneficiaries, this may not be prudent. These beneficiaries look at the list as a shopping list and seek all kinds of items they will not use or need. Further, if the assets in the SNT are limited, it may be better to limit the beneficiary's options.

These discussions will aid the trustee in understanding what the expectations are for use of the funds. It will also allow the trustee to set appropriate expectations. If there are unrealistic expectations, they should be corrected immediately. The trust document should also be read (and any memorandum of intent reviewed) to see how the person setting up the trust intended for trust assets to be used to enhance the quality of life of the beneficiary. Regardless of the amount held in trust, the trustee will protect him or herself by setting up a budget, sticking to it, and, if circumstances change, having the flexibility to modify it.

> **Example:** SNT trustee meets with beneficiary and his girlfriend to discuss a budget. The beneficiary wants to use the funds to buy a car for him and one for his girlfriend, pay for rent on a

two-bedroom apartment where he and his girlfriend will live, buy furniture, a home gym, and a computer, supply a monthly allowance of $1,000, and in a couple of years pay for school.

The trustee can immediately set the proper expectations. The trustee can explain that because this is a first-party SNT, the trustee is not allowed to use any funds for the girlfriend, because distributions are only allowed for beneficiary's sole benefit, that payment of rent will reduce the amount of SSI the beneficiary will receive (which may or may not be in his best interest), and that a cash allowance directly to the beneficiary is not allowed, as it will eliminate SSI and increase share of cost for Medi-Cal. They should then discuss whether it is realistic to buy all these items immediately, given that the beneficiary wants to pay for school. The budget meeting allows the trustee to set the whole tone of the administration. It is best done as early as possible so a beneficiary does not get frustrated if he or she expects to receive things and keeps getting rejected without explanation.

The budget itself requires the trustee to delve into the entire financial background of the beneficiary. Depending on the cooperation of the beneficiary, this can be quite simple or very frustrating.

If the beneficiary is not cooperative and may not have friends or family who will support the person with a disability, the trustee may be able to obtain information from the beneficiary's school records, such as an Independent Education Plan (IEP), or from the Regional Center's Individual Program Plan (IPP). It may be difficult for the trustee to obtain these reports, but if there is a caseworker or care manager for the beneficiary, it may be possible to review.

If the SNT assets came from a litigation recovery, the beneficiary's personal injury attorney may have obtained a "Life Care Plan" as part of the litigation. These plans are an excellent way to obtain information about the care and services the beneficiary will require throughout his or her life.

The trustee can only do as much as he or she can with the information at hand. It would still be a good idea to set a budget even if the beneficiary does not cooperate. It will provide direction when deciding on making distributions and preserving assets for expected future disbursements.

To aid the trustee, a worksheet is set forth in Appendix E of this book. The worksheet provides a list of commonly addressed income and expense items that should be reviewed. It is recommended that this budget be reviewed periodically (perhaps once a year while doing the accounting) to make any changes and updates to it.

Helpful Hint: For further assistance, several companies have online financial calculators that will give an estimate of the estimated costs of taking care of a person with a disability. Merrill Lynch provides such a calculator at http://www.totalmerrill.com/TotalMerrill/calculators/snc/start.asp.

SHOULD A TRUSTEE SET UP A SYSTEM FOR MAKING DISBURSEMENTS?

Yes. The number one complaint by SNT beneficiaries about an SNT trustee is his or her lack of communication concerning SNT disbursements.

The disbursement procedure should be established very early with the beneficiary (or his or her advocates) to determine how disbursements may be requested. The procedure should explain whether disbursements can be made—for example, only during business hours, on weekdays, or within twenty-four hours from a written request. The procedure should be in writing and given to the beneficiary, any legal guardians, and those friends and family willing to participate. Following these steps will go a long way in eliminating future friction with the beneficiary during the administration.

The trustee can provide a form to the beneficiary in which a written request for disbursement can be made. A sample SNT distribution request form can be found in Appendix F of this book.

The trustee should also clearly communicate his or her decision on each disbursement request. While the trustee has the sole and absolute discretion to make (or not make) a disbursement, a clear statement as to why he or she has refused to make a specific disbursement will be much better for the trustee in the long run.

> **Critical Pointer:** It is a good idea for a trustee to either require the beneficiary to email in a disbursement request or purchase a fax machine for a beneficiary or his or her caregiver. This way, the trustee will have a written record of what was requested and what action was taken.

How Does a Trustee Make Appropriate Disbursements?

There are several ways for an SNT trustee to make SNT disbursements that will not interfere with the beneficiary's public benefit eligibility:

1. The safest way is to distribute these services or goods directly to the beneficiary personally.[165] In other words, the trustee can pay for a computer and personally deliver it to the beneficiary.
2. The trustee can purchase the items or services directly.[166] For example, trustee purchases kitchen appliances online (like at Amazon.com or Overstock.com) and has the item delivered to beneficiary's address.
3. The trustee can reimburse a friend or relative who pays for the service. For example, the beneficiary's best friend purchases tickets to a baseball game. The trustee can then reimburse the friend for the beneficiary's ticket.

   Warning: The trustee cannot reimburse the beneficiary directly for purchases he or she makes, even if the item or service would be a perfectly acceptable disbursement. If the SNT trustee reimburses the beneficiary, the amount of money distributed to the beneficiary will be counted as SSI "unearned income" and reduce the beneficiary's SSI payment dollar-for-dollar.

4. The trustee may purchase a gift card or certificate for the beneficiary. However, a gift card or certificate must meet certain legal requirements as described later in this chapter and in chapter 5.
5. The trustee may pay the beneficiary's credit card bills. The trustee must continue to exercise his or her discretion over each charge made—for example, if the trustee pays the whole bill and certain items were for food or shelter purchases, then in-kind support and maintenance (ISM) may be triggered. This is discussed in detail later in this chapter.

---

[165] 20 C.F.R. §416.1103(g); POMS SI 00815.400; POMS SI 00815.550.
[166] 20 C.F.R. §416.1103(g); POMS SI 00815.400; POMS SI 00815.550.

CAN AN SNT TRUSTEE USE A GIFT CARD OR GIFT CERTIFICATE FOR AN SNT BENEFICIARY?

The trustee could purchase a gift card or certificate and distribute it to the beneficiary. However, the gift card or certificate must meet two very important requirements:[167]

1. The gift card or gift certificate cannot ever be used to buy food or shelter. It does not matter if food or shelter was actually purchased with the card or certificate, only if the card or certificate holder has the ability to purchase these items directly (for example, a gift card or certificate to a restaurant, grocery store, Wal-Mart—which sells food—or Visa gift card). As described in detail in chapter 5, the SSA will treat the gift card as SSI unearned income (not ISM), meaning that if a gift card was purchased that could be used for food or shelter, the SSI recipient would lose the entire value of the card (less the $20 any income exclusion) from his or her SSI check.

   Critical Pointer: It is commonly misunderstood that if a gift card or gift certificate pays for food or shelter items, it will be treated as ISM income. This is wrong. It is treated as SSI "unearned income" and will reduce the SSI payment "dollar-for-dollar" after the first $20.[168]

2. The gift card or gift certificate also must include a legally enforceable prohibition against selling the card for cash. If it fails to have this prohibition, it will also be counted as unearned income for the full amount of the value of the card or certificate in the month of receipt, just as if SNT trustee had distributed cash to the beneficiary. The SSA states that absent evidence to the contrary, presume a gift card or certificate can be resold. For example, evidence to the contrary may include a legally enforceable prohibition on resale or transfer of the card imposed by the card issuer merchant printed on the card.

---

[167] POMS SI 00830.522.

[168] 20 C.F.R. §416.1124(c)(12); POMS SI 00810.420, 01120.200(E)(1)(a).

Generally, gift cards or certificates for stores such as Macy's, clothing stores, bookstores, or electronics stores cannot be redeemed for food or shelter items. However, the trustee must also make sure that the card has the beneficiary's name on it somewhere and has some kind of legal prohibition against resale. It is very difficult (if not impossible) to find a gift card or gift certificate that qualifies under both of these SSI rules.

> **Critical Pointer:** In the author's experience, he has not yet found a gift card or gift certificate that meets the SSI requirements and would caution any trustee who attempts to utilize this method that he or she is treading on very dangerous ground.

CAN THE TRUSTEE PAY THE BENEFICIARY'S CREDIT CARD BILLS?

Yes. This surprises many trustees given some of the other SNT restrictions the trustee must follow. The reason it works is that the trustee is directly paying a valid debt of the beneficiary. A trustee must however, still exercise his or her discretion over each item in the credit card bill.

> **Example:** Paul Parry, an SNT beneficiary uses his credit card to buy a cell phone for $100, appliances for $40, concert tickets for $60, and groceries for $50 at Safeway. The SNT trustee can pay for the cell phone, appliances, and concert tickets, but if he or she pays the $50 for groceries, that portion of the bill will be counted as ISM against the beneficiary. If ISM is not an issue because the trustee is already paying Paul's rent, then it would be okay to pay for the food as well.

It is also important to know if the SNT beneficiary is a first-party SNT, the trustee must make sure that each payment is made for the sole benefit of the beneficiary. In the above example, if the concert tickets were for Paul Parry and a friend, the trustee could only pay for Paul's share of the ticket price. The other ticket would have to be paid from either Paul's public benefits money or by his friend.

Some commonly encountered problems with an SNT trustee agreeing to pay the beneficiary's credit card bills is the beneficiary abusing the credit card or the beneficiary failing to qualify for a credit card. The beneficiary may qualify if he or she has a cosigner on the account. This leads to the other issue that commonly arises—the SNT beneficiary abusing the use of the card. This may be alleviated by having a low credit limit on the card, like $500.

While the SNT trustee can make payments on the credit card, the trustee still has a fiduciary duty to make sure that such disbursements are in the best interest of the beneficiary. Thus, it is important to communicate with the beneficiary about the types and amounts of disbursements that will be approved.

> **Example:** Mitch Schroeder, an SNT beneficiary, uses his credit card to buy a Jet Ski for $3,500. The purchase of the Jet Ski would cause Mitch to lose his SSI due to excess resources. (See chapter 5 on Vehicles.) The SNT trustee refuses to pay for it. Mitch cannot afford to pay even the minimum balance of the credit card bill from his monthly SSI check. Mitch goes into default, loses his credit card, and loses his credit. In a worst-case scenario, he could have to declare bankruptcy and lose SSI until he sold the Jet Ski.

Another issue arises if the beneficiary takes a cash advance on the credit card. The cash will not be counted as income in the month of receipt. This is because it will be treated as a loan.[169] However, if the beneficiary holds onto the cash until the first day of the next calendar month, it will be treated as a resource and could jeopardize eligibility if the loan is over $2,000 (for individual) or $3,000 (for couple).[170]

CAN THE TRUSTEE GIVE THE BENEFICIARY A BANK DEBIT CARD FROM AN SNT ACCOUNT?

No. If this happens, it is treated as if the beneficiary receives a resource of the amount of cash held in the bank account. This situation is different from a credit card, described in the prior question, because it simply provides unfettered access to all the cash in the bank account. This would then be a countable

169 POMS SI 00815.350.
170 POMS SI 01120.220(D)(3)(a).

resource to the beneficiary and would likely eliminate eligibility for both SSI and Medi-Cal.

CAN THE TRUSTEE GIVE CASH (OR AN ALLOWANCE) TO THE BENEFICIARY OR REIMBURSE THE BENEFICIARY?

The trustee can distribute cash to the beneficiary, but it generally would not be prudent to do so. The reason is that it will directly affect the beneficiary's public benefits. If the beneficiary receives SSI, the receipt of cash will reduce the SSI check dollar-for-dollar after the first $20 (SSI any income exclusion). If the beneficiary is a Medi-Cal only recipient, it will increase the beneficiary's share-of-cost by the amount of cash received by the beneficiary.

Thus, for either SSI or Medi-Cal recipients, distributing cash to the beneficiary is not a good idea.

> **Example:** Sarah VanPelt an SNT beneficiary wishes to receive $250 to buy a television set and asks for an ongoing monthly allowance of $600 for living expenses. If the trustee agrees to do so, Sarah will lose $830 from her SSI check in the month of receipt of the $850 or, if she is only a Medi-Cal recipient, will owe an additional $850 as a share-of-cost before Medi-Cal will begin to pay her medical expenses. For every month thereafter, if Sarah is an SSI recipient, she will lose $580 from her SSI check ($600 unearned income less $20 any income exclusion), and if a Medi-Cal-only recipient will have an increased $600 share-of-cost for Medi-Cal.

The Medi-Cal share of cost calculations are more complicated than stated in these examples but are to provide the basics of the effects on Medi-Cal when cash is provided to a Medi-Cal recipient.

This is true even if the beneficiary is only seeking reimbursement for purchases made, which will also be treated as SSI unearned income regardless if the reimbursement was for items that are exempt or not counted by SSI.

> **Example:** George Borges, an SNT beneficiary, purchased San Francisco Giants baseball tickets for $200. He asks the trustee to reimburse him for the tickets. If the trustee agrees

to do so, George will lose $180 from his SSI check or, if he is a Medi-Cal-only recipient, will owe an additional $200 as a share-of-cost before Medi-Cal will begin to pay his medical expenses. This is true even though purchasing baseball tickets would be an acceptable distribution if made directly by the trustee.

This may be the hardest rule to follow for many trustees, especially if prior trustees (often family members) were providing such an allowance to the beneficiary. The prior trustee may have been able to get away with the improper disbursement, but it will only be a matter of time before the agencies that run the public benefit programs catch on and seek an SSI "overpayment" of benefits paid or deny Medi-Cal eligibility. Thus, a prior trustee's violation of the rules is no excuse for a current trustee to fail to refuse to follow existing rules.

> **Example:** The SNT trustee has been distributing $500 per month to the beneficiary for a year. The SSA was never informed. The beneficiary during his annual review tells the SSA worker that he has been receiving this money. The SSA seeks an overpayment reimbursement from the beneficiary of $5,760 ($480 x 12) for the unearned income.

CAN THE TRUSTEE LEND SNT MONEY TO THE BENEFICIARY?

Yes, but certain rules must be followed. If a loan is made, the cash will not be counted as income in the month of receipt. This is because it will be treated as a bona fide loan.[171] However, if the beneficiary holds onto the cash until the first day of the next calendar month, it will be treated as a resource and could jeopardize eligibility if over $2,000 (for individual) or $3,000 (for couple).[172] See chapter 5 for further discussion.

In order for the SNT trustee to make a loan, the loan must be bona fide. This means the loan agreement must be valid under California law, in effect at time of transaction, beneficiary acknowledgment that cash will be repaid, and

---

[171] POMS SI 00815.350.

[172] POMS SI 01120.220(D)(3)(a).

a specified repayment plan that is feasible.[173] Because of these restrictions, it is difficult to envision many situations when a loan to a beneficiary would be in the best interests of the beneficiary.

> **Example:** An SNT beneficiary asks for a loan to pay for his or her food shelter of $900 per month while awaiting a determination on his application for SSI and Medi-Cal. Repayment will be made when the SSA repays for the months it took to determine SSI eligibility. The SNT trustee and beneficiary enter into a loan transaction. For six months, the SNT trustee lends the beneficiary the money. On the sixth month, the SSA approves eligibility for SSI and pays a lump-sum amount to the beneficiary for the six-month wait. The beneficiary repays the SNT the amount that was loaned. There is no effect on SSI for this transaction.

> **Example:** The SNT trustee has been distributing $500 per month to the beneficiary for a year. The SSA was never informed. The beneficiary during his annual review tells the SSA worker that he has been receiving this money. The SSA seeks an overpayment reimbursement from the beneficiary of $5,760 ($480 x 12) for the unearned income. In defending the request, the beneficiary suggests that trustee should characterize disbursement as a loan. This will not work, because the loan is not bona fide. While it is possible to enter into an oral contract valid under California law, the loan was not entered into at the time the money was spent. Also, it would be difficult to show a feasible repayment plan.

HOW TO MAKE DISTRIBUTIONS FOR SNT BENEFICIARY WHO RECEIVES SECTION 8

As described in chapter 5, certain Public Housing Agencies (PHA) in California are taking the position that SNT disbursements will be treated as income, thereby reducing or eliminating Section 8 eligibility. In order to reduce the effect

---

[173]   POMS SI 01120.220(C).

of this position, the SNT trustee should try to make disbursements that are exempt from being counted as Section 8 income.

> **Note**: A recent California case (decided after the author wrote this section) may also be used by an SNT trustee to prevent the loss of Section 8 by SNT beneficiaries. In *Finley v. City of Santa Monica* (Cal.Sup. Ct. County of Los Angeles, No. BS 127077, May 25, 2011), a California trial court determined that distributions of principal from a special needs trust are not countable income for purposes of calculating a Section 8 recipient's rent because the principal of the trust would not be a countable asset if held directly by the Section 8 recipient. This is great news for SNT beneficiaries who also receive Section 8. Check the author's website for further discussions on this topic.

The easiest types of distributions to make (that will not be counted as Section 8 income) are those that are "temporary, nonrecurring, or sporadic."[174] However, this definition is vague. Some PHAs will take the position that even a once-a-year distribution will be counted as regularly recurring, if paid each year. Others will only count monthly disbursements if made each month for the same item. For example, the monthly cell phone bill. Fortunately, most large distributions are in their nature "nonrecurring or sporadic," such as automobiles, vacation trips, and purchases of computer equipment. Therefore, these disbursements should have no effect on Section 8 eligibility.

To eliminate all regularly recurring payments from the SNT, the SNT trustee could create a chance element on deciding when to make payment. For example, assigning different monthly bill to the roll of a dice (2-4 = cell phone; 5-10 = club membership; 11-12 = no payment made, etc.) and making a decision on whether to pay the bill only when the appropriate number comes up. This sounds silly, but it is one way to make sure such payments are sporadic and nonrecurring.

> **Example:** SNT beneficiary receives Section 8 housing, which is essential to his living in the community. If he lost his

---

[174]   24 C.F.R. §§5.609(c), 982.316.

Section 8 voucher, his SSI check and SNT assets would be insufficient to provide housing, and he would be forced to move into an institution. The SNT trustee makes sure that all SNT disbursements would not be counted as Section 8 income. The trustee does not make any regularly recurring disbursements from the trust. Thus, all monthly payments must be paid for from the beneficiary's SSI check. The SNT trustee agrees to pay all one time purchases and on different months rolls the dice to see if one or more of monthly expenses will be paid.

Other types of disbursements that would not be counted as income are medical expense reimbursements or amounts received by the family that are specifically for, or in reimbursement of, the cost of medical expenses for any family member and for payment of a live-in-aide. See the list of noncountable income for Section 8 purposes in chapter 5.

HOW DOES THE TRUSTEE MAKE A PURCHASE FOR A HOME USING SNT ASSETS?

The purchase of a home by the SNT trustee may be the biggest purchase an SNT trustee will make. As described in chapter 5, a home is an exempt asset for both SSI (of an unlimited value) and for Medi-Cal (up to $750,000), so it can generally be owned by either the SNT or the beneficiary without interfering with public benefits.

Typically, the trustee has the legal authority to use trust assets to purchase a home.[175] The SNT trustee should, however, check the trust document to see if there is an express prohibition against the purchase of real estate. If there is, the SNT trustee cannot make the purchase absent a court order.

Likewise, in certain first-party SNTs that are under continuing court jurisdiction, the trustee should determine whether the local probate court will require a court order to purchase the home. It would be prudent for a trustee to seek a local attorney to assist in determining whether court authorization is required. See chapter 11 on how to find legal assistance for SNTs.

---

[175] Probate Code §16226.

Critical Pointer: Due to the high cost of homes in California, the trustee will want protection from later second-guessing by other beneficiaries, judges, or entities. In order to protect the trustee, he or she can file a Probate Code §17200 petition for instructions (as described in chapter 11) seeking authorization for the purchase of a home. With appropriate notice, a hearing, and a court's order, the trustee will be protected from any future potential future liability.

Once it is determined that the SNT trustee has the legal authority to purchase the home, the next decision that needs to be made is who will own the home, the beneficiary or the trustee of the SNT?

There are both practical and legal issues that should be considered by the trustee in making this decision. Below are a list of advantages and disadvantages to home ownership by a beneficiary and by a trustee.

Advantages of direct home ownership by the SNT beneficiary:

- Self-determination by the beneficiary with a disability to own and control a valuable asset.
- The ability to create an estate plan leaving the home to the heirs of the beneficiary's choice.
- A step-up in basis on the value of the home at the death of the beneficiary with a disability. This benefit applies only if the SNT that makes the distribution is not a grantor trust (see chapter 9, on taxation, which describes grantor trust status).
- Providing equity for collateral to a loan for the beneficiary with a disability.
- Minimizing the recovery claim by the Department of Health Care Service (DHCS) in a first-party SNT if the beneficiary is under the age of fifty-five at death and not an inpatient in a nursing home.[176] see chapter 10 on Medi-Cal recovery claims for first-party SNTs.

Disadvantages of direct home ownership by the SNT beneficiary:

---

[176]   Welfare & Institutions Code §14009.5.

- If the beneficiary is unable to manage his or her own financial affairs, a conservatorship of the estate may need to be opened to manage the home.
- The beneficiary will be required to manage all home ownership issues, such as insurance, maintenance, and general upkeep. This may be an issue for some beneficiaries due to their disabilities.
- If the beneficiary is vulnerable to predators, he or she might be persuaded to sign the house over to someone else.
- If the distribution is to a minor, then many of the minor's dealings with the property are limited by law. A minor cannot delegate a power or enter into a contract relating to an interest in real property and may disaffirm most other contracts. Therefore, brokers, transfer agents, title companies, and others will not knowingly deal with a minor, and unless the minor is emancipated, a guardian may have to be appointed to deal effectively with a minor's property.
- The home will be subject to the personal creditors of the beneficiary. If the home was owned by a third-party SNT, it would be protected from most of the beneficiary's creditors.
- If the beneficiary sells the home, he or she will have only three months to purchase a new home without an SSI penalty.[177] If the beneficiary does not find a new home or, if after the purchase of a new home, there are assets in excess of $2,000, the beneficiary will lose SSI and Medi-Cal due to excess resources, unless those assets are transferred to a first party SNT. If the home in the SNT was sold, the sales proceeds would not be counted against the beneficiary.
- If home is rented, the rental income will count against the beneficiary's SSI and Medi-Cal eligibility.

Warning: There may be an issue with making a distribution of a home from a first-party SNT to a beneficiary. The distribution of a personal residence from a first-party SNT may be considered a circumvention of the Medi-Cal payback requirement to the DHCS. This may invite a DHCS lawsuit against the trustee upon the beneficiary's death. To alleviate this concern, a notice of proposed action should be prepared and served on DHCS, or

---

[177] POMS SI 01130.110(A)(1).

a trustee could seek a petition for instructions under Probate Code §17200 (as described in chapter 11) and provide notice to DHCS. This should provide the trustee with protection from liability.

Advantages of home ownership by the trustee of the SNT:

- The trustee can control the ownership of the home, meaning that the trustee is assured that taxes are paid, insurance is paid, and the home remains in repair.
- The trustee can diversify trust investments to include real property.
- The trustee can rent the home without any effect on beneficiary's SSI or Medi-Cal.
- The trustee can protect the home from the beneficiary's creditors in certain circumstances. Generally, much better protection in a third-party SNT.
- The trustee can own the property on behalf of a minor or adult who lacks capacity without having to obtain a guardianship or conservatorship.
- The trustee can control what persons are allowed to live in the home with the SNT beneficiary and protect the beneficiary from predators who would attempt to take advantage of the beneficiary.
- The trustee can sell the home without it interfering with the beneficiary's public benefits.

Disadvantages of home ownership by the trustee of the SNT:

- The trustee must make sure that all property taxes are paid.
- The trustee must make sure all fire, earthquake, and home owners insurance is paid.

   Note: Trustee should have regular appraisals done on property to make sure insurance coverage is adequate.

- The trustee must make regular inspections of property and make sure all maintenance and repairs are being made.
- The trustee must collect rental payments and enter into rental agreements with others living in the property. This also means that

if rental payments are not made, eviction proceeds may need to be instituted.

- The home may not receive a basis step-up on the death of the beneficiary if it is owned by a nongrantor trust, like third-party SNT.
- The home becomes part of the first-party SNT property for payback recovery by DHCS during trust termination. See chapter 10 for discussion of first-party SNT payback.

SHOULD AN SNT TRUSTEE CONSIDER JOINTLY OWNING REAL PROPERTY?

It depends. An SNT trustee may be asked to jointly own real property when the beneficiary has an existing home, has sold it, and wants to buy a new home but does not have enough money to do so or a parent (or other relative) wishes to buy a home for the person with a disability but needs more money to do so.

As long as the SNT trustee has the authority to purchase real estate, the trustee can use SNT assets to jointly own property. To protect the beneficial interest in the distribution, an SNT trustees will often make sure that the SNT (or the beneficiary) takes title to the pro-rata amount of the contribution. As described in chapter 5, the ownership of the real property (as long as for the beneficiary's principal place of residence) is an exempt asset for both SSI and Medi-Cal purposes.

The real problems that arise with joint ownership are practical ones. For example, the trustee is often at the mercy of the joint owner, who stops making mortgage, insurance, or maintenance payments because of financial hardship, the joint owner dies, or the joint owner decides to sell and begins a partition action (a legal proceeding to force a sale of the home). It is important that the trustee come up with a plan (in advance) to solve any of these problems that may arise.

> **Example:** SNT trustee is asked to contribute $200,000 for the outright purchase of principal residence for beneficiary. The beneficiary's parent will contribute the remaining $100,000. The SNT trustee and parent execute a deed with SNT owning two thirds of property and the parent owing one third of property. A separate agreement is entered into so that all expenses are shared pro rata, based on percentage ownership. After several years, while the beneficiary is residing in the home, the parent

had paid all the expenses and the beneficiary was well taken care of. However, in year seven, the parent dies. In the parent's estate plan, he left his share of the home to his nondisabled child, the beneficiary's sibling. The sibling decides that she does not want to own the property and wants to sell. The SNT does not have enough money to buy the sibling out and refuses to sell. The sibling could force a sale through a partition action, and when sold, the beneficiary would need to move from the home.

CAN A TRUSTEE MAKE DISTRIBUTIONS FOR HOME MODIFICATIONS ON REAL PROPERTY NOT OWNED BY SNT OR BENEFICIARY?

If the trustee of either a first party or third party SNT is asked to make a modification to a home not owned by the trustee, the trustee is generally allowed to do so if it is in the best interests of the beneficiary. See chapter 5 for more discussion on the effect on SSI of paying for home modifications.

Typically, the type of modifications requested are for accessibility to a bathroom, adding a ramp, adding an elevator, or widening doorways or hallways. However, it could be something less obvious, such as adding a therapy room, a pool, or a sauna to the home. In general, adding ramps, widening doors to accommodate wheelchairs, and installing disability modifications to a bathroom add little significant value to the home. However, modifications that add several hundred square feet to a bedroom, a therapy room, a swimming pool, or a bathroom may add significant value.

> **Example:** The beneficiary is renting property. He had some mobility issues but was able to remain mobile until recently and now needs a wheelchair for all mobility needs. The beneficiary has permission from the landlord to make the bathroom accessible. He asks trustee to make the requested modifications at a cost of $8,000. The SNT trustee may make the modifications without any effect to beneficiary's SSI or Medi-Cal.

The SNT trustee will need to carefully consider approving a modification if there are no protections in place. For example, the homeowner may either evict the beneficiary or sell the property once the distribution is made. If that happens, the beneficiary is without a home and the SNT has lost assets. Another issue that may arise is if the homeowner dies and the heirs evict the beneficiary or sell the home. There may be unforeseen creditor issues by the homeowner and even foreclosure. Thus, the SNT trustee will need to be careful in making a significant disbursement if any of the above concerns arise.

> **Example:** Same facts as prior example, but as soon as the modifications are done, the landlord evicts the beneficiary. The SNT trustee has no recourse for the $8,000 distribution.

The trustee should find a way to protect the disbursements that do add substantial value to the home or are a very large disbursement from trust. Protections include the beneficiary receiving a life estate in the home, beneficiary entering into an occupancy agreement binding on owner and heirs, beneficiary (or SNT) obtaining a pro-rata co-ownership interest in home, or SNT obtaining a secured interest in home equal to the amount of the distribution. Before making such a distribution, the trustee should consult an attorney to make sure these protections are included to protect trust assets.

> **Example:** The trustee is asked to make expenditures of $50,000 in the residence of the beneficiary to make accessibility modifications to bathroom and add a saltwater sauna. The home is owned by the beneficiary's brother.

The trustee believes that the beneficiary will benefit from accessibility modifications so he can use the bathroom. Plus, a doctor has given a recommendation that a sauna will ease the beneficiary's pain to his limbs and provide therapy to beneficiary's body. The trustee agrees to make distribution but will only do so if brother deeds 20 percent interest in home, which is valued at $250,000, to protect the disbursement.

HOW SHOULD THE TRUSTEE MAKE PURCHASE OF AN AUTOMOBILE?

A SNT trustee can purchase a vehicle of any value without any effect on public benefits. See chapter 5 for more information on the effect of purchasing an automobile. The SNT trustee will need to decide whether the vehicle should be owned by the trust or by the individual.

If the beneficiary has capacity and there is little concern over predators, it is best if the automobile is owned by the individual. Otherwise, the trustee and the assets of the trust may be liable if the beneficiary or a third-party driver is negligent and causes an accident. The trustee could then be a defendant in a lawsuit and the assets of the trust subject to the driver's creditors. If the individual is the owner, then only assets held outside trust would be subject to these creditors.

The trustee of the SNT should still be named as a lienholder on the automobile so that the individual with ownership cannot sell or borrow against the vehicle without the permission of the SNT trustee.

> **Helpful Hint**: If an SNT beneficiary requires more than one automobile, the SNT can purchase and retain ownership of any additional automobiles and maintain SSI and Medi-Cal eligibility. Remember, these programs allow beneficiary to own only one vehicle. In these circumstances, it may be prudent to establish a separate SNT to hold title to any additional automobiles. This way, if the automobile is involved in an accident, the trust that holds the beneficiary's other assets is not subject to any accident victim creditors.

CAN AN SNT TRUSTEE HIRE A CAREGIVER FOR BENEFICIARY?

Yes. Hiring a caregiver is often the most important service an SNT trustee can provide to a person with a disability. A caregiver can allow a beneficiary to remain at home or simply provide services to enhance the beneficiary's life.

It is never a good idea to hire someone casually to help with caregiving services for the beneficiary. When a person is hired, many trustees assume they can simply pay an hourly wage directly to the caregiver. This assumption is far too simplistic. Many trustees will get into trouble for failing to recognize that what he or she thought was a simple arrangement was instead a legal employer/employee relationship. The result could be that the trustee is personally responsible for failing to comply with a host of employment laws and incur significant liability for a caregiver's injuries and unpaid taxes.

The issues involved in hiring caregivers can be deceptively difficult. The following are the types of questions the trustee must be able to answer:

- Is the caregiver status as employee or independent contractor clearly understood and documented?
- Is the proposed caregiver someone who can be hired, e.g., someone who does not have a criminal record or has proper United States documentation to work?
- Is the compensation reasonable given the assets available to the trustee?
- Is the proposed caregiver trained and capable of providing the required level of care?

Helpful Hint: A rich source of data on all aspects of caregiver hiring, training, and selection is found at www.caregiver.org. Any trustee considering hiring a caregiver should review this website.

Warning: The hiring of a caregiver will greatly increase the potential for abuse by the caregiver. The caregiver will oftentimes have the most unfettered personal contact with the beneficiary, which can lead to serious issues later. The SNT trustee should consider all aspects of protecting the beneficiary from abuse during the caregiver hire and while managing the caregiver.

HOW SHOULD A TRUSTEE HIRE A CAREGIVER?

There are really three basic ways to hire a caregiver.

1. The trustee hires a care management or professional home care agency.
2. The trustee uses a registry of available help and selects a caregiver.
3. The trustee hires the caregiver themselves.

In order for the trustee to better understand the available options, below is a summary description of the various types of caregiving services:

- **Home Care Agency/Organization**

  The term home care agency is very broad. Most often it indicates that a home care provider is certified or licensed by the state or federal government. However, in some instances, certification or licensing is not a legal requirement. Thus, it is important for the trustee to understand what the home health agency's credentials are in deciding whether to use them.

Home health agencies usually provide a plethora of skilled and unskilled caregivers. For example, some agencies provide services through physicians, nurses, therapists, social workers, homemakers, durable medical equipment and supply dealers, and volunteers. Home health agencies recruit and supervise their own personnel. As a result, the home health agency will assume liability for all care and employment matters.

In general, this is the most expensive option, but is also the safest for the trustee if care is taken in selecting an appropriate agency. Some benefits of using a home health agency are

o   Agencies will make sure that all applicable state and federal labor, health, and safety laws and regulations, including payroll tax and social security withholding requirements are followed.
o   Agencies generally have rigorous screening procedures and provide training for their employees.
o   Agencies can usually provide a caregiver on short notice in an emergency, or they can provide several candidates to choose from.
o   If the caregiver hired through the agency does not work out, the agency will provide someone else.
o   Agencies will typically provide caregiver supervision 24/7 for any crisis.
o   Agencies may also include on staff professional certified care managers that can help an SNT trustee.

- **Registries**

Most communities have attendant registries which are a good resource for finding in-home help. These registries usually are not licensed or regulated by government. When calling an attendant registry, it is important to inquire about their particular screening process or training requirements. The trustee should also inquire about the fees charged. Fees for using a registry can vary greatly, from free to thousands of dollars.

There are also nonprofit community agencies that maintain lists of individuals available to perform all kinds of household tasks, from cleaning and laundry to repairs and gardening. It is a good idea to shop around and obtain the best service for the lowest fee.

The trustee will select and supervise the work of a registry-referred provider. The trustee must also pay the caregiver and comply with all applicable state and federal labor, health, and safety laws and regulations, including workers' compensation, payroll tax, and social security withholding requirements as described below.

- **Individual selected by trustee**

A trustee can just hire someone to be the beneficiary's caregiver. The screening process is generally easier if the trustee uses a registry, but using one is not necessary. Independent caregivers can be anyone the trustee can find, including friends, family, nurses, therapists, aides, homemakers, or privately employed chore workers.

The trustee will select and supervise the work of the caregiver. The trustee must also pay the caregiver and comply with all applicable state and federal labor, health, and safety laws and regulations, including payroll tax and social security withholding requirements, as described below.

Some benefits of using an individual:

- ○ Can hire a trusted family member or friend of the beneficiary who knows the beneficiary and who the beneficiary trusts
- ○ Generally costs less to hire someone directly

Helpful Hint: A sample caregiving contract is attached as Appendix K to this book. It can be used when the SNT trustee is hiring a caregiver directly.

SHOULD A TRUSTEE USE A HOME CARE AGENCY OR HIRE A PRIVATE INDIVIDUAL?

It depends. The real goal is to find the right person for the job. Thus, each situation will be different, depending on the

- type of care required;
- availability of a trusted individual to serve;
- amount of SNT's assets to pay for services; and
- ability to manage either an individual or agency.

In general, if the assets justify it, hiring a home care agency is often the preferred method for an SNT trustee. It is better because the trustee will not have to be involved in the day-to-day administration of the caregiver and will generally be protected against liability as long as appropriate steps were taken in the selection and periodic review of the agency. In selecting an agency, it is important that the trustee make sure that the agency is licensed, bonded, and insured. Plus, home health agencies costs vary widely. A trustee should check around to see if he or she can find the one that provides the best expertise with a good reputation at the best price.

However, if the trustee only has limited trust assets to work with, then hiring an individual may be the only affordable option. If there is no family member or friend available to serve, then it may be prudent to review a local registry of available workers as described in the previous question. You can also look within the caregiving circles of people who have a family member with a similar disability as the SNT beneficiary, or ask the beneficiary's doctor, physical therapist, hospital or nursing home personnel, church members, and not-for-profits that serve the community of persons with disabilities. It is very important that the trustee do an adequate background check and reasonably review the qualifications of a potential caregiver. Failure to do so can result in a trustee being sued and may place the beneficiary in a very dangerous situation.

See, Appendix J for a checklist for hiring and managing a caregiver and Appendix K for a sample caregiving agreement.

CAN A TRUSTEE HIRE A PROFESSIONAL CARE MANAGER INSTEAD OF A HOME CARE AGENCY?

Instead of hiring a home care agency or personally supervising the caregiver, a SNT trustee can hire a professional case manager to supervise the privately hired caregiver.

A professional care manager can assist the SNT trustee as well as the beneficiary and his or her family by providing a plethora of services that the SNT trustee may not be competent to provide. Care managers are professionals—trained to evaluate and recommend care for persons with disabilities. A care manager might be a nurse, social worker, psychologist, or public benefits expert who specializes in assessing the abilities and needs of persons with disabilities.

Care managers can assist the trustee and serve in any of a number of functions. For example, a care manager may

- Assess the level and type of care needed and develop a care plan
- Take steps to start the care plan and keep it functioning
- Make sure care is in a safe and disability-friendly environment
- Resolve family conflicts and other issues with long term care
- Become an advocate for the care recipient and the caregiver
- Manage care for a loved one for out-of-town families
- Conduct ongoing assessments to implement changes in care
- Oversee and direct care provided at home
- Coordinate the efforts of key support systems
- Provide personal counseling
- Help with Medi-Cal qualification and application
- Arrange for services of legal and financial advisers
- Provide placement in assisted living facilities or nursing homes
- Monitor the care received in a nursing home or in assisted living
- Assist with the monitoring of medications
- Find appropriate solutions to avoid a crisis
- Coordinate medical appointments and medical information
- Provide transportation to medical appointments
- Assist families in positive decision making
- Develop care plans for older loved ones not now needing care

The services offered will depend on the educational and professional background of the care manager, but most are qualified to cover items in the list above or can recommend a professional who can. Fees may vary. There is often an initial consultation fee that is followed by hourly fees for services. The hiring of a case manager is an appropriate expenditure of an SNT.

WHAT QUESTIONS SHOULD BE ASKED OF A POTENTIAL HOME CARE AGENCY?

Not all home care agencies are equal. The SNT trustee should assess which agency is best for his or her beneficiary. If the SNT trustee is uncertain how best to match an agency with the beneficiary, the trustee should hire a professional care manager to assist in matching an appropriate agency with the beneficiary. The following is a list of issues that should be considered by the trustee when hiring a care agency:

- When discussing hiring an agency, the trustee should be very clear about the beneficiary's care needs, emotional needs, personality traits, cognitive status, and nonpersonal needs (such as travel) for improved screening.
- The trustee should be very specific about dates and times when care will be needed.
- The trustee should seek a full description of agency caregiver screening and employment process. The more sophisticated the agency, the more sophisticated the screening process the agency will employ. A good one should provide a criminal background check, DMV checks with regular review, fingerprinting, proof of US employment eligibility, skills testing and thorough reference checks.
- The trustee should seek a written explanation of all of the agency's services and fee structure.
- The trustee should ask the agency to assess the client's needs in person and create a plan of care with written caregiver instructions that will be updated as needed.

WHAT QUESTIONS SHOULD BE ASKED OF A POTENTIAL CAREGIVER?

In selecting an appropriate caregiver, a trustee should create a job description for the type of care that the SNT beneficiary will require, as well as information about the hours and wages. The trustee will then have a good idea of what questions should be asked based on the needs of the beneficiary.

Example: <u>Sample Job Description</u>
Position: Home care worker for person with disability
Reports to: SNT trustee
Hours: Monday through Friday, 9:00 a.m.-1:00 p.m.
Minimum Requirements: 1-2 years of experience in home care, good interpersonal skills
Responsibilities: 1. Assist with dressing, 2. Bathing, 3. Preparing lunch, 4. Shopping

In preparation for the caregiving interview, the trustee should have a list of questions pertinent to the job description and a sample work contract ready for the applicant to read. A sample caregiving agreement is attached as Appendix K to this book. The following are some suggested questions for the interview:

- Why are you interested in this job?
- Where have you worked before?
- Why did you leave?
- What were your duties?
- How do you feel about caring for a person with a disability?
- What do you find to be the most difficult part of working in home care?
- How do you handle people who are angry, stubborn, or fearful?
- Tell me about a time your client did not want to comply with medical orders?
- What would you do if your client started yelling or screaming at you?
- What would you do in case of an emergency such as _____?
- Do you have a driver's license?
- Do you have a car?
- Would you be able to transfer someone from a wheelchair into a car or onto a bed?

- Is there anything in the job description that you are uncomfortable doing?
- What time commitment are you willing to make to stay on the job?
- Can you give me two work-related and one personal reference?

Immediately after the interview, it is important for the trustee to write down first impressions and, if possible, discuss these with another family member or friend. It also would be best before hiring the person for the person with a disability to meet with them.

The trustee should also check the references of at least two final applicants. If the offer is accepted, the caregiver and the in-home helper should set a date to sign the contract and begin work. Both employer and employee should keep a copy of the contract.

> **Helpful Hint**: It is always prudent to run a background check when hiring individuals to assist a person with a disability. One service, for around $100, will provide criminal searches, identity verification, reference check, and several qualification confirmations. See, http://www.choicetrust.com. Another option is to utilize a professional screening company. Some additional resources on how to safely screen, hire, and check on new employees is located at www.esrcheck.com.

WILL THE CAREGIVER HIRED BE AN EMPLOYEE OR INDEPENDENT CONTRACTOR?

In general, no matter how careful an SNT trustee is, the caregiver will nearly always be an employee. The distinctions between the two are as follows:

- For federal payroll tax purposes, an employee is "any individual who, under the usual common law rules applicable in determining the employer-employee relationship, has the status of employee."[178] The federal employment tax regulations set out these common law rules.[179] In general, an employer-employee relationship will exist

---

[178] Internal Revenue Code ("I.R.C.") § 3121(d)(2).

[179] See Treasury Regs. §§ 31.3121(d)-1, 31.3306(i)-1, and 31.3401(c)-1.

when the person for whom the services are performed has the right to control and direct the worker who performs the services.[180] This is called the "control test" and is set forth in more detail below. For California's workers' compensation matters, employee is defined as "every person in the service of an employer under any appointment or contract of hire or apprenticeship, express or implied, oral or written, whether lawfully or unlawfully employed."[181]

- A person is an "independent contractor" if he or she is not an "employee" of the SNT. The presumption is that the relationship is one of employer/employee. It is up to the trustee to prove that the relationship is that of an independent contractor.

One of the primary factors the IRS and California EDD consider in determining whether a worker is an employee (as opposed to an independent contractor) is whether the employer has the right to control the manner in which services are performed. Other factors that the IRS considers in determining whether a worker is an employee are discussed in IRS Publication 15-A. Other factors that the EDD considers in determining whether a worker is an employee are discussed in EDD Publication DE-44. If the worker meets many of the following factors, the IRS will find an employer/employee relationship exists between the SNT trustee and the caregiver:

1. The worker is required to comply with the employing entity's instructions.
2. The employing entity or another must train the worker.
3. The employing entity integrates the worker's services into its business operations.
4. The worker must render his or her services to the employing entity personally.
5. The employing entity hires, supervises, and pays any assistants to the worker.
6. There is a continuing relationship between the worker and the employing entity.
7. The worker must devote substantially full time to the employing entity's care.

---

[180]   Treasury. Reg. § 31.3121(d)-1(c)(2).
[181]   Cal. Labor Code§3351.

8. The worker does not work for more than one employer at a time.
9. The worker performs work on the employing entity's premises.
10. The worker must perform services in the order or sequence that the employing entity sets.
11. The worker must submit oral or written reports to the employing entity.
12. The employing entity pays the worker by the hour, week, or month.
13. The employing entity pays the worker's business and/or traveling expenses.
14. The employing entity furnishes significant tools, materials, and other equipment to the worker.
15. The employing entity invests in facilities that he or she uses in his work.
16. The worker does not realize a profit or suffer a loss because of his or her services.
17. The worker does not make his or her services available to the public on a regular and consistent basis.
18. The employment entity has the right to discharge the worker.
19. The worker does not have the right to end his or her care relationship with the employing entity at any time he or she wishes without incurring liability.

Some examples where the IRS determined there was an employee/employer relationship:

- A worker managed the convalescent's personal needs, entertained the "convalescent," lived in the convalescent home, accompanied the convalescent on trips, and provided any other services necessary for the comfort or well-being of the convalescent.[182]
- A brother engaged his sister, who is independent of his financial support, to act as his housekeeper and companion and to perform minor nursing services for him in his home during regular hours and according to his instructions.[183]

---

[182] Revenue Ruling 56-109, 1956-1 C.B. 467.
[183] Revenue Ruling 54-572, 1954-2 C.B. 341.

- Relatives were retained to provide personal care in the home of a family member and were paid, in part, by a welfare agency.[184]
- A hospital resident retained a private attendant to perform services of a domestic nature for the resident where the resident hired that attendant from a list provided by the hospital.[185]

The most common ways that trustees get into trouble is when the caregiver files a wage and hour claim as an employee, when the caregiver is injured while working, and when there is an IRS audit. In these instances, if the SNT trustee has not complied with the myriad tax reporting and employment laws, he or she will be subject to serious penalties.

> **Warning:** Some trustees illegally pay the caregiver cash without reporting the employment to anyone. An SNT trustee will be subject to severe penalties, and large fines will arise if taxes go unpaid or if wage and hour laws and workers' compensation requirements are ignored. The SNT trustee will likely have to pay these fines from his or her own pocket. It makes little sense for a trustee to put themselves in such jeopardy.

WHAT EMPLOYMENT ISSUES MUST THE SNT TRUSTEE UNDERSTAND?

It depends on whether the SNT trustee hired a home care agency or hired an individual from a registry or an individual.

1. If the SNT trustee decides to hire a home care agency, the home care agency is the caregiver's employee and the company manages all employment related issues.
2. If the SNT trustee uses a registry or hires an independent trustee, the SNT trustee will be required to address a number of issues, including wage and hour laws, notice and recordkeeping requirements, safety, liability, immigration laws, insurance issues, and withholding procedures, which are described below.

---

[184] Private Letter Ruling 9309026 (December 4, 1992).
[185] Revenue Ruling 74-388, 1974-2 C.B. 325.

As described in the previous answer, caregivers are hired as either employees or independent contractors. The legal distinction between the two is enormous, but the practical difference can be miniscule. However, nearly all caregivers hired to take care of an individual with a disability will be employees.

When a SNT becomes an employer, the trustee must register with the California Employment Development Department within fifteen days. A regular employer should use EDD Form DE1. A household employer should use EDD Form DE1-HW. The SNT will be assigned a state employer identification number.

A newly hired caregiver should be asked to complete IRS Form W-4, "Employee's Withholding Allowance Certificate," and US Citizenship and Immigration Services (USCIS) Form I-9, "Employment Eligibility Verification." The SNT trustee also must verify that the caregiver may legally work in the United States.

The following is a list of the most common (but not nearly all) employment issues that must be resolved by an SNT trustee who has hired a caregiver:

- **Liability.** When home care is provided, the SNT trustee must protect the SNT assets and himself or herself from liability resulting from injury of the caregiver or losses from caregiver theft. A trustee should examine existing homeowner's liability and casualty insurance to see if adequate caregiver coverage is provided. If not, insurance should be purchased. Further, liability may attach to an SNT trustee as employer under a legal doctrine called *respondeat superior* for injuries caused by an employee's negligent or wrongful operation while acting within the scope of the employment.[186] For example, if the caregiver causes an automobile accident on the way to the store to pick up groceries for the SNT beneficiary, the SNT trustee as employer may be liable. An insurance broker should be consulted for each policy to confirm caregiver coverage.

- **Workers Compensation.** In California, policies providing comprehensive personal liability coverage must include workers' compensation benefits for household employees, unless the benefits are otherwise covered or the employee's services are performed in

---

[186] Civil Code §2338.

connection with a trade, business, or occupation.[187] The SNT trustee should consult with his or her insurance broker to make sure that workers' compensation is provided.

- **Minimum Wage/Overtime.** The minimum wage and overtime laws are very complex and differ depending on the nature of the work. Generally, a live-in employee must be paid one and one-half times the regular rate for all hours worked over twelve hours (rather than over eight hours) in one workday (for five workdays; on the sixth and seventh day, the overtime rate for time worked in excess of nine hours per day is double the regular pay).[188] Special exemptions apply to domestic companions for the aged or infirm.[189] However, each worker's situation must be examined for proper compliance.
- **Social Security/Medicare Withholding.** The SNT trustee will be required to withhold Social Security and Medicare (commonly called FICA) on wages for domestic help hired to provide care if the worker is paid more than specific limits.[190] Generally, 7.65 percent of the paycheck is withheld, and the employer pays another 7.65 percent on the employee's behalf.[191]
- **Unemployment.** An SNT trustee must pay unemployment tax (commonly called FUTA). Withholding is required if a care worker is paid compensation above specific limits during any quarter of the current or preceding calendar year.[192] There are also state unemployment, disability insurance, and employment training taxes to be considered.

For further discussion on the taxation obligations of a caregiver, see chapter 9.

> **Helpful Hint:** Unless the SNT trustee is very experienced in employment issues, it is strongly recommended that the

---

[187] Insurance Code §§11590-11593.
[188] Wage Order No. 15-2001(3)(A)-(B) (8 Cal Code Regs §11150(3)(A)-(B)).
[189] 29 U.S.C. §213(a)(15).
[190] I.R.C. §§3102(a), 3121.
[191] I.R.C. §§3101, 3111.
[192] I.R.C. §3306.

trustee hire a payroll service to pay appropriate taxes. One such company, Paychex (at http://www.paychex.com) provides support in the employee/employer relationship.

WHAT HAPPENS IF THE TRUSTEE FAILS TO COMPLY WITH EMPLOYMENT LAWS?

In general, the SNT trustee will be responsible to pay the taxes and will be subject to penalties. The SNT will be responsible for all unpaid income, FICA, and FUTA taxes.[193] The federal tax penalty for failure to withhold income taxes is 1/5 percent (3 percent if no informational returns were filed) of the wages subject to income tax withholding. The social security tax penalty is 20 percent (40 percent where no informational returns were filed) of the social security taxes required to be withheld.[194] The trust will also be responsible for interest on unpaid taxes at the statutory rate.[195]

There may also be fines assessed the trustee for failing to withhold and may also seek penalties for failure to file a tax return.[196]

> **Warning:** If it is found that the trustee willfully failed to collect and pay taxes may be personally liable for the total amount of the uncollected tax under the "100% penalty provisions of the Internal Revenue Code.[197]

There may be ways to alleviate some of these penalties and fines by showing that the employer relied on existing practice. However, the findings must be in good faith with reliance on long-standing employment practices.

California may add additional penalties beyond the IRS California imposed liability for unpaid personal income, unemployment insurance, and state disability insurance taxes. In addition, California imposes a 10 percent penalty on any employer that, without good cause, fails to pay any contribution

---

[193] I.R.C. §§3304, 3102, 3301.

[194] I.R.C. §3509.

[195] I.R.C. §6601.

[196] I.R.C. §6651.

[197] I.R.C. §6672.

required of it or its employees.[198] If the Employment Development Department of California (EDD) determines that the employer willfully engaged in fraud in misclassifying its workers, instead of a 10 percent penalty, the EDD has discretion to issue a 50 percent penalty.[199] Plus, the EDD can issue a personal liability tax assessment against the trustee that failed to make payment. California will also require interest be paid on any unpaid contributions.[200] Unpaid personal income tax is generally assessed at a rate of 6 percent of wages subject to withholding.

Again, California has some opportunities to find relief from these penalties and fines on findings that the employer innocently and honestly believed that workers were independent contractors and not employees.

HOW MUCH SHOULD A CAREGIVER BE PAID?

A home care agency will have its own fee schedule. The cost of fees will depend greatly on the type of services needed.

An individual caregiver is generally paid an amount equal to the prevailing wage for similar services performed in the community where the services will be performed. Thus, if the caregiver is only providing home cleaning services, shopping, and preparing meals, the pay should equal what it would generally cost to hire someone to perform these tasks. One way to determine these costs is to check Craigslist to see what similar services are being offered in the beneficiary's community. Thus, a trustee should have a good idea what others in the area charge for similar services.

The minimum wage and overtime laws are very complex and differ depending on the nature of the work. Generally, a live-in employee must be paid one and one-half times the regular rate for all hours worked over twelve hours (rather than over eight hours) in one workday (for five workdays; on the sixth and seventh day, the overtime rate for time worked in excess of nine hours per day is double the regular pay).[201] Special exemptions apply to domestic

---

[198] Cal. Unempl. Ins. Code §1112.
[199] Cal. Unempl. Ins. Code §1128(a).
[200] Cal. Unempl. Ins. Code §1113.
[201] Wage Order No. 15-2001(3)(A)-(B) (8 Cal Code Regs §11150(3)(A)-(B)).

companions for the aged or infirm.[202] However, each worker's situation must be examined for proper compliance.

> **Warning:** Sometimes an SNT trustee is asked to pay a premium to the beneficiary's family members or friends to provide caregiving services. A trustee is breaching his legal duty if he or she pays more than those services are worth. Further, if a trustee hires his own family, he or she could be liable for self-dealing and be liable for breach of fiduciary duty unless the trust document authorizes this type of hiring or there is a court order authorizing this expenditure.

WHAT CAN AN SNT TRUSTEE DO TO REDUCE CAREGIVING COSTS?

Home health care can be very expensive. According to a 2009 study by Genworth Financial, the median annual cost in the San Francisco Bay Area for in-home nonmedical services is $52,624, based on forty-four hours per week. The cost from a Medicare-certified (home health) agency would be $217,360 and the cost of a private room in a nursing home would be $102,018. Thus, it is imperative that the trustee understand and control caregiving costs as much as possible.

It is the rare SNT that has sufficient assets to pay for all of a beneficiary's needed caregiving services throughout his or her lifetime. Thus, many trustees struggle to make sure that assets will stretch out as far as possible. Here are some suggestions for stretching out the dollars for caregiving:

1. **Check for Long Term Care Insurance.** While rare, a beneficiary of an SNT may be eligible to have a long term care insurance pay for a home care agency.
2. **Negotiate the rate**. If the trustee has hired a home care agency, it can often find more affordable ways to meet the SNTs budget by using less expensive caregivers. For example, an expensive RN should not be handling services an unskilled worker can manage.

---

[202]   29 U.S.C. §213(a)(15).

3. **Cutback hours**. The trustee can sometimes reduce hours without jeopardizing care. It is important to continually assess the beneficiary's needs to determine if a cutback in hours can provide an almost equal level of care. A trustee should also be wary of agencies that continually "suggest" that more hours are needed. Before agreeing, make sure that more hours are truly needed.

4. **Discuss with doctor**. The beneficiary's doctor may know of less expensive resources for nonmedical care.

5. **Discuss with place of worship**. A beneficiary's place of worship, or the trustee's, may sometimes know volunteers willing to help people with disabilities in the community.

6. **Discuss with beneficiary's family and friends**. The trustee may be able to reduce fees by having family or friends taking over some of the duties that the trustee has to pay for, like cleaning or shopping.

7. **Visit disability centered not for profits**. There are many not-for-profits that assist persons with disabilities. For example, the Centers for Independent Living have centers all around the state that can help. To find the local agency, see http://www.ilru.org/html/publications/directory/california.html.

8. **Seek other nonprofit resources**. For example, Family Caregiver Alliance (www.caregiver.org) provides grants to those needing respite (family caregiver relief) care, which can offset some of the costs.

9. **Apply for government resources**. California Medi-Cal provides In-Home Support Services (IHSS), which can provide funds to pay for, or at least supplement, nonmedical caregiving services.

10. **Shop separate services around**. If both medical care and personal care are needed, make sure that if one agency is handling both that a less expensive personal care agency is not available to pay for the personal care. Oftentimes, if one agency handles both, the personal care is much more expensive.

11. **VA Benefits**. If the beneficiary is a veteran, he or she may qualify for aid and attendance benefit. Check with a local VA agency to see if beneficiary qualifies.

WHAT OTHER RESOURCES CAN AN SNT TRUSTEE REVIEW TO ASSIST IN HIRING CAREGIVERS?

The following books will help a trustee understand the incredible pressures and difficulties that many caregivers face and provide solutions that will assist both the SNT trustee and those providing care.

D. Jeanne Roberts. *Taking Care of Caregivers*. San Mateo: Bull Publishing Company, 1991.

James R. Sherman. *The Caregiver Survival Series.* Golden Valley: Pathway Books, 1994.

Helping Yourself Help Others: A Book for Caregivers. New York: Times Books, 1994.

Nancy Mace and Peter Rabbins. *The 36-Hour Day.* Baltimore: The Johns Hopkins University Press, 1991 edition.

Angela Heath. *Long-Distance Caregiving.* Lakewood: American Source Books, 1993.

The following websites can help trustees manage a caregiver.

AARP's website has a caregiver resource center that provides exceptional assistance in hiring, training, and retaining a caregiver at http://www.aarp.org/relationships/caregiving-resource-center.

Eldercare Services' website and blog has information, education, and caregiver services at www.eldercareanswers.com.

Family Caregiver Alliance's website provides information and education on a variety of caregiver issues at www.caregiver.org.

H.E.L.P.'s website offers some wonderful caregiving tools. H.E.L.P. also provides classes for those who are helping the elderly and disabled. http://www.help4srs.org/healthcare/caregiving.

Legally Nanny's website offers advice to individuals hiring elder care providers on legal and tax advice. For a fee, they will assist in handling the legal and tax requirements of hiring an at home caregiver. http://www.legallynanny.com.

Social Worker/Advocate Erin Vogt prepared an excellent guide on hiring home health-care workers. The article goes through much of the same information in this chapter and also provides several checklists and forms that will aid a trustee of an SNT in hiring a caregiver. http://duttoncaseylaw.com/uploads/Guide%20to%20 Hiring%20In-Home%20Help%20FINAL.pdf.

CAN THE SNT TRUSTEE HIRE THE BENEFICIARY'S PARENTS TO SERVE AS CAREGIVER?

Generally yes, but certain issues must be resolved by the SNT trustee before agreeing to pay a parent. It often makes sense to hire a parent to be the beneficiary's caregiver. Parents are aware of their child's needs, often provide better care, and typically cost less than a third party. Further, the parent may have given up a job to care for their child and may need the funds to allow them to continue to provide care.

The SNT trustee may need to address the following issues:

- If a minor child beneficiary is receiving SSI, the payment of caregiving income to the parent may reduce or eliminate the child's eligibility for SSI under a concept called SSI deeming.[203] This concept is discussed in chapter 4 more fully, but the basic idea is that a parent must use his or her income to support those dependent on them. The SNT trustee must make sure that any payments to a parent will not interfere with the child/SNT beneficiary's SSI eligibility.
- If the parents are trustees, they may have a conflict of interest in hiring themselves as employees of the trust that they administer. If the SNT document does not expressly allow them to hire themselves

---

[203] 20 C.F.R. §416.1160 for the rules about how a parent's income is "deemed" to be that of a minor child for SSI eligibility purposes.

as caregiver, then court instruction should be obtained through a court petition to approve the hiring and setting the amount of their compensation. This petition is further discussed in chapter 11.

- If the beneficiary is a minor, the parents have an existing duty to pay for that child's support that the SNT's assets cannot be used to offset. Parents have a general obligation to support their minor children "in the manner suitable to the child's circumstances."[204] Parents also have equal responsibility to support "to the extent of their ability, a child of whatever age who is incapacitated from earning a living and without sufficient means."[205] The parents' duty of support does not necessarily end with the furnishing of mere necessities. A minor child is entitled to be maintained in a style and condition consonant with his or her parents' position in society, and this duty of support continues even if the child is "possessed of ample means" of his or her own.[206] Because of their general duty of support, parents will be expected to provide some level of care for the beneficiary without compensation or reimbursement. However, SNT trustees have been successful in allowing trust assets to pay for items that go beyond the mere duty of support and constitute exceptional needs. SNT trustees have also been successful in paying for items when the parents are unable to afford these items due to unemployment as described below.

There is an exception to this general rule. When the parents are unable to afford basic support a child's assets can be used to pay for the support or, in certain circumstances, supplement the parents' basic support to provide a higher standard of living for the child:

> . . . that a parent possessing adequate financial resources has a duty to provide his or her child with basic support regardless of the child's independent resources. Such a rule serves the dual purposes of assuring that a child's independent income is preserved for use of the child during his or her adult years, and at the same time permitting, in an

---

[204] Family Code §3900.

[205] Family Code §3910.

[206] *Chapin v Superior Court* (1966) 239 Cal.App.2d 851.

appropriate case, such income to be used to supplement the parents' contribution so that the child might enjoy a higher standard of living during minority than the parents could otherwise afford. In the absence of a clear contrary trust purpose or the inability of the parents reasonably to provide any support, we conclude that this approach both respects the parents' statutory obligations of support mandated by . . . . Thus, to pay a parent for caregiving, the trustee must make sure that the parent is being compensated for things that are greater than the parent's support obligation.[207]

Example: Jonathan is the trustee of his adult friend Simon's first-party SNT. Simon's mother, Alene, has been taking care of Simon since the accident that caused his disability. Alene asks Jonathan to pay a monthly amount to provide caregiving to Simon. Jonathan may authorize such payments as long as the fee is reasonable. Jonathan checks with area caregivers and provides a salary commensurate with that of the city they live in. Jonathan further will have to comply with all employment obligations, so he hires Paychex to do all employment withholding. He further consults with his insurance broker to make sure that all insurance is in place to protect the SNT.

Example: Father is the trustee of a first-party SNT that is under ongoing court jurisdiction for his minor son. He has quit his job to take care of his son and is living on a very limited income. Son is receiving SSI and Medi-Cal due to Father's limited resources and income. Father would like to pay himself as son's caregiver. Father must file a petition with court to determine whether he will be able to make these disbursements. The court petition will need to address the issue of his legal duty of support, his earning capacity, and the amount of the compensation. If court agrees, he can pay himself for these services. However, Father must be careful to not pay himself too much income, because

---

[207]   *Armstrong v Armstrong* (1976) 15 Cal3d 942, 947.

doing so would eliminate his son's SSI due to SSI deeming to a minor child. See chapter 4 for further discussion on deeming.

CAN THE SNT TRUSTEE HIRE THE BENEFICIARY'S IHSS WORKER AS A CAREGIVER?

Yes, but the SNT trustee cannot simply supplement the pay of the IHSS worker and instead must pay for additional work performed by the IHSS worker.

> **Note:** IHSS stands for In-Home Supportive Services, which provides at home caregiver service paid for by Medi-Cal and is described in more detail in chapter 4.

It is often a good idea to hire the beneficiary's existing IHSS caregiver because he or she will already understand the beneficiary's needs and may be less expensive than hiring a third-party agency caregiver. If IHSS caregivers are doing a good job, it may also be prudent to find a way to provide them additional pay so they do not leave. Due to the recent budget problems, IHSS worker's hours have been cut and the amount of pay they receive has been drastically cut. This has caused many of the best IHSS workers to leave to find better employment opportunities.

While an IHSS worker's pay cannot be directly supplemented, the worker can be paid for services beyond those funded by the program or for services not funded by the program.[208] In order to property structure the pay for an IHSS worker, the SNT trustee should know what services the IHSS worker has been hired to provide and how many hours a month are being paid for by the government.

In general, IHSS provides personal care services, which include assistance with ambulation, bathing, oral hygiene, grooming, and dressing; care and assistance with prosthetic devices; bowel, bladder, and menstrual care; skin care; repositioning, range-of-motion exercises, and transfers; feeding and assurance of adequate fluid intake; respiration; paramedical services; and assistance with self-administration of medications.[209] In addition to the personal

---

[208] 42 C.F.R. §447.1; MPP Regs §30-767.4; Welfare & Institutions Code §§12300(h) (2), 14132.95(j).

[209] Welfare & Institutions Code §14132.95(d)(1).

care services described above, ancillary services, such as meal preparation and cleanup, laundry, food and other shopping, and domestic services, are available as long as they are subordinate to personal care services.[210]

Currently, a beneficiary who needs more than 20 hours per week of personal care services from an individual provider, the maximum available is 283 hours per month.[211] For a recipient who needs fewer than 20 hours per week of personal care from an individual provider, the maximum is 195 hours per month.[212]

Thus, to property hire an IHSS worker, he or she should be hired for hours in addition to those hours already authorized by the government and for services not already being paid for.

> **Example**: If IHSS is paying a caregiver $10 an hour for ten hours a month, a trustee cannot augment the worker's salary by paying an additional $5 hour on top of the $10. However, the trustee can hire the IHSS caregiver for additional hours and pay a premium wage for those hours. For example, if the IHSS worker is being paid $10/hour for ten hours, the SNT can pay $20 an hour for an additional ten hours helping the beneficiary, which brings the IHSS's worker pay up to $15 an hour for all the work provided.

Note, however, that the services provided during the hours paid by the trustee must be different from the services authorized by IHSS. If the services are the same, the hours provided by IHSS may be reduced. For example, if IHSS pays for two baths a week and the trustee agrees to pay for five baths a week, then IHSS will cease paying for the two baths a week, because it sees a need for only two.

> **Warning:** All numerical figures are valid up to year 2011. These numbers may change with future changes in the law.

---

[210] Welfare & Institutions Code §14132.95(d)(2).

[211] Welfare & Institutions Code §12303.4(b)(1).

[212] Welfare & Institutions Code §12303.4(a)(1).

ONCE A CAREGIVER IS HIRED, WHAT SHOULD THE TRUSTEE DO TO MONITOR THE CAREGIVER?

The SNT trustee should do the following to make sure that the caregiving arrangement continues to be in the best interest of the beneficiary:

- Make sure that there is a personal care agreement between the trustee as employer and the caregiver as employee. An example of a caregiver agreement is set forth in Appendix K.
- Make sure that there is a written care plan or caregiver instructions that identify the trustee's expectations for care, the beneficiary's specific needs, and the caregiver's roles and tasks to resolve those needs.
- Make sure there is a communication log or notebook where caregivers will document beneficiary care follow up and communicate with each other (if there is more than one caregiver).
- Make sure that the caregivers can communicate with each other if the notebook/log is insufficient by providing needed numbers to all caregivers.
- Make unannounced visits to ensure that caregiver is providing needed care.
- Communicate immediately with caregiver if expected needs are not being met.
- Provide ongoing training and professional support for caregiver as needed.
- If there is a problem, be certain of it before attempting to correct problem, unless the beneficiary's safety is at issue.

  Note. There is no caregiver that cannot be replaced (even family members). It is the beneficiary's safety and quality of life that must be maintained.

Chapter 6 Summary

- ✓ A trustee should set up a budget to assist the trustee in complying with his or her legal duty.
- ✓ Appendix C of the book provides a checklist to assist the trustee in setting up a budget.

- ✓ A trustee should set up a system of making distributions for the benefit of the beneficiary that is communicated as early as possible to the beneficiary.
- ✓ A trustee must be careful in making disbursements, because doing it wrong could jeopardize the beneficiary's eligibility for public benefits.
- ✓ A trustee can provide a gift card or gift certificate but must follow specific rules; failure to follow these rules will result in the gift card being counted as cash and reduce SSI eligibility dollar for dollar.
- ✓ A major consideration on distributions is whether it will interfere with the beneficiary's eligibility for public benefits.
- ✓ A trustee can pay the credit card bills of the beneficiary but must still exercise discretion on what is purchased so the trustee does not inadvertently cause a reduction or loss of SSI or Medi-Cal due to excess resources or in-kind support and maintenance.
- ✓ A trustee should not give the beneficiary a bank debit card as this will be counted as cash.
- ✓ A trustee should never give cash or an allowance directly to an SNT beneficiary who is receiving SSI or Medi-Cal.
- ✓ Distributions to beneficiaries on Section 8 must be planned carefully.
- ✓ A Section 8 recipient should not receive a regularly recurring payment from the SNT unless the trustee knows how the distribution will affect Section 8 eligibility.
- ✓ A SNT trustee can make a purchase of a home for the beneficiary.
- ✓ There are advantages and disadvantages to whether the SNT should own the home or a distribution made to the beneficiary of the home.
- ✓ A trustee can pay for home modifications of a residence not owned by the beneficiary but should consider the effect of doing so.
- ✓ A trustee may purchase an automobile for the beneficiary but should not have the SNT own the automobile due to liability reasons.
- ✓ The trustee should make the SNT a lienholder on the car so the beneficiary will not sell it without permission of trustee.
- ✓ The trustee can make disbursement for caregivers for the beneficiary which may be the most important distribution that can be made but is also fraught with lots of potential for harm.
- ✓ The trustee can either do a private hire or use a home care agency when hiring a caregiver.
- ✓ The trustee can hire a professional care manager who can supervise a privately hired caregiver.

- ✓ The trustee can find caregivers through a registry, word of mouth, places of worship, not for profits, doctors/nurses, and others.
- ✓ The trustee should run a background check on the caregiver and enter into a written contract for services.
- ✓ If the trustee does a private hire, the trustee is responsible for all employment responsibilities including tax reporting, withholding, immigration, and liability.
- ✓ If the trustee does a private hire, he or she should hire a payroll agency to help with the employment relationship.
- ✓ If the trustee hires a home care agency the agency will be responsible for all employment responsibilities.
- ✓ A trustee should always check that insurance covers the caregiver in case of injury or theft.
- ✓ A parent can be hired as caregiver but care should be taken to not pay a parent who already owes a duty to support a minor child or adult with a disability.
- ✓ A parent serving as trustee should file a separate petition to the court to determine if it is ok to hire themselves as caregiver.
- ✓ A trustee should consider hiring the IHSS worker for additional hours if needed.
- ✓ The trustee cannot supplement the pay of the IHSS worker nor pay for services that are already being paid for by IHSS.

CHAPTER 7

Keeping SNT Records and Providing Accounting

This chapter will describe the trustee's obligation to keep records of trust transactions and when (and to whom) the trustee will be required to account and report. The trustee's responsibility to account will increase depending on whether the SNT is under continuing court jurisdiction.

> **Note:** Most SNTs are not under court jurisdiction. The ones that are generally include those first-party SNTs established by a court for a beneficiary who lacks capacity. If not sure what type of SNT is being administered, the SNT trustee should consult chapter 2 for a discussion of the different types of SNTs or review chapter 11 to find a special needs planning attorney who can assist in making this determination.

There are two different account and report requirements, depending on whether the SNT is under court jurisdiction:

- A trust under court jurisdiction will require an accounting be prepared in a very formal way as set forth in the Probate Code, reviewed by court staff (often called examiners), and then reviewed again by a judge. Depending on the county, court examiners and judges may not understand how an SNT is supposed to operate. Oftentimes, this will lead to trustees being very reluctant to make appropriate disbursements in fear of a court finding them at fault. It is important that SNT trustees and the attorneys that represent them be willing to fight for the beneficiary's rights.

- A trust not under court jurisdiction will typically require an accounting at least once a year. However, an SNT document may waive this requirement. Regardless of the waiver, an SNT trustee may decide to prepare an account to begin the running of the statute of limitation. Further, an SNT trustee will always have a duty to keep beneficiaries reasonably informed of trust transactions. This duty is not waivable and will require much of the same information that would be required in an account. Thus, doing an account (even if there is a waiver) may still be a good idea.

WHAT IS THE TRUSTEE RECORD KEEPING RESPONSIBILITIES?

Trustees have a legal duty to maintain accurate records of all trust business.[213] Records should be thorough, legible, and easily accessible and should provide a full description of the trustee's administration. Keeping detailed and accurate records ensures that the trustee can fulfill his or her duties to provide information, file tax returns, and submit complete accounts and reports. For example, an SNT trustee may be asked to provide information to the Social Security Administration if the beneficiary is on SSI. The SNT trustee must be able to determine whether distributions from the SNT are considered SSI income, not income, in-kind income or in-kind support and maintenance. To be certain that SNT distributions from the trust fall into the desired category, the trustee should include a short description of the purpose of each distribution.

Keeping good records also provides the best means of protecting trustees against liability in case a beneficiary questions the propriety of an administrative act. If proper records are not kept at the same time as the actions taken, it can be incredibly difficult to go back and recreate records months (or even years) later. Waiting to try and recreate records is more costly and will cause a trustee numerous headaches and problems.

The record-keeping requirement is relatively easy for a naturally organized person. However, if this is not an accurate description of trustee, then the trustee

---

[213] See Probate Code §§16060, 16062, and 16064.

should hire someone to assist in keeping records—oftentimes a bookkeeper can serve that role.

WHAT INFORMATION SHOULD BE RECORDED?

In general, the trustee should set up a system that keeps the following information available:

- Cash and assets received. Cash amounts spent. Plus, the allocation of the assets between principal, income, or both.
- Inventory of all trust assets, including,

  1. current valuation of trust assets;
  2. cost basis (the amount paid for an asset, e.g., if person paid $50,000 for a home, the cost basis in real property is $50,000 even if its value has increased to $100,000);
  3. periodic market valuations of securities; and
  4. gains and losses incurred on sale of assets and other dispositions.

- Records of all transactions must be retained and organized so as to reflect their connection to the above data, e.g.,

  1. canceled checks, paid invoices, and receipts;
  2. bank statements;
  3. explanation of each disbursement made;
  4. trust and beneficiary income tax returns (sometimes called fiduciary tax returns); and
  5. tax audit reports.

- Other documents that should be maintained:

  1. Investment policy statement and ongoing updates
  2. Quarterly investment reviews
  3. Updates to health records and care plans
  4. Trustee annotations of conversations with professional advisers and interested third parties
  5. Pertinent e-mails and letters related to trust activity

6.   Court documents and orders

WHAT IS THE PROCEDURE FOR KEEPING RECORDS?

There is no one right way to keep records. Whatever procedure is selected, the trustee should keep a record of each disbursement as it is made, keep the receipt for the disbursement, and review the records monthly. The trustee should review the records again at the end of the year.

The individual trustee may maintain trust records with a system of folders. A separate folder is maintained for each of the following categories:

1.   A copy of the trust agreement and all amendments
2.   A copy of the beneficiaries public benefit program eligibility letters and notices
3.   Notices sent by trustees to beneficiaries and others
4.   Cost-basis information
5.   Completed discretionary action forms and information regarding to whom and why the discretionary payments were made, or why the transfer between principal and income was made
6.   Information evidencing compliance with the Prudent Investor Rule
7.   Bank statements and canceled checks
8.   Deposit slips and other income items
9.   Paid bills
10. Copies of tax returns
11. Status of assets (or, depending on their number and complexity, one folder for each asset), including confirmations of purchases and sales
12. Transactions of any business operated by the trust
13. Correspondence and memoranda of a routine nature
14. All correspondence and memoranda in connection with the above or other actions of the trustee that might be called into question later

Helpful Hint: Because most SNTs last for years, it would also be prudent for a trustee to purchase a software accounting system like *Quicken* or *QuickBooks* to keep track of the ongoing trust transactions. This will aid the trustee greatly when he or she is preparing end-of-the-year accountings. The cost of the software and any training programs the trustee wishes to take can be paid for from trust assets.

WHAT HAPPENS IF A TRUSTEE FAILS TO KEEP PROPER RECORDS?

If an SNT trustee fails to keep appropriate records, he or she will be unable to provide an accurate account of trustee actions to the beneficiary, public benefit agencies, to a court, and to other government agencies, like the IRS.

A trustee can be removed if he or she fails to keep proper records, because a court may find that a trustee who fails to keep adequate records is unfit for the office.[214] Further, trustees who fail to keep proper records can also be held liable for breach of fiduciary duty, contempt, damages, and, where appropriate, attorney fees.[215] It also means that if a trustee is questioned in court and has failed to keep proper records, all presumptions will be made against the trustee and all doubts arising from the failure to keep records will be resolved against the trustee.

> **Example:** A trustee has been using trust cash each month for beneficiary's acupuncture treatments. The trustee fails to make a note of the transactions, obtains no invoices, and gets no cash receipts. Two years later, the trustee's actions are being questioned in court. If the trustee is unable to provide accurate records of these transactions, he or she will be presumed to have misused the funds and could be required to pay back the trust money from his or her own personal funds, called a surcharge.

WHO IS ENTITLED TO REVIEW TRUST RECORDS?

The trustee has an affirmative duty to keep the beneficiaries of a trust reasonably informed of the trust and its administration.[216] A trustee is required to provide

---

[214] See Probate Code §§15642, 16420, 17200(b)(10).

[215] See Probate Code §§16060, 17200(b)(7), 17211(b); Code Civil Procedure §1209(a)(5).

[216] Probate Code §16060.

the beneficiary with a report of information about the assets, liabilities, receipts, and disbursements of the trust, the acts of the trustee, and the particulars relating to the trust that are relevant to the beneficiary's interest.[217] This duty cannot be waived.[218] This duty is in addition to any duty to account as described later in this chapter.

The obligation to disclose information to a beneficiary also includes the beneficiary's legal representative (like an attorney, conservator, or agent under power of attorney) if their legal authority covers that request. A major exception to this rule is matters subject to an attorney-client or attorney-work-product privilege. Thus, any document that includes communications between the SNT trustee and his or her attorney should not be disclosed.

If the beneficiary (or his or her legal representative) wants to review records, the beneficiary must give sufficient notice to the trustee. It would be prudent for the SNT trustee to be present when the beneficiary is reviewing the files to make sure nothing is taken and that all files have been provided. If the beneficiary wants copies of trust records, trust assets can be used to pay for it.[219]

The SNT trustee may also be required to show government agencies (e.g., the Social Security Administration or the Department of Health Care Services—the agencies that run SSI or Medi-Cal) copies of trust records to show that administration of the SNT has been appropriate. If the SNT trustee refuses, the beneficiary could lose eligibility for these programs.

WHO IS NOT ENTITLED TO REVIEW TRUST RECORDS?

As part of a trustee's duty of confidentiality, he or she has a duty to not disclose to any third parties information acquired as trustee when the trustee should know that the effect of the disclosure will be detrimental to the beneficiary's interest.

There are exceptions to this duty to not disclose. One is if a trustee is a party to litigation, the civil litigation rules override the basic duty of confidentiality.[220]

---

[217] Probate Code §§16061, 17200(b)(7).

[218] Probate Code §16068.

[219] See Probate Code §15684.

[220] See *Coberly v Superior Court* (1965) 231 Cal. App. 2d 685.

However, even if there is a pending litigation, documents protected by the attorney-client privilege are protected.

Another exception is if a government regulations to which the trust is subject suspends the duty of confidentiality. For example, if the beneficiary is receiving SSI and the Social Security Administrations wants to review the trust to see if it meets the legal requirements of being a trust, the trustee will be required to give a copy to the agency to make sure it complies with its internal rules. Failure to provide the trust or trust records will jeopardize the beneficiary's eligibility for public benefits.

Another common exception is when a specific statute requires the disclosure. For example, many first-party SNTs are established by court order, including ongoing court jurisdiction over the trust. The trustee will be obligated to provide records to the court during court accountings.

> **Helpful Hint**: It is important that a trustee know when it is appropriate to disclose confidential trust information and when it is not. Whether the trustee is allowed to do this depends on the terms of the trust, who is asking for the information, why they are seeking the information, and whether there is some legal requirement for disclosure. If the trustee is uncertain, he or she should see an attorney experienced in trust administration to make sure that valuable privacy rights are not lost by improper disclosure. See chapter 11 on where to go for help.

What Are the Trustee's General Accounting Requirements?

SNT trustees have a general duty to account to beneficiaries and to maintain and provide them with information about the trustee's administrative decisions and acts.[221] The type of account the trustee must provide depends on whether the SNT is under continuing court jurisdiction or is not being supervised by the court.

- Non-court supervised SNTs generally include all third-party SNTs and some first-party SNTs. The first-party SNTs that are not court

---

[221] Probate Code §§16060, 16062, and 16064.

supervised generally include those established for beneficiaries who are disabled but still have mental capacity to manage their own affairs.
- Court-supervised SNTs are generally first-party SNTs established through a conservatorship or with the beneficiary's litigation proceeds for those beneficiaries who are disabled and lack the mental capacity to manage their own legal affairs.

However, these are generalities; the trustee should make sure he or she knows if the SNT is under continuing court jurisdiction or not, because it makes a big difference on what type of accounting is required.

> **Critical Pointer:** Not all court-established first-party SNTs are court supervised. A first-party SNT may be court established and not require court-supervised accountings. It is imperative that the trustee review the trust document and the court's order establishing the first-party SNT for direction on whether the trust must file accounts and reports for court approval. If the trustee does not feel comfortable making that decision, he or she should review chapter 11 to find an attorney to see if the SNT requires a court supervised account.

WHAT ARE THE ACCOUNTING REQUIREMENTS FOR A NON-COURT SUPERVISED SNT?

An SNT trustee of an SNT that is not under court supervision typically must account at least once a year to each beneficiary to whom distributions are authorized to be currently distributed.[222] This is typically only to the SNT beneficiary. The terms of an SNT may waive the account requirement for the SNT trustee.[223] The trustee should check the terms of the trust to see what is required.

> **Note:** Even if there is a waiver of account, as described in previous questions in this chapter, the SNT trustee must still

---

[222]   Probate Code §16062.
[223]   Probate Code §16064(a).

comply with the duty to keep a beneficiary reasonably informed of trust actions. Because an SNT beneficiary is entitled to receive disbursements based on the trustee's discretion, it could be argued that the trustee has an obligation to disclose much of the information that would typically be included in an account regardless of a waiver of account.

As described below, the typical accounting format is very informal. However, an SNT trustee may submit an accounting to the court.[224] In such a case, the accounting must be submitted to the court in a specific format. See discussion on filing court supervised account for the format and form of a court accounting. The benefit of petitioning a court for approval is to limit the period of time during which a beneficiary may challenge the actions of the trustee.

The beneficiary may also compel the trustee to account if the trustee has failed to submit a required or requested report or account within sixty days after written request of the beneficiary, and no report or account has been made within six months preceding the request.[225]

WHO SHOULD PREPARE NON-COURT SUPERVISED ACCOUNTINGS?

The trustee has the overall duty to prepare the account.[226] Many SNT trustees will prepare the account personally. This process can be simplified if the SNT trustee uses an accounting software program, such as *Quicken* or *QuickBooks*, which can generate a year-end report that can be included with the account.

If the account will be complicated or the SNT trustee does not wish to prepare it, the trustee is authorized to hire someone to assist in preparation of the account. In locating someone to assist, the SNT trustee should make sure that person has experience in preparing a trust account, because it can be different than doing most other types of financial accounting. Professionals who can assist the SNT trustee with the account generally include an attorney, a paralegal, and a CPA. However, if there are relatively few transactions, hiring a bookkeeper may be less expensive.

---

[224]   Probate Code §17200(b)(5).

[225]   Probate Code §17200(b)(7).

[226]   Probate Code §16062(a).

Remember that if the trustee hires a professional to assist with the account, the responsibility of the account remains with the SNT trustee.[227]

WHAT MUST AN ACCOUNTING IN A NON-COURT SUPERVISED ACCOUNT INCLUDE?

In general, there is a cover letter that will state that the SNT trustee is providing this account to a beneficiary. There is certain language in this cover letter that an SNT trustee will wish to include to shorten the statute of limitations on trustee actions. See Appendix I for a sample of such a cover letter.

Either in the cover letter, or as part of an attachment, the account should contain the following information. It is recommended that the SNT trustee put each one on a separate schedule, on a separate page:

1) A statement of receipts of principal and income that have occurred during the last year of the trust, or since the last account;

SNT RECEIPTS   AMOUNT

Fremont Bank, Checking Account #123456789

1/10/2010	Marathon Oil Dividend	$1.00
4/23/2010	Myers Note Payment	$100.00
5/23/2010	Myers Note Payment	$150.04
6/23/2010	Myers Note Payment	$150.04
12/23/2010	Marathon Oil Dividend	$50.00
	Total Receipts	$400.08

2) A statement of disbursements made of principal and income that have occurred during the last year of the trust, or since the last account;

SNT DISBURSEMENTS

Fremont Bank, Checking Account #123456789   Amount

---

[227] Probate Code §16012.

1/9/2010	Rent—Petaluma Estates	$2,500.00	
2/23/2010	Atty Fees: Urbatsch	$600.00	
3/23/2010	Telephone	$100.00	
4/26/2010	Caregiver Exp.	$300.00	
5/26/2010	Best Buy—Television	$1,620.00	
6/30/2010	Bus Pass	$50.00	
7/28/2010	AT&T cell phone	$180.00	
12/26/2010	MOMA (Year Pass)	$550.00	
	Total Disbursements		$5,900.00

3) A beginning statement of the assets on hand of SNT;

BEGINNING SNT ASSETS ON HAND

Asset Description	Value as of January 1, 2011
Fremont Bank, Checking Account	
#123456789	$50,000
Myers Note	$10,000
Marathon Oil Stock	$10,000
Total Assets	$70,000

4) An ending statement of the assets on hand as of the end of the period covered by the account;

ENDING SNT ASSETS ON HAND

Asset Description	Value as of January 1, 2011
Fremont Bank, Checking Account	
#123456789	$47,000
Myers Note	$8,000
Marathon Oil Stock	$10,000
Total Assets	$65,000

5) The trustee's compensation for the last complete fiscal year of the trust or since the last account;

SNT Trustee Compensation

Fremont Bank, Checking Account #123456789		Amount	
1/9/2010	Trustee Fees	$500.00	
2/23/2010	Atty Fees: Urbatsch	$500.00	
3/23/2010	Telephone	$500.00	
4/26/2010	Caregiver Exp.	$500.00	
5/26/2010	Best Buy—Television	$500.00	
6/30/2010	Bus Pass	$500.00	
7/28/2010	AT&T cell phone	$500.00	
12/26/2010	MOMA (Year Pass)	$500.00	
	Total Disbursements		$4,000.00

6) The agents hired by the trustee, their relationship to the trustee (a sample of this statement is typically placed in cover letter, See Appendix I), if any, and their compensation, for the last complete fiscal year of the trust or since the last account;

SNT Compensation of Agents Hired By Trustee		Amount	
1/9/2010	Atty Fees: Urbatsch	$500.00	
2/23/2010	Atty Fees: Urbatsch	$600.00	
3/23/2010	Cons.: Huyck	$100.00	
4/26/2010	CPA Fes: Kasten	$300.00	
7/28/2010	Atty Fees: Urbatsch	$550.00	
	Total Disbursements		$2,0500.00

7) A statement that the recipient of the account may petition the court under Probate Code §17200 to obtain court review of the account and the trustee's acts (a sample of this statement is typically placed in cover letter; see Appendix I);

8) A statement that claims against the trustee for breach of trust may not be made after the expiration of three years from the date the beneficiary receives an account or report disclosing facts giving rise to the claim (a sample of this statement is typically placed in cover letter, See Appendix I);[228] and

9) A statement of the names and last-known addresses of all contingent beneficiaries.[229]

WHAT TYPE OF FORMAT MUST THE ACCOUNTING BE IN?

As long as the items in the previous question are present, the accounting does not have to be in any specified format. This makes it easier to attach receipts and disbursement schedules produced by financial management programs, such as *QuickBooks* or *Quicken*.

Attached in Appendix I there is a sample accounting cover letter to an SNT beneficiary covers the needed information.

HOW CAN A TRUSTEE SHORTEN THE LENGTH OF TIME HE OR SHE IS LIABLE FOR HIS OR HER ACTIONS AS TRUSTEE?

A concern that many trustees have (or should have) is shortening the amount of time they can be sued for actions made as a trustee. If no accounts are delivered to trustees, then trustees can be responsible for their actions as long as they are alive. This means that a trustee could have been negligent in year 2012, and because the beneficiary did not discover it until 2031, that beneficiary could still sue the trustee. Imagine how difficult it would be for a trustee to file a good defense—especially if that person was no longer serving as trustee and had thrown away or lost trust records. Remember, if the trustee does not have records, all presumptions are made against the trustee, presuming he or she did something wrong.

A primary reason for doing annual accountings is the triggering of the statute of limitations. In general, if the trustee provides an accurate account that adequately disclose any item in the account or report, a beneficiary can

---

[228] Probate Code §16063(a).

[229] Rules of Court 7.902.

only file a lawsuit on those actions for the next three years.[230] The three-year statute can only be started for an incapacitated adult and minor beneficiaries by service of the account on the legal representative, guardian, or parents.[231]

To start the three-year period running, the account or report must include a prescribed form of notice, in twelve-point boldface type, informing the beneficiaries of their right to object within the specified time, the manner in which to object, and the commencement of the three-year period:[232]

> **You are entitled, under Probate Code §17200, to petition the court to obtain a court review of the account and of the acts of the trustee. Claims against the trustee for breach of trust may not be made after the expiration of three years from the date you received an account or report disclosing facts giving rise to the claim.**
>
> **Helpful Hint:** Attached as Appendix I is a cover letter to beneficiaries that complies with the legal requirements of a non-court supervised accounting that will trigger the three-year statute of limitations.

There is a chance that the terms of the SNT will shorten the three-year statute of limitations even further. If the SNT document contains language relieving the trustee of liability for a breach of trust when a beneficiary fails to object to a trustee's account within a specified period of time (the law says it cannot be shorter than 180 days), then that is allowed.[233] However, even if the trust instrument contains a waiver, a court may require an accounting if it can be shown that it is reasonably likely that a material breach of trust has occurred.[234]

---

[230] Probate Code §16460(a)(1).
[231] Probate Code §16460(b).
[232] Probate Code §16461(c)(3).
[233] Probate Code §16461.
[234] Probate Code §16064(a).

> **Example:** A sample SNT provision limiting liability might state something like, "If a beneficiary has received an interim or final account in writing, or other written report, that adequately discloses the existence of a claim against the trustee, the claim is barred with respect to that beneficiary unless the beneficiary delivers a written objection to the trustee within 180 days after receipt of the account or report by the beneficiary."

A trustee is not protected from an SNT waiver of liability (no matter how broadly stated) if his or her own actions for breach of trust were committed intentionally, with gross negligence, in bad faith, with reckless indifference to the beneficiary's interest, or for any profit the trustee derived from a breach of trust.[235]

WHO SHOULD GET A COPY OF THE NON-COURT SUPERVISED ACCOUNT?

The SNT beneficiary should receive a copy of the accounting. If he or she is a minor or lacks capacity and has a legal representative, such as a conservator, guardian or custodial parent, they should each receive a copy of the accounting.

Generally, these are all the people who are legally required to receive an account. However, if the trustee is concerned that the people named as a remainder or contingent beneficiaries may later complain about trustee actions, he or she may provide a copy to these beneficiaries to trigger the statute of limitations against them, just as described for the primary beneficiary in the previous question.

> **Helpful Hint:** The trustee should have the beneficiary, if competent, sign approvals of the annual accountings as they are delivered. If beneficiary does not have capacity, consider having the legal guardian or conservator sign on behalf of the beneficiary. The trustee has the option of asking a court to review and approve the accountings if the beneficiary does not approve them.

---

[235]   Probate Code §16461(b).

CAN A BENEFICIARY WAIVE A TRUSTEE'S ACCOUNT REQUIREMENT?

Yes. An SNT beneficiary may waive (in writing) the right to a report or account that is not under court jurisdiction from the trustee.[236] However, the beneficiary can withdraw this written waiver at any time "as to the most recent account and future accounts."[237] A beneficiary's waiver of account would not begin the statute of limitations on actions taken by trustee. Finally, a beneficiary's waiver has no effect on the beneficiary's right to petition for a report or account under Probate Code §17200. See chapter 11 for a discussion of petitions under Probate Code §17200.

> **Helpful Hint:** Because a beneficiary has the right to withdraw his or her waiver, the statute of limitations does not begin to run, and the cost and expense of an account is not overly burdensome, it would probably be best for an SNT trustee to do an accounting rather than seek a waiver.

WHAT IS A COURT-SUPERVISED ACCOUNT?

A court account is a filing with the probate court that has jurisdiction over the SNT; it includes detailed financial information about the SNT for a specified period. Court accountings are very different from what most people think of as accountings. Instead of tracking assets by their tax cost basis, a court account tracks the "carry value" of assets from the last accounting period.

Court accounts must comply with a strict set of rules set forth in Probate Code. Thus, it is important that the trustee either be very familiar with these rules or hire someone to assist in the preparation of these accounts.

The effect of a court order approving an account is conclusive on all persons, assuming proper notice has been given, actions were properly disclosed by trustee, there was no fraud, and the order so finds.[238] Thus, it is important that the SNT trustee provide a thorough description of trustee

---

[236] Probate Code §16064(b).

[237] Probate Code §16064(b).

[238] Probate Code §1260(c).

matters so the broadest number of issues can be conclusively resolved by court order.

> **Helpful Hint**: Costs related to preparing court accountings can be dramatically reduced by minimizing the volume of individual security transactions in the trust's investment portfolio. This is because each individual transaction must be separately identified in the account.

WHAT TYPE OF SNT MUST FILE A COURT ACCOUNT?

Typically, only an SNT under continuing court jurisdiction is required to file a court account. This type of SNT is generally a first-party SNT that has been established through a court petition for a beneficiary who lacks the capacity to manage his or her own affairs. Mostly, these SNTs are established from a litigation recovery[239] or through the beneficiary's conservatorship from an inheritance or the existing assets of the beneficiary.[240]

A trustee should know if the SNT is under ongoing court jurisdiction. It would be the rare trustee who agreed to serve in an SNT, under ongoing court jurisdiction, who had not been appointed through a court petition. If unsure, the trustee should contact an attorney to see if there is such a requirement.

An SNT trustee may still be required to file a court account in a non court-supervised trust, if ordered to by the court, or may choose to do so to shorten any statute of limitations period.[241]

WHO SHOULD FILE A COURT-SUPERVISED ACCOUNT?

The SNT trustee is responsible for filing an account. A court account can be complex and very challenging. It is strongly recommended that an attorney experienced in administering SNTs and filing fiduciary accounts with the court represent the trustee. A CPA may be of assistance in preparing the court authorized accounting schedules, but very few CPAs do this type of work. It is

---

[239] Probate Code §§3600-3613.

[240] Probate Code §2580.

[241] Probate Code §17200(b)(5).

very different from preparing other types of accounts, and it is recommended that, just as with attorneys, the trustee find a CPA experienced in preparing just these types of account schedules. Chapter 11 provides information on locating such an attorney.

WHAT ARE THE LEGAL REQUIREMENTS FOR A COURT-SUPERVISED ACCOUNT?

Generally, the trustee must account one year after the trust is established and every two years thereafter, unless the court orders a different timeframe.[242] All accounts filed with the court under the Probate Code must include a financial statement and a report of administration as provided in the law[243] and also the names and addresses of beneficiaries.[244] Further, the account must state the period covered[245] and contain a summary showing all of the following, to the extent applicable:

- property on hand at the beginning of the period covered by the account (all inventories);
- assets received during the accounting period, excluding property listed in an inventory;
- receipts, excluding items listed under items (1) and (2) or receipts from a trade or business; net income from a trade or business;
- gains on sales;
- disbursements, excluding disbursements for a trade or business or distributions;
- loss on sales;
- net loss from a trade or business;
- distributions to beneficiaries, the ward, or conservatee; and
- property on hand at the end of the accounting period, stated at its carry value (fiduciary acquisition value).[246]

---

[242] Probate Code §2620(a).
[243] Probate Code §§1060-1064.
[244] Cal Rules of Court 7.902.
[245] Cal Rules of Ct 7.901(a).
[246] Probate Code §1061(a).

The accounts must be in very a specific format, set forth by statute, including a series of schedules that are attached to the account. These schedules (as described below) primarily come from the Judicial Council of California forms.

The Probate Code defines the two types of accounts as either a "standard accounting" or a "simplified accounting."[247] The difference between the two is that a standard accounting lists receipts and disbursements by subject-matter category, with each receipt and disbursement category subtotaled, whereas a simplified accounting lists receipts and disbursements chronologically, by receipt or payment date, without subject-matter categorization.

> **Note:** Unless the court account is rather simple, nearly all court accounts are prepared using the standard format.

A SNT trustee must use a standard accounting if

1. the SNT assets contain income real property;
2. the SNT assets contain a whole or partial interest in a trade or business;
3. the appraised value of the SNT assets is $500,000 or more, exclusive of the beneficiary's personal residence;
4. either the receipts schedule or the disbursements schedule prepared in simplified accounting format is more than five pages long, in which case the excessively long schedule must be prepared in standard accounting format, although the balance of the accounting can be prepared as a simplified accounting; or
5. the court directs that a standard accounting be filed.[248]

If the SNT contains none of these items, the trustee can prepare a simplified accounting. In many cases, even an experienced preparer might choose the simplified accounting in an appropriate case, e.g., if there are very few different expense categories and if it is possible to automate the transfer of totals from the schedules to the summary form. To do so, however, the person preparing the accounting must use the mandatory Judicial Council account forms, as described in the next question.

---

[247] Probate Code §2620(a); Cal Rules of Court 7.575.

[248] Cal Rules of Court 7.575(b).

WHAT ARE THE JUDICIAL COUNCIL FORMS?

The Judicial Council of California is the policymaking body of the California courts. Among its several duties is promulgating rules of court administration, practice, and procedure. As part of this responsibility, the Judicial Council provides sample forms that are sometimes mandatory and sometimes optional. A complete list of all these forms can be found at http://www.courtinfo.ca.gov/forms/.

For court-supervised accounts, the Judicial Council has created thirty-four forms and one worksheet to be used for standard (categorized) accounts and simplified (chronological) accounts. These specific forms can be found at http://www.courtinfo.ca.gov/cgi-bin/forms.cgi. Once at that page, the trustee will need to scroll down to the forms which begin at Judicial Council Form GC-400 and proceed through Judicial Council Form GC-405.

> **Note:** The forms are titled under Guardianship and Conservatorships but still must be used for SNTs under continuing court jurisdiction.

WHAT JUDICIAL COUNCIL FORMS MUST BE USED IN A COURT-SUPERVISED ACCOUNTING?

Only one form, Summary of Account—Standard and Simplified Accounts (Judicial Council Form GC-400(SUM)/GC-405(SUM)), is mandatory for a simplified or standard accounting. (For a copy of the form, see http://www.courtinfo.ca.gov/forms/documents/gc400sum.pdf.)

If the trustee wishes to use the simplified accounts (chronological) method, he or she must use some of the Judicial Council forms. The following Judicial Council forms are mandatory for simplified accounts and may be used in standard accounts at the SNT trustee's option:

- GC-400(PH)(1)/GC-405(PH)(1): Cash Assets on Hand at Beginning of Account Period
- GC-400(PH)(2)/GC-405(PH)(2): Noncash Assets on Hand at Beginning of Account Period*
- GC-400(AP)/GC-405(AP): Additional Property Received During Period of Account*
- GC-400(B)/GC-405(B): Gains on Sales*

- GC-400(OCH)/GC-405(OCH): Other Charges*
- GC-400(D)/GC405(D): Losses on Sales*
- GC-400(DIST)/GC-405(DIST): Distributions to Conservatee*
- GC-400(OCR)/GC405(OCR): Other Credits*
- GC-400(E)(1)/GC-405(E)(1): Cash Assets on Hand at End of Account Period
- GC-400(E)(2)/GC-405(E)(2): Noncash Assets on Hand at End of Account Period*
- GC-400(F)/GC-405(F): Changes in Form of Assets*
- GC-400(G)/GC-405(G): Liabilities at End of Account Period*
- GC-405(A) Receipts-Simplified Account; and
- GC-405(C) Disbursements-Simplified Account

Of the forms listed above, those marked with asterisks may be omitted if the accounting has no information for those forms.

In addition to those forms above, the following optional forms may be used only in standard accounts and cannot be used in a simple account:

- GC-400(A)(1) through (A)(6): Receipts

  - (A)(1): Dividends
  - (A)(2): Interest
  - (A)(3): Pensions, annuities, and other regular periodic payments
  - (A)(4): Rent
  - (A)(5): Social Security, veteran benefits, other public benefits
  - (A)(6): Other receipts

- GC-400(C)(1) through (C)(11): Disbursements

  - (C)(1): Conservatee's caregiver expenses
  - (C)(2): Conservatee's residential or long-term care facility expenses
  - [(C)(3) is for guardians only: minor's education expenses]
  - (C)(4): Fiduciary and attorney fees
  - (C)(5): General administration expenses
  - (C)(6): Investment expenses
  - (C)(7): Living expenses

- o   (C)(8): Medical expenses
- o   (C)(9): Property sales expenses
- o   (C)(10): Rental property expenses
- o   (C)(11): Other expenses

- •   GC-400(NI): Net income from trade or business
- •   GC-400(NL): Net loss from trade or business
- •   GC-400(A)(C): Receipts and disbursements worksheet (do not file)

Experienced trustees may have already developed their own forms prior to the Judicial Council releasing these accounting forms. These trustees are allowed to continue to use their forms as long as their forms provide the same information as required by the Judicial Council forms and as long as they [249]

- •   provide receipts and disbursements in the subject-matter categories specified in the optional Judicial Council forms for receipts and disbursements schedules;
- •   provide the same information about any asset, property, transaction, receipt, disbursement, or other matter that is required by the applicable Judicial Council accounting form; and
- •   provide the information in the same general layout as the applicable Judicial Council accounting form, except that instructional material contained in the form and material contained or requested in the form's header and footer need not be provided.

Obviously, if a trustee is doing his or her first account, it would be best to use the judicial council forms, as they are already established.

WHAT OTHER INFORMATION MUST BE PROVIDED IN A COURT ACCOUNT?

In addition to the Judicial Council forms that are included as attachments to the court petition, the court petition itself must include certain information during the court accounting. These include

---

[249]   Cal Rules of Court 7.575(e)(2).

1. **Description of Financial Transactions**. The trustee should inform the court of the financial activities of the SNT that are not readily understood from the schedules described above.[250] This includes any problems encountered with investments or any changes made in the overall investment plan of the trust.

2. **Explanation of Unusual Items**. The trustee should explain any usual items in the account.[251] It is common that after a year (or two years) some transactions may look unusual in retrospect. These can include payments of cash, disbursements to third parties for reimbursements of different transactions, or payments to professionals for services that may appear unusual without an explanation.

3. **Disclosure of Family Relationships**. The trustee is required to disclose any family or affiliate relationships of any trust transactions. Family is defined very broadly to include a relationship created by blood or marriage. Affiliate is defined as an entity that directly or indirectly through one or more intermediaries controls, is controlled by, or is under common control with the trustee.[252] For example, if the trustee hired his brother to make modifications to real estate owned by the trust. The trustee must disclose this relationship to the court. While not improper, the court will review these transactions more closely to make sure that these transactions are reasonable and are not disguised gifts to family members.

4. **Allegations of Cash Investments**. This is a simple statement that all cash has either been invested or maintained in interest-bearing accounts, except for an amount of cash that is reasonably necessary for the orderly administration of the SNT.[253]

5. **Requests for Compensation**. The petition should disclose any compensation paid from SNT assets during the accounting period to the trustee, the advisory committee members (if there is one), or the trustee's attorney. There may have been compensation allowed under a prior court order or for periodic payments of compensation

---

[250]   Probate Code §1064(a)(1).

[251]   Probate Code §1064(a).

[252]   Probate Code §1064(c).

[253]   Probate Code §1064(a)(5).

in a court order. This must also be disclosed.[254] This is a requirement because oftentimes an SNT under continuing court jurisdiction does not allow the trustee, his attorney, or any member of the trust advisory committee to receive compensation without a court order. To obtain compensation, it is best that the trustee and his attorney complete a declaration that shows all the hours that were spent on the trust administration during the accounting period.

Note: A sample petition for first account and report is attached as Appendix N.

In addition to the petition, with each court account, the trustee must also provide some of the original financial statements of accounts held as part of the trust estate. The statement must show the account balance as of the close of the accounting period and, in the case of an account that closes during the accounting period, the closing statement of each such account as well as the opening statement of any new accounts. With the first account filed by the trustee, he or she must also provide the original statements showing the balance immediately preceding the date of appointment.

A private professional trustee must file all original account statements for all periods of the accounting.[255] This requires the filing of all original statements received during the accounting period and not just at the end or beginning of the accounting. While the statute speaks of conservators, it would be prudent for a private professional trustee to comply with this rule also. If a statement contains confidential information, it must be filed with a separate affidavit describing the character of the statement, captioned "CONFIDENTIAL FINANCIAL STATEMENT" in uppercase letters.

The accounting petition will also generally require that a proposed court order be filed with the paperwork. Different counties will have different rules about this, so the trustee should check the local rules to see what a proposed order should include. For example, some will require that the order include all factual statements made in the petition, while some will only want all rulings issued by the court.

---

[254] Cal Rules of Court 7.755, 7.903(8).

[255] Probate Code §2620(c)(3).

HOW DOES SNT TRUSTEE FILE COURT ACCOUNT?

The person filing the paperwork should bring copies of all documents. All documents typically include

- Petition for Account & Report (with all attached schedules)
- Notice of Hearing
- Declarations of Attorney (or sometimes trustee) in support of fees
- Proposed Order Approving Account

    Note: The Judicial Council has a form that can be used to provide notice to all parties called: Notice of Hearing-Probate (Judicial Council Form DE-120) a copy of which can be found at http://www.courtinfo.ca.gov/forms/documents/de120.pdf.

Typically (some counties may differ), the court will provide a hearing date. The original will be filed with the court, but the filing clerk will file stamp the papers to show the date they were filed with the court. Some counties will allow the person filing the paperwork to select the hearing date. It is important to keep these documents as part of the SNT trustee's file.

There is a filing fee that can be paid for from the trust. Currently, the filing fee for trust accountings for SNTs established through court petitions is $200.[256] Most counties are not aware of this exception for these types of SNTs and will attempt to charge the full filing fee of $395-$415.

Once the case is filed, the SNT trustee will be given a Notice of Hearing. This Notice must be served on all parties as described in the next question.

HOW MUST NOTICE BE GIVEN BY THE TRUSTEE OF THE COURT-SUPERVISED ACCOUNT?

At least thirty days before the date of the hearing, the trustee must provide notice of the time and place of the hearing to all those who are entitled to notice.[257]

---

[256] Government Code §70652(d).

[257] Probate Code §17203(a).

Notice is required to be provided to all nonpetitioning trustees, all nonpetitioning beneficiaries who are entitled to notice, and any person who requested special notice.[258] The trustee may also want to consider providing notice to the State Director of Health Care Services, the Director of Mental Health, and the Director of Developmental Services. While not required by law, it should trigger the statute of limitations for any trust actions.

Typically, the only document that is served is a copy of the Notice of Hearing and not a copy of the Petition or other filed documents.

WHAT HAPPENS AT THE COURT HEARING?

In most counties, a probate examiner will review the paperwork a few days before the hearing to see if all of the technical requirements have been followed in submitting the accounting. Generally, the examiner will review the paperwork to see if all schedules are there, notice was sent, and all information is included. Some counties will let their examiners also ask questions about the substance of the account. The examiner will then inform the trustee (or his or her attorney) of any technical defects in the accounting submission and if there are any questions about the petition.

The attorney or trustee at this time has the opportunity to respond to the examiner's notes. This may require a continuance of the hearing date. Once the notes are cleared, the hearing may be pregranted, or the attorney or trustee may have to address an issue with the probate judge and a hearing will take place. At the hearing, the judge will ask the trustee or the trustee's attorney questions on any issues that have arisen because of the account. The judge will then issue a ruling on the petition and the account.

> **Helpful Hint:** It may be surprising to learn that many judges and court examiners have little understanding of SNTs and will ask questions or issue rulings that bear no relation to the law. Some judges believe that the SNT is to be very narrowly construed and can only pay for certain things, like medical equipment. One judge refused to allow a trustee to buy a fax machine for the beneficiary to make disbursement requests from the trust and made the trustee pay back the cost of the

---

[258]   Probate Code §17203(a).

fax machine to the trust. Thus, it is a good idea to find out by talking to local attorneys how a judge is likely to rule on a certain case.

It is important that the trustee and his or her attorney do not let these misperceptions interfere with the purpose of these trusts and educate these judges about how the trust should work. Many judges will second-guess the trustee on disbursements made or not, investments made, and other actions by the trustee. Judges legally do not have the right to second-guess the trustee of an SNT unless the trustee acts in bad faith or in disregard of the purposes of the trust.[259] This being said, it is still important to remember that court hearings are expensive and fights with the court are counterproductive for the beneficiary, so it may be best to limit the fights the trustee will make with the court to only those that are important.

WHAT IS THE EFFECT OF THE COURT SIGNING AN ORDER ON A COURT-SUPERVISED ACCOUNT?

Once a judge has signed the order approving and settling the accounting, the order is conclusive against everyone who has been given notice. This means that those persons can no longer sue the trustee for any acts disclosed in the accounting.[260]

If the trustee does nothing with the order, the order is final after 180 days from the date of entry of the order. However, if the trustee feels that it is important to cut off the right to appeal sooner, he or she can provide notice of entry of judgment, which cuts off the time to appeal at sixty days.[261]

Chapter 7 Summary

✓ The trustee is legally obligated to keep records of the trust administration that are clear and concise.

---

[259] *Estate of Genung* (1958) 161 Cal. App. 2d 507; Probate Code §16081(a).
[260] Probate Code §1260(c).
[261] Probate Code §1300(b); Cal Rules of Court 8.104(a).

- ✓ If a trustee fails to keep good records, he or she may be liable for damages, costs, fines or sanctions, removal as trustee and (if serious) possibly held in contempt of court.
- ✓ The trustee should keep records for practical reasons, because to do so will allow an easier and cheaper administration when preparing tax documents and preparing accountings.
- ✓ Excellent trust records will also protect a trustee if someone sues him or her, because a failure to have records will be held against the trustee.
- ✓ Trust records are private documents and only certain people or entities are entitled to review them.
- ✓ Trustee is legally obligated to account and provide information about trust administration.
- ✓ A trustee's legal obligation to account will depend on whether the SNT is under continuing court jurisdiction.
- ✓ If SNT is *not* under ongoing court jurisdiction, the trustee is generally required to account at least once a year, unless waived by trust document.
- ✓ A trustee account is the responsibility of trustee, but he or she may delegate it to a professional if needed.
- ✓ The trustee's account for non-court supervised trusts should include all transactions made, amounts held in trust, agents hired by the trustee, investment, compensation received, and any issues that have arisen in the past year.
- ✓ The trustee's account for non-court supervised trusts does not need to be made in any specific format; however, certain disclosures do need to be made in account concerning right to object.
- ✓ The trustee's account for non-court supervised trusts can trigger statute of limitations for all person receiving copy of account, which, depending on terms of trust, can vary from three years to 180 days.
- ✓ Trustees of first-party SNTs under continuing court jurisdiction have a much more comprehensive accounting requirement.
- ✓ Trustees of court-supervised SNT must account to the court one year after establishment of the trust and every two years thereafter.
- ✓ The trustee has to follow a very specific format for the account schedules, which can be found under the Judicial Council Forms.

- ✓ The trustee can use either a standard accounting or simplified accounting, depending on a variety of factors, although most trustees use the standard accounting.
- ✓ In addition to accounting schedules of financial transactions, the trustee must account to the court on a variety of transactions, including unusual disbursements, hiring of family or affiliates, financial transactions, investment of cash, and compensation of trustee and attorney.
- ✓ A court hearing will be held where a judge will issue a ruling after reviewing the filed account schedules and report of trustee
- ✓ Once court issues ruling on court accounting, it is conclusive on all parties at least 180 days after the issuance of the order, or 60 days after the trustee or his or her attorney serve a notice of entry of judgment on all parties.

CHAPTER 8

Managing SNT Investments and Assets

This chapter will cover the trustee's duty to invest and manage trust assets. It will start with the general rules concerning the trustee's duty to invest trust assets, then discuss investment standards based on the type of SNT the trustee is managing, provide a summary of the types of proper asset classes for an SNT, discuss the use of professional money advisers to assist the trustee, and cover questions that arise when hiring a professional money adviser, and describe the best way to provide ongoing investment monitoring.

Investing trust assets is a challenge for those with little investment or financial background. In its simplest sense, investment involves allocation of SNT assets among existing assets of the trust (which may be nontraditional), bonds, equities and cash equivalents. The nature of the allocation depends on risk tolerance, economic and market conditions, time horizon (short term or long term), income needs, liquidity requirements, and tax and legal issues (investments only in certain types of investments). Aside from assets that may already be a part of the SNT (e.g., a family business, home, or existing real estate), the three general types of investments are as follows:

- **Cash**: Cash provides for immediate or short-term needs and is available for scheduled distributions or any unplanned emergency that may arise. Penalty-free certificates of deposit, money market accounts, treasury bills, and savings accounts are examples of investments that are considered to be "cash" or "cash equivalents."
- **Fixed Income**: Investments in this category feature predetermined returns that may or may not be taxable depending on the entity issuing the bonds. Investment vehicles in this category may include (but

are not limited to) bonds, notes, certificates of deposit, and annuity benefits. These types of investments are most often utilized to provide for predictable future needs or to protect against market volatility.

- **Equities**: This category may include stocks, mutual funds, real estate, or other investments purchased with the intension of a later sale at higher price. Equities are most appropriate to be purchased as a long-term investment and can be held for five to ten years or more.

A trustee should always remember that, in general, he or she will be held to a higher standard of care and fidelity than if the trustee were investing his or her own funds. Thus, the trustee cannot be overly aggressive in investing the trust's assets. Not surprisingly, courts often over-reward conservative investment styles. When in doubt, less risky investments, even at a lower rate of return, would be less likely to be challenged by a beneficiary or their representative.

As a result of this fear of court challenge, most people believe that trust investments should be made conservatively; however, do not make this mistake: investing only in safe and conservative (but low yielding) investments is also a challengeable act. The problem with investing too conservatively for a trust that is supposed to last a long time is that the investment income will not cover the annual cost-of-living increases over that period, and the trustee will not have enough money to provide for the future needs of the beneficiary.

The discussion in this chapter on trustee investment and management only scratches the surface of the variety of situations that may arise during a trustee's administration. It is nearly always prudent to hire a professional to assist in the trustee's investment of trust assets. The end of the chapter contains a more detailed discussion about hiring professionals to assist in investing trust assets.

WHAT IS THE TRUSTEE'S GENERAL DUTY WHEN INVESTING AND MANAGING TRUST ASSETS?

In general, a trustee has a duty to invest trust property, preserve trust assets, and make the assets productive.[262] This means that a trustee has a legal obligation to gather the trust assets that are (or should be) owned by the trust,

---

[262]   Probate Code §§16006-16007.

review the asset composition in order to develop an investment plan, provide protection for the trust assets, and make the assets productive, typically by investing cash or renting out real property.

> **Warning:** Some trustees believe that if the trustee does not take a fee, the trustee will not be held responsible for his or her negligent acts. This is wrong. A trustee's duty of care remains whether or not he or she receives a fee.[263] This means that if the trustee breaches one of the following duties, he or she will be held *personally* responsible even if the trustee never got paid.

A number of trustee responsibilities arise when investing and managing assets:

1. Duty to Review Assets and Make Productive.

When a trustee takes control of an SNT, he or she must, within a reasonable time, review the trust assets and make decisions concerning the assets so that the assets are protected and productive.[264] The trustee must review whether each asset should be retained or disposed of to comply with the purposes, terms, distribution requirements, and circumstances of the trust.[265]

This means that a trustee is not allowed to hold cash or assets without investing them or making them productive in some way. Thus, keeping all of the assets in a non-interest bearing checking account or owning a home that is vacant and habitable without trying to rent it out would be violating the trustee's duty.

The trust may contain language that alters this duty—for example, if the trust language permits investment in specific unproductive assets appropriate for a situation (like a vacation home), then the

---

[263] Probate Code §16041.
[264] Probate Code §16007.
[265] Probate Code §16049.

trustee would be allowed to do so without necessarily maximizing the yield from that asset.

2. **Duty to Consider Beneficiaries' Needs**.

The trustee must consider the interests and needs of all of the beneficiaries in making investment decisions within the terms of the trust instrument.[266] "Impartially" does not necessarily mean "equally." People who set up trusts frequently express intent to favor one beneficiary (e.g., the person with a disability) over another (e.g., the remainder beneficiaries, or those who would inherit if the person with a disability died). In such cases, the terms of the trust control and one beneficiary can have priority over another.[267]

In nearly every SNT administration, the only beneficiary's interest that must be considered is the person with a disability, who is the primary beneficiary. The trustee should understand what assets will be needed to care for this person and invest accordingly. A few trusts may require that investment decisions also consider remainder beneficiaries. If that is the case, investment decisions must take into account the interests of these remainder beneficiaries, which may alter some of the investment strategies of the trustee. If the trustee is not sure of which type of beneficiary should have priority over another type of beneficiary, the trustee should contact an attorney. See chapter 11 for a discussion on how to find assistance from a special needs planning attorney.

3. **Duty to Diversify**.

A trustee has a general duty to diversify the investments of the trust unless, under the particular circumstances surrounding the administrations, it would not be prudent to do so.[268] For example, the trustee is probably not under a duty to diversify if the trust is extremely

---

[266] Probate Code §16003.

[267] Probate Code §16000.

[268] Probate Code §16048.

small, if it will only be around a short time, or if general economic conditions are so unstable that the trustee would be wise to invest all the trust funds in a single safe-asset class (e.g., fixed-income government securities from solvent government entities).

The idea of diversification is to spread risk among various types of investments and to provide a rate of return without incurring undue risk. For example, if the trust assets are heavily weighted or exclusively invested in fixed investments (such as bonds), it may be prudent to balance the portfolio through the purchase of securities to provide a greater chance of a higher rate of return.

Upon becoming an SNT trustee, the trustee need not *immediately* diversity the trust assets if other factors would prove harmful to the trust. For example, large capital gain positions, if sold, might cause large tax liabilities. A plan to diversify assets over multiple tax years—if property documented and approved by the court—should satisfy the trustee's duty to diversify.

> **Note:** It is important for the trustee to review the trust document. The duty to diversify can be expanded, restricted, eliminated, or altered by a statement in the trust.[269] Thus, if the trust document allows it, a trustee can invest in an undiversified portfolio.

4. Duty to Keep Beneficiaries Informed.

As described in the previous chapter, the trustee must keep the beneficiaries "reasonably informed of the trust and its administration."[270] This generally includes providing a report on investments made and how well the investments performed. When there is a duty to disclose, the disclosure must be full and complete, and any material concealment or misrepresentation will amount to

---

[269] Probate Code §16046(b).

[270] Probate Code §16060.

fraud sufficient to entitle the injured party to bring an action against the trustee.[271]

5. Duty to Keep Trust Assets Separate.

The trustee has a duty to keep trust assets separate and identified.[272] This means that the trustee should not mix his or her own personal assets with the beneficiary. Doing so would be a breach of trust and lead to consequences for the trustee.

Further, because assets are held in an SNT, the trustee should make sure that the person with a disability's own assets (typically from SSI or SSDI) are not commingled with the trust's assets. This can be a problem if the trustee is also serving as the representative payee for the beneficiary. If these assets are commingled, it could jeopardize continued public benefits eligibility.

6. Duty to Avoid Self-Dealing, Impropriety, and Conflicts of Interest.

If an investment may benefit trustee personally, or if the trustee wishes to invest in property in which the beneficiary has an ownership interest (or that the trustee already owns), a conflict of interest may be created. Situations in which the trustee participates with the beneficiaries or self-deals inherently call into question a trustee's duty of loyalty. Some of these situations are discussed below:

- **When a trustee buys an asset or sells an asset to the beneficiary**. For example, self-dealing can occur if the SNT trustee is asked to buy the beneficiary's automobile so that he can receive a new one. It is not absolutely improper for the trustee to buy from or sell to a trust beneficiary.[273] However, a trustee may be challenged if there is a dispute over the proper value of the asset. To protect him or herself, the trustee should employ a professional, disinterested professional to set the market value. Further, the trustee could petition a court for

---

[271] *Werschkull v United Cal. Bank* (1978) 85 Cal. App. 3d 981.

[272] Probate Code §16009.

[273] Probate Code §16004.

instructions and obtain permission for the particular transaction.[274] This would be the safest thing a trustee could do to protect him or herself from later second-guessing.

- **When a trustee is asked to participate on the trust's behalf in an investment with the beneficiary**. An SNT trustee may, for example, be asked to help the beneficiary buy real estate with the beneficiary. If the trustee makes an independent evaluation that the investment is proper, there is nothing wrong with this.[275] In this case, it is good practice to disclose the investment and the beneficiary's interest to all other interested parties. If the trust is subject to continuing court supervision, the court should be advised. This type of disclosure will protect the trustee from possible breaches of duty if the investment does not perform as planned.

- **When a trustee is asked to delegate decision-making authority to a beneficiary on investment and asset management.** The fact that the trust and a beneficiary share ownership of an asset does not give the trustee a right to delegate ultimate decision-making authority over the asset to the beneficiary or to anyone else.[276] In such situations, the trustee and beneficiary should negotiate an arm's-length, written management agreement, as if they were cotrustees. If such an agreement cannot be reached, the trustee can sell the trust's share to the beneficiary, purchase the beneficiary's share, or, by agreement, put the property on the market. This can happen sometimes during an SNT administration when the beneficiary co-owns the home they live in with the SNT.

- **When a trustee profits from the use of trust property or obtains some benefit from transactions using trust property.** A trustee may be held responsible when the trustee profits from the use of trust property, participates in transactions adverse to the beneficiary, or attempts to enforce a claim against trust property that the trustee purchased after appointment as trustee.[277] If the trustee moves into a home owned by the SNT or exclusively uses

---

[274] See Probate Code §17200.

[275] Probate Code §§16002, 16012.

[276] Probate Code §16012.

[277] See Probate Code §16004(a)-(b).

Kevin Urbatsch

a car purchased for the beneficiary, this could violate the trustee's duties.

ARE THERE ANY EXCEPTIONS TO THE TRUSTEE'S GENERAL DUTY TO INVEST AND MANAGE ASSETS?

Yes. If the trust document limits the trustee's duty to invest and manage assets, then the trustee may rely on the trust document to negate these duties. Thus, if the trust document says that all investments must be in a certain stock portfolio or that real estate may stay vacant, then the trustee may follow that advice without getting in trouble, but only up to a point.

A trustee cannot blindly follow the trust document's terms and be completely free from potential liability. If there is significant loss in the assets because the trustee blindly follows the trust instrument's instructions, he or she could still be found liable if he or she could have done something to stop the losses. There is no bright line test to say when a trustee should do something, but if there are significant losses, the trustee should do something. Preferably, the trustee would petition a court for instructions on what to do. Once a court rules on the issue, the trustee would be protected.

SHOULD A TRUSTEE BUY AND MAINTAIN INSURANCE ON TRUST ASSETS?

Yes. It is vitally important to insure against the risks of owning property. As described elsewhere, the trustee has a duty to protect trust assets. Insurance is the primary way to do this. It is obvious that all real property, automobiles, and other trust assets must be insured. If the beneficiary is renting an apartment, the trustee should also consider renter's insurance.

The trustee should make sure that there is sufficient liability insurance to protect the trust assets from a lawsuit. This should be one of the first items a trustee will consider if, for example, a residence is held for the use of a beneficiary, an automobile has been purchased for the beneficiary's use, or a business is being run inside the trust.

WHAT SHOULD A TRUSTEE DO TO PROTECT

BENEFICIARY'S PERSONAL PROPERTY?

A trustee is also responsible for any tangible personal property in the trustee's possession.[278] As describe above, the trustee should insure against any loss of personal property.

If a beneficiary goes into a board and care or some type of skilled nursing facility, the trustee should safely store the beneficiary's belongings. The appropriate type of storage depends on the asset: furniture may be stored in a warehouse; paintings and stamps require specialized storage to prevent deterioration; jewelry, coins, and other small valuables should be stored in a safe deposit box in the trustee's name.

The storage facility should be inspected occasionally to ensure that it is secure and meets the trustee's storage requirements. The trustee should maintain a written record of these inspections, noting the inspection date, the trustee's impressions of the property's condition, and any other considerations affecting a decision to retain or dispose of the property. These reports should be kept in the appropriate asset file.

IS A TRUSTEE ALLOWED TO INVEST TRUST PROPERTY ANY WAY HE OR SHE WANTS?

No. There is always a limitation on how trust property may be invested. The standard of investment will depend on a couple of factors (described more fully below):

- If the SNT is a court supervised first-party SNT, then the trust will generally be required to invest in a limited way, as set forth in the Probate Code and as described in the next question and answer.
- If the SNT is not court supervised, then the trustee will invest trust assets in one of two ways: (1) if the SNT document is silent or if it states that the trustee shall invest as authorized by California law, then the default investment standard will be the prudent investor rule; or (2) if the SNT document sets forth an investment standard, that standard is what will be used when investing assets.[279]

---

[278] Probate Code §16047.

[279] Probate Code §16200(a).

WHAT CAN A TRUSTEE INVEST IN WITH A COURT SUPERVISED FIRST-PARTY SNT?

There is a special investment standard for first-party SNTs. An SNT under ongoing court jurisdiction is generally one that was established for a beneficiary that has lost capacity. These are mostly SNTs that are established through a conservatorship or with litigation proceeds. See chapter 2 to learn how to distinguish these types of trusts.

Unless good cause is shown, such a trust must allow only the following types of investments:[280]

1. Direct obligations of the United States, or of the State of California, maturing not later than five years from the date of making the investment.

2. United States Treasury bonds redeemable at par value on the death of the holder for payment of federal estate taxes, regardless of maturity date.

3. Securities listed on an established stock or bond exchange in the United States that are purchased on the exchange.

4. Eligible securities for the investment of surplus state moneys as provided for in Government Code §16430 (i.e., generally most California municipal bonds, notes, and some commercial papers).

5. An interest in a money market mutual fund registered under the Investment Company Act of 1940[281] or common trust funds under 12 CFR §9.18, the portfolios of which are limited to United States government obligations maturing not later than five years from the date of investment and to repurchase agreements fully collateralized by United States government obligations.

6. Units of a common trust fund described in Financial Code §1564, which fund has as its objective investment primarily in short-term fixed income obligations and will be permitted to value investments at cost under regulations of the appropriate regulatory authority.

---

[280] Probate Code §2574.

[281] 15 U.S.C. §§80a-1—80a-64.

The trustee can expand the available investments for good cause by obtaining court permission. Petitioning the court is generally a good use of trust funds if the trust has significant assets because of the very peculiar (and narrow) choice of authorized investments.

> **Critical Pointer:** There is some concern among attorneys that the above authorized investments do not allow investment in traditional mutual funds (a type of investment that builds in diversity of investment and increased rates of return). Other attorneys believe that because the permitted investments authorize investments into individual securities, this by implication also authorizes investments in mutual funds. It is surprising how little some judges understand even basic investment concepts, such as using such funds to decrease risk and increase returns. Nevertheless, the safest course in many instances is to petition the court to expand the trustee's investment authority to include investment in mutual funds. See chapter 11 for a discussion on petitioning the court.

> **Warning:** It may be that the trustee has been a trustee of a court-supervised SNT for many years and has been investing in things that are not authorized in the acceptable investment list (in technical violation of the California Probate Code). If the trustee is unsure of the SNTs investment standard, he or she should visit an estate planning attorney to discuss the matter. See chapter 11 for a discussion on how to find an attorney.

WHAT CAN A TRUSTEE INVEST IN WITH NON-COURT SUPERVISED SNTS?

Many SNTs do not include an overall investment standard; the ones that do typically state that the trustee is obligated to follow California law on the subject. If that is the case, then the general rule for trusts is that the trustee must invest under the prudent investor rule.[282] The California prudent investor rule states,

---

[282] Probate Code §16046(a).

1. A trustee shall invest and manage trust assets as a prudent investor would, by considering the purposes, terms, distribution requirements, and other circumstances of the trust. In satisfying this standard, the trustee shall exercise reasonable care, skill, and caution.
2. A trustee's investment and management decisions respecting individual assets and courses of action must be evaluated not in isolation but in the context of the trust portfolio as a whole and as a part of an overall investment strategy having risk and return objectives reasonably suited to the trust.[283]

The prudent investor rule superseded the old law that some investments are improper *per se* and permits a trustee to invest in any kind of property or type of investment, as long as the trustee exercises reasonable care, skill, and caution.[284] In determining whether or not a trustee is in compliance with the prudent investor rule, a number of factors are relevant. The court will evaluate compliance with the following duties:

*   duty to select risk and return objectives reasonably suited to the particular SNT;[285]
*   duty to diversify;[286]
*   duty to investigate facts relevant to investing and managing assets;[287]
*   duty to evaluate investments in the context of the portfolio as a whole;[288]
*   duty to avoid unreasonable or inappropriate costs;[289] and
*   duty to consider tax consequences.[290]

[283] Probate Code §§16045-16054.
[284] Probate Code §16047(a).
[285] Probate Code §16047(b).
[286] Probate Code §16048.
[287] Probate Code §16047(d).
[288] Probate Code §16047(b).
[289] Probate Code §16050.
[290] Probate Code §16047(c)(3).

In general, a trustee should not "place all the trust's eggs in one basket." For example, if all of the trust assets are invested in an airline stock and there is a terrorist attack that results in huge losses for the airline industry, the value of the trust assets would be compromised. Thus, a trustee needs to diversify the trust assets and minimize the risk that the trust could be impoverished by a downturn in any one stock or any one market sector.

However, when a court is determining whether a trustee has followed the prudent investor rule, such a determination is made in light of the facts and circumstances existing when a trustee made his or her investment decisions.[291] This is important, because the trustee will not want to be judged in hindsight. For example, if trustee invested in an airline stock (as part of a larger portfolio) and that stock suffered a decline due to an unanticipated strike, then the trustee will not be held responsible for that particular loss in value of the stock—if the overall investment strategy is done prudently. Thus, a trustee may lose money in investments from time to time and nevertheless be complying with the prudent investor rule.

If a trustee lacks the knowledge or experience to carry out his or her duties, prudent investing may require the trustee to delegate investment decisions to (or at least receive advice from) an investment expert.[292] Assuming delegation is done prudently with respect to costs, selection of the expert, terms of the delegation, and periodic review, the trustee will not be liable for the expert's actions.[293] In the questions below, there is a discussion on selecting an appropriate investment adviser.

WHAT IF THE TRUST DOCUMENT OR A COURT ORDER SPECIFIES HOW A TRUSTEE SHOULD INVEST IN A WAY THAT CONTRADICTS THE PRUDENT INVESTOR RULE?

There are two situations when a trustee is not required to follow the general prudent investor rule.

---

[291] Probate Code §16051.
[292] Probate Code §16052(a).
[293] Probate Code §16052(c), See also Probate Code §16401.

1. where the trust document modifies the investment standard. This allows the trustee to follow the trust description of how investments should be managed;[294] or
2. where a court order requires a different duty of investment, the trustee must follow the court order. This can happen in SNTs when a court establishes a first-party SNT for a person with a disability who also lacks capacity.[295] In this case, the permitted investments are very narrow, and any expansion of investment authority must be done by court permission, as described in the previous question and answer.

A trustee is not liable to a beneficiary for the trustee's good faith reliance on the trust's express provisions.[296] Thus, if the trust document authorizes investments that would otherwise not be approved if the trustee were required to follow the prudent investment standard, the trustee may follow the terms of the trust and still be complying with his or her fiduciary duty.

> **Example:** If the trust document stated that the trustee shall invest 20 percent of the assets in the trust in Fabrinet stock. Generally, investing 20 percent of trust assets in the stock of one company would be a violation of the prudent investor rule. However, if the trust document specifically authorizes such an investment (and it would not be really dangerous to do it), a trustee may do so without worrying about being sued for violating the investment standard.

However, even if a trust document allows a trustee to invest in a particular way, if it would be dangerous to do so, the trustee can still be sued for following the terms of the trust.

> **Example:** If the trust document stated that the trustee shall invest all trust assets with ABC Corporation and ABC Corporation had, due to factors within the reasonable knowledge of the trustee, lost 50 percent of its value each of the last three years,

---

[294] Probate Code §§16000, 16046(b).
[295] California Rules of Court 7.903(c)(4).
[296] Probate Code §16046(b).

a trustee could be sued for continuing to invest trust assets with ABC Corporation. This is true even though the trust document authorized this investment. A trustee's reliance on a trust term cannot excuse every decision made by the trustee. This is especially true when factors within the reasonable knowledge of the trustee suggested a different course of action. In this case, the trustee would be better served investing the money elsewhere.

The safest course for the trustee in this situation would be a petition for instructions. See chapter 11 on how to do this.

WHAT ARE THE CONSIDERATIONS IN DEVELOPING AN OVERALL SNT INVESTMENT STRATEGY?

Regardless of the investment standard of the trust, a trustee will need to develop an investment strategy. An appropriate investment strategy will take into account specific circumstances of the trust and its beneficiaries, the factors listed in the Prudent Investor Act, and the costs of various investments. The factors that should be considered are

1. General economic conditions
2. The possible effect of inflation or deflation
3. The expected tax consequences of investment decisions or strategies
4. The role that each investment or course of action plays within the overall trust portfolio
5. The expected total return from income and the appreciation of capital
6. Other resources of the beneficiaries as known by the trustee
7. Needs for liquidity, regularity of income, and preservation or appreciation of capital
8. An asset's special relationship or special value, if any, to the purposes of the trust or to one or more of the beneficiaries[297]

---

[297] Probate Code §16047(c).

A full analysis of all factors relevant to developing investment strategies is beyond the scope of this book. Indeed, such an analysis would likely fill many books. The appropriate strategy will likely depend on the intended level of current distributions and the expected duration of the trust.

The factors in developing an investment strategy include consideration of and balancing the beneficiary's future as well as current needs. For instance, a $1 million trust account seems like a large amount of money to most people. However, a beneficiary with a disability may need to depend on that fund for a lifetime—the balance of which could well be eighty years. Even a withdrawal of $50,000 a year will mean that the size of the fund will likely decline over the years in terms of purchasing power. If the withdrawals are limited to $30,000 a year in the first few years, the trust fund could be expected keep up with inflation. To see how that works out, let's do the math:

Let's assume that (1) the trust will have an average annual return of 7 percent, including interest, dividends and capital appreciation, (2) trustee fees and other expenses will be 1 percent a year, and (3) inflation will average 3 percent per year. Different assumptions will, of course, lead to different results. Any distribution policy can reflect actual returns and costs after several years. But here are the results after ten, twenty, and thirty years given distributions of $50,000 a year in the first example and of $30,000 a year growing with the growth of the trust fund in the second example:

	Example 1	Example 2
Year 1		
Trust fund	$1 million	$1 million
Annual distributions	$50,000	$30,000
Year 10		
Trust fund	$1.1 million	$1.3 million
Annual distributions	$50,000	$39,000
Year 20		
Trust fund	$1.2 million	$1.75 million
Annual distributions	$50,000	$52,000
Year 30		
Trust fund	$1.45 million	$3.3 million
Annual distributions	$50,000	$99,000

Belt-tightening in the first several years of a trust can reap some significant results for the trust and for the beneficiary's later years. However, this must be balanced against the beneficiary's likely lifespan, likely future needs, and potential benefit of current spending. For instance, there is little need to preserve capital in a trust whose primary beneficiary has a terminal illness. Similarly, it is a dilemma for a young client where extra tutoring may help a child achieve educational success that may make the difference between learning an employable skill in later life and having to depend on the trust for support. Of course the future is not clear to see, but if the expenditure was reasonably likely to produce the desired result, one would not withhold payment in such case, even if it would mean exceeding the normal safe threshold for trust expenditures.

The foregoing example illustrates that the SNT trustee must make financial decisions based on the beneficiary's personal needs. Often the best results require professional and family member cotrustees, or trust advisers and trust protectors, to reach a consensus based on both financial and a careful assessment of the beneficiary's current and future needs and current and potential future resources, as opposed to a blanket standard for all SNTs in all situations.

If the persons who receive trust income (known as current income beneficiaries) are different from those who will receive the principal when the trust terminates (known as remainder beneficiaries), trust records should classify all receipts and disbursements as either income or principal. In most cases, there will be no difficulty with this. Things like rent, ordinary dividends, and interest are clearly income; generally, proceeds from the sale of an asset are principal.

WHAT STEPS CAN A TRUSTEE DO TO DEVELOP AN INVESTMENT STRATEGY?

When developing an investment strategy for an SNT, it is imperative to focus on the short—and long-term needs and goals of the SNT beneficiary. The determination begins by taking an inventory of the current and future needs of the client and ranking them by priority. Such a "Wish List" can aid the trustee and financial adviser in evaluating what is probable, possible, or unattainable for the SNT beneficiary. The next step is allocating the assets to provide the best possible chance of earning the income needed to accommodate the beneficiary's ongoing special needs. Finally, there needs to be a system to review the ongoing investment strategy so changes can be made when the beneficiary's circumstances are different or the market conditions require change.

While this task might seem daunting, there is legal shelter for trustees under the law governing trust investments, known as the Uniform Prudent Investment Act. The essence of the UPIA is that risk can be legally viewed in totality for the portfolio, rather than on each invested security. It therefore allows for prudent diversification of the client's investment assets. The UPIA's focus is on the *process* of how investments are determined and implemented, not the result of independent investments.

As an SNT trustee, it is central to compliance with the UPIA to draft an investment policy statement (IPS) for the trust. An IPS outlines the client issues, risk level, restrictions, parameters, and goals for the SNT related to investments. The IPS serves as the "game plan" for the SNT investments and expenditures. In Appendix M, there is a sample IPS that was established in a different matter.

In order to develop the investment strategy, a trustee should follow the following steps:

- **Setting the Budget:** The first step is to develop a budget for the client. Obviously, the amount being used to fund the SNT will generally serve as a barrier to pay for the beneficiary's entire budget. Thus, it is important to manage client expectations in regard to what is a feasible, sustainable annual budget.

  In order to manage expectations, some trustees do not allow the beneficiary to create a "Wish List." These trustees do not want to have to explain why certain items on the list cannot be paid for. It is up to the individual trustee's discretion to decide if the beneficiary should participate in developing the budget.

  Some common examples of typical SNT needs/wants are

  - Home/personal residence purchase (and ongoing expenses related to home maintenance)
  - Home adaptations related to disability access
  - Adaptive automobile
  - Adaptive disability equipment, e.g., wheelchairs, telephone equipment, lavatory, speech

○ Computer and video equipment and software
○ Related physical therapies, clinics, providers, etc.
○ Caregivers, paid family caregivers
○ Travel and fuel expenditures
○ Companion Travel expenses
○ Clothing and specialized wear, shoes, etc.
○ Prosthetics, catheters, etc.
○ Educational expenses
○ Parental respite care
○ Clothing
○ Trusteeship, legal and administrative expenses
○ Benefits disqualifying distributions—primarily rent

Helpful Hint: In some first-party SNT cases where the funds came from a litigation recovery, the personal injury attorney may have paid for a Life Care Plan for the SNT beneficiary. The Life Care Plan goes over all the future needs and costs of the beneficiary. It can be a good starting point for determining client needs.

• **Testing the Likelihood of Earning Enough to Meet Budget:** Once there is a target budget determination, it is crucial to create forward-looking financial planning projections to "test" the likelihood of attaining the proposed budget. As all costs of providing equipment and services are likely to increase with inflation over time, the trustee must account for this in the analysis if the trustee is to continue to maintain the client's lifestyle in the future. Taxation of earnings and benefits must also be accounted for, as well as variability and uncertainty of future investment returns.

There are special needs planning calculator programs freely available on the Internet to aid in budgeting and financial forecasting:

• Merrill Lynch Special Needs, found at (http://www.totalmerrill. com/totalmerrill/pages/SpecialNeedsFinancialServices.aspx)
• MetDesk, at http://www.metlifeiseasier.com/metdesk/

Note: While these can be a great starting point, it is generally preferable to employ a financial professional with experience and expertise related directly to beneficiaries with disability cases to evaluate and prepare the client budget. In order to locate such a financial professional, please review chapter 11.

- **Investing and Allocating Assets:** The next step is properly investing the available SNT assets. Obviously, the needs, circumstances, age, and financial risk tolerance of the beneficiary will determine the appropriate risk level of the client's SNT investments. This concept is the basis of the prudent investment laws related to investing as an SNT trustee.

  As risk and return are inherently related, it is ultimately a trade-off between stable, low-risk investments (a low "fear factor"), and achieving a higher annual budget to improve the beneficiary's lifestyle and combat the effects of inflation (a reasonable return on investment assets). Most practical investment solutions will combine safety and surety for short-term needs with higher yielding investments dedicated to achieving long-term goals.

  Example: A first-party SNT may be the recipient of a structured settlement annuity that pays a guaranteed monthly amount into the SNT. An investment adviser may include short-term bonds and high quality stocks to provide a comprehensive investment program to achieve the beneficiary's lifetime goals. This allocation between bonds, annuities, and stocks provides the basis for a prudent investment plan.

  Using the financial planning projection systems discussed earlier, the SNT trustee can test various budget scenarios involving a multitude of investment risk levels. Each will provide insight as to how likely the proposed budget is to be attained over the life expectancy of the beneficiary. An annual budget can then be adopted based upon the most likely scenario with the least amount of risk. This directly determines the risk level for the SNT assets and allows the SNT trustee to implement an investment program, which matches the client's need to their necessary risk matrix.

For some first-party SNTs (as discussed in prior question/ answers), certain state laws under the Probate Code limit allowable SNT investments. If an SNT is created by a court (as in most personal injury claims or through a conservatorship), California Rule of Court 7.903 requires that investments in the SNT comply with the more stringent standards of California Probate Code §2574. The practical implications of these regulations are that these SNT's may not invest in

- Traditional mutual funds or unit investment trusts
- US Treasury bonds greater than five years in maturity
- Corporate bonds of any type or maturity
- OTC stocks
- And many other "risky" investments

Note: If the SNT trustee wishes to expand investment authority even for these types of first party SNTs, he or she is allowed to do so with court permission. A special needs planning attorney can assist with the filing of a petition to probate court. See chapter 11 to find a special needs planning attorney.

- **Plan for Ongoing Review of Investments.** The final step of any investment strategy is to develop a plan for reviewing the investment strategy implemented. Beneficiaries are human beings who undergo myriad changes over time. Markets and investments are continuously evolving due to volatile economic conditions. The trustee should continually monitor and adjust the IPS and investments based upon changes in

-

  ➢ Actual vs. projected trust expenditures
  ➢ Health changes of the SNT beneficiary
  ➢ Aging of the beneficiary, particularly attainment of majority age
  ➢ Parental caregiver aging or incapacitation
  ➢ Changes to the living situation of the beneficiary

> Investment performance
> Additional caregiver expenses
> Health-care adjustments
> Social Security Administration and Medi-Cal or Medicare policy changes

Brokerage account statements should be audited for transactions and reconciled monthly. Care should be taken to conduct investment performance reviews of the trust accounts at least quarterly.

Ongoing investment management of the SNT assets requires periodic review of transactions and investment performance. Brokerage account statements should be audited for transactions and reconciled monthly. Care should be taken to conduct investment performance reviews of the trust accounts at least quarterly. In evaluating the trust performance, the trustee might utilize the following data:

- Basic performance measures showing market gain or loss, dividends and interest received.
- Relative performance comparisons to market indices, such as the Standard and Poor's 500 Index or the Blackrock Aggregate Bond Index, or a combination of these.

Proper record keeping, quarterly investment reviews and annual IPS and financial plan updates are imperative to continued compliance with the UPIA.

CAN THE TRUSTEE DELEGATE THE INVESTMENT RESPONSIBILITIES TO ANOTHER?

Yes, a trustee is allowed to delegate investment and management functions as prudent under the circumstances.[298] This is contrary to the general rule.

---

[298]   Probate Code §16052(a).

Other than investment and management functions, a trustee cannot delegate his or her other responsibilities to others[299] For a trustee who has little to no experience in investing or managing assets, it would likely be a breach of that trustee's duty to not consult with investment counselors, real estate brokers, accountants, tax attorneys, and other specialists as necessary in managing trust assets.[300]

If a trustee decides to delegate investment or management responsibilities, the trustee must still exercise prudence in (1) selecting the agent, (2) establishing the scope and terms of the delegation of authority, and (3) periodically reviewing the agent's overall performance and his or her compliance with the terms of the delegation.

WHAT PRINCIPLES SHOULD A TRUSTEE UNDERSTAND WHEN HIRING A FINANCIAL/ INVESTMENT PROFESSIONAL?

Hiring a financial professional for the special needs trust should not be done haphazardly. It is important that the trustee find the right person to help the special needs beneficiary meet their expected future goals. Thus, it is imperative that the financial planner not only have the experience in managing assets, and in particular, experience in managing assets for a person with a disability.

Below is a very brief summary of who the financial players are.

1. Types of Financial Professionals

There are generally three types of financial professionals that can be hired to assist a trustee:

- **Investment adviser** refers to any individual or firm providing investment advice for compensation as part of a regular business of giving investment advice. An investment adviser must register with the Securities and Exchange Commission (SEC) or appropriate state securities agencies as an investment adviser, unless specifically exempted from registration. Investment advisers may recommend

---

[299]   Probate Code §16012.
[300]   Estate of Gump (1991) 1 Cal. App. 4th 582, 595.

stocks, bonds, mutual funds, partnerships, or other SEC-registered investments for clients. To register, an applicant must file a Form ADV (Adviser) detailing educational and professional experience with either the SEC or the state(s), stating the basis for their compensation and disclosing whether he or she has ever been the subject of disciplinary action. This form or its equivalent must be shown to potential clients prior to the commencement of a professional engagement.

- **Financial adviser** is a generic term used broadly by consumers and financial services professionals to describe an individual engaged in providing financial advice, services, or products to a client for compensation. The term "financial adviser" covers a broad spectrum of financial professionals, including financial planners, insurance agents, registered representatives, money managers, investment advisers, and individuals who sell, or advise people on, financial products.
- **Broker/Dealer** is a term used to describe an individual or a company that is licensed to buy and sell investment products for or to clients. Some broker/dealers are large companies that sell securities that they own (thus, the term "dealer"), while others are firms that only buy and sell securities on behalf of investors (thus, the term "broker"). To be in the US securities business, an individual or a company must be a broker/dealer or an individual must be affiliated with a broker/dealer as a registered representative. There are different types of brokers, including full service firms like Merrill Lynch and discount brokers like Charles Schwab.

2. How Financial Professionals Are Paid

Investment advisers and financial planners can be compensated in a number of ways:

- An hourly rate
- A flat fee to complete a specified project
- A quarterly or annual retainer fee
- A fee charged as a percentage of assets that they manage on your behalf (Typically anywhere from .50% per year to 2.50% per year. The more assets there are, the lower the fee.)

- Commissions paid to them from financial or insurance products purchased through them
- A combination of fees and commissions

3. Types of Financial Professional Designations

There are a whole host of designations for financial advisers. Some are well recognized and respected, while others are merely made up to aid in marketing products, like selling annuities to seniors. The designation pecking order includes the CFP (certified financial planner) designation. Other designations, like the ChFC (chartered financial consultant) and CLU (chartered life underwriter), are focused on specific segments of the financial advisory field. Below are a few of the most respected designations that a SNT trustee may want to see from a financial professional being hired:

1. **Certified Financial Planner** (CFP)

This is perhaps the most widely recognized credential in the financial planning industry. The academic requirement consists of five courses covering insurance, estate, retirement, education, tax and investment planning, plus ethics and the financial planning process. Once that is complete, students must sit for the board exam. This is a ten-hour, 285-question test that spans two days and includes two comprehensive case studies. Once a passing grade has been achieved, prospective certificants must also complete at least three years of professional experience plus a bachelor's degree in order to obtain the CFP designation. To find a CFP in your community, go to, http://www.cfp.net/search. Certified financial planners owe their clients a fiduciary duty—the highest duty in the law, and similar to the duty a trustee owes to a beneficiary.

2. **Chartered Financial Analyst** (CFA)

This designation is generally considered to be one of the most difficult and prestigious credentials in the financial industry, at least in terms of investment management. The academic requirements for this designation are second only to those for CPAs. Three years of coursework must be completed, covering a range of topics and disciplines, such as technical and fundamental analysis, financial accounting, and portfolio theory and analysis. Those who earn this designation often become portfolio managers or analysts for various types of financial institutions. However, such a designation does not necessarily impose a fiduciary duty upon individual investors.

3. **Chartered Financial Consultant** (ChFC)

This designation is used by financial professionals—including accountants, attorneys, bankers, insurance agents and brokers, and securities representatives—who have earned the ChFC designation by completing the American College's eight-course education program, met experience requirements, and agreed to uphold a code of ethics.

4. **Registered Investment Adviser** (RIA)

This designation applies to those who have taken and passed a test and filed a Form ADV IV with the SEC. Generally, RIAs owe to their clients a fiduciary duty. An individual who works with a registered investment adviser is sometimes called an investment advisory representative (IAR).

5. **Registered Representative**

A registered representative is a designation given to stockbrokers who represent a broker/dealer. Their duty is circumstantial to a specific case; thus they do not necessarily owe their clients a fiduciary duty.

6. **Insurance Agent**

Many life insurance agents hold themselves out to be "financial advisers." Life insurance agents owe a duty of reasonable care—the care commonly exercised by others in their industry. As such, it is generally acknowledged that insurance agents have the lowest hurdle with regard to the duty they owe to their clients. Some insurance agents are extraordinary, and one should not judge a specific professional based solely upon his or her particular license.

7. **Agencies in Charge of Financial Adviser Oversight**

The trustee should review any financial advisers' background through online access to the agencies that oversee them. The following is a list of useful websites of these agencies:

- The Securities and Exchange Commission (SEC) provides useful information to research adviser licensing. Their main page is http://www.sec.gov. On the SEC homepage, look for "Investor Information—Check Out Brokers and Advisers," at http://www.sec.gov/investor/brokers.htm.
- The Financial Industry Regulatory Authority (FINRA), formerly known as the National Association of Securities Dealer, Inc. (NASD), has a separate system for monitoring securities dealers. Go to http://www.finra.org/Investors/ToolsCalculators/BrokerCheck.
- In addition, the CFA Institute http://www.cfainstitute.org (formerly the Association for Investment Management and Research, or AIMR) provides background about the roles of securities analysts and brokers. They also offer an insightful guide on financial adviser selection at http://www.cfainstitute.org.
- You can find more information on licensing at the state level on state government websites. To find state securities regulators, go to the North American Securities Administrators Association, Inc. (NASAA) website at http://www.nasaa.org, and select "Find a Regulator" on the left panel.
- To find state insurance regulators, go to the National Association of Insurance Commissioners (NAIC) at http://www.naic.org. The NAIC provides an interactive map of "State Insurance Department Web Sites" at http://www.naic.org/state_web_map.htm.

WHAT STEPS SHOULD A TRUSTEE TAKE WHEN HIRING A FINANCIAL ADVISER?

The trustee should be in control in the selection process. It is acceptable to obtain the advice of the beneficiary and the family of the beneficiary, but the trustee has the ultimate responsibility (and liability) in the selection process.

Screening several advisers may appear to be a lot of effort, but remember that a trustee will be legally required to engage the services of a competent professional; meeting with just one (unless the trustee has worked with them before and has previously made comparisons) will not allow the trustee the opportunity to compare services.

1. Before Meeting with Financial Adviser

A trustee should do as much online research as possible on the prospective adviser. Reviewing their website is a good first step, but the trustee should dig a bit deeper. There are ways to get information on the investors' references and credentials.

According to the SEC's website:

Most investment advisers must fill out a form called "Form ADV." They must file their Form ADVs with either the SEC or the state securities agency in the state where they have their principal place of business, depending on the amount of assets they manage.

Form ADV consists of two parts. Part 1 contains information about the adviser's business and whether they've had problems with regulators or clients. Part 2 outlines the adviser's services, fees, and strategies. Before you hire someone to be your investment adviser, always ask for, and carefully read, both parts of Form ADV.

You can get copies of Form ADV from the investment adviser, your state securities regulator or the SEC, depending on the size of the adviser. You can find out how to get in touch with your state securities regulator through the North American Securities Administrators Association, Inc.'s (NASAA) website or by calling (202) 737-0900. Ask your state securities regulator whether they've had any complaints about the adviser, and ask them to check the CRD (Central Registration Depository).

If the SEC registers the investment adviser, you can get a copy of the Form ADV by accessing How to Request Public Documents. In addition, at the SEC's headquarters, you can visit our Public

Reference Room from 10:00 a.m. to 3:00 p.m. to obtain copies of SEC records and documents.[301]

There are also websites where you can check the background of your financial adviser. The California website that helps to locate these websites for California financial advisers is http://www.corp.ca.gov/about/adviser.asp. The trustee may also check out the SEC website at http://www.sec.gov/investor/ brokers.htm. Some other agencies that collect information on financial advisers include

1. Certified Financial Planner Board of Standards, Inc. 888-237-6275—www.CFP.net/
2. North American Securities Administrators Association 202-737-0900—www.nasaa.org
3. National Association of Insurance Commissioners 816-842-3600—www.naic.org
4. Financial Industry Regulatory Authority (FINRA) 800-289-9999—www.finra.org
5. National Fraud Exchange (fee involved) 800-822-0416

2. The Initial Meeting

Most advisers will meet personally with the trustee at no charge for between one half hour to one hour. The primary purpose of an initial meeting is introduction and mutual assessment. The trustee should make the most of this meeting.

Attached as Appendix H is a list of questions a trustee should ask during this meeting with space for providing answers. In the alternative, a trustee can use the form provided by the SEC at http://www.sec.gov/complaint/callform.htm.

> **Critical Pointer:** When the trustee asks questions, make sure to use the forms provided to write down the answers he or she receives from the prospective adviser and the basis of the decision the trustee made. Also, let the prospective financial

---

[301]   http://www.sec.gov/investor/pubs/invadvisers.htm.

professional know that you are taking notes so that it will keep them honest.

The trustee should not expect an initial meeting to result in any specific recommendations from the prospective adviser about how to handle trust assets. A good adviser must do extensive investigation of the beneficiary's situation before making any specific recommendations. Even if a prospective financial adviser seems to meet all of the beneficiary's needs, the trustee should not discount his or her gut reaction to meeting with the person. If the trustee does not feel comfortable with the financial adviser then he or she should not hire the adviser.

3. Preparing and Signing the Agreement

The terms of the agreement with the financial adviser should be in writing. In establishing the scope and terms of the delegation, the trustee and the agent should prepare written guidelines that include
- a summary profile of the trust and its purposes;
- the investment objectives for the assets delegated to the agent, including a statement of risk tolerance;
- asset allocation targets;
- a description of acceptable asset class characteristics;
- a description of how performance will be measured;
- income and/or cash flow requirements for the beneficiaries;
- investment time horizon;
- other liquidity needs for the trust for payment of taxes, fees, or other expenses;
- a description of the tax status of the trust; how taxes are allocated, and whether there are (or should be) any special restrictions on trust investments as a result of the trust's tax status;
- an agreement of how transactions will be reported to the trustee; and, ideally,
- a summary description of how communications will be transacted between the agent and the trustee and how investment transactions will be approved.

CAN A TRUSTEE STILL BE HELD RESPONSIBLE FOR BREACHES IF HE OR SHE DELEGATES THE DUTY OF

Investment to a Professional?

Yes. As already discussed, the trustee may delegate the financial and management functions of the trustee's job to a professional. However, this does not end the trustee's responsibility. He or she must still monitor the ongoing performance of the financial adviser.[302]

If the trustee fails to continue monitoring the adviser's performance and the adviser is not performing his or her job appropriately, the trustee may still be held liable.[303] Further, a trustee found liable for the acts or omissions of an agent is liable for any loss or other adverse consequences affecting trust property as a result of the act or omission of the agent, if that act or omission would be a breach of the trust if committed by the trustee.[304] Thus, if the financial adviser is not following the appropriate investment standard set forth in the trust document, both the financial adviser and the trustee will be held liable.

What Type of Monitoring of the Financial Adviser Should a Trustee Do?

As described in the previous question and answer, the failure to review the financial adviser's performance can lead to the trustee being sued if the adviser has done something wrong. Thus, it is critically important to continually review the investment adviser's performance. The trustee should review investment performance no less frequently than quarterly.

At a minimum, the trustee should have a copy of the investment strategy that was decided upon and regularly receive the adviser's financial statements.

> **Practice Pointer:** If the trustee does not have experience in reading these types of statements, the SEC has provided a Beginners' Guide to Financial Statements at http://www.sec.gov/investor/pubs/begfinstmtguide.htm.

---

[302] Probate Code §§16052(a)(1) and (a)(3).
[303] Probate Code §§16401, 16052.
[304] Probate Code §16401(b).

WHAT SHOULD A TRUSTEE DO IF HE OR SHE SUSPECTS WRONGDOING BY A FINANCIAL ADVISER?

It is imperative that the trustee act promptly.[305] Depending on the type of wrongdoing suspected, the trustee should take reasonable steps in solving the issue. This can include immediate termination, reporting to appropriate entities (courts and financial oversight groups) and possibly (in more serious matters) filing a lawsuit against the adviser.

If there is only a suspicion of wrongdoing, then a suggested course of action that may solve the problem:

1. Talk to the financial professional and explain the problem. Where is the fault? Were communications clear? Refer to the trustee's notes. What did the financial professional tell the trustee?
2. If the financial professional cannot resolve the problem, then talk to the financial professional's supervisor (which, for brokers, is often the firm's branch manager).
3. If the problem is still not resolved, write to the compliance department at the firm's main office. Explain the problem clearly, and how it should be resolved. Ask the compliance office to respond within thirty days. If trustee is still not satisfied, contact the appropriate regulatory agencies and file a complaint. For example, if the SEC is the appropriate agency, the trustee can file a complaint at

Office of Investor Education and Advocacy
US Securities & Exchange Commission
100 F Street, NE
Washington D.C. 20549-0213
Fax: (202) 772-9295 http://www.sec.gov/complaint.shtml

If there is more than suspicion of wrongdoing, then the following course of action may solve the problem:

1. Fire the financial professional.

---

[305] Probate Code §16401(b)(6).

2. If court supervised, immediately bring the wrongdoing to the court's attention.
3. Report the financial professional to appropriate regulatory agencies and file a complaint. For example, if the SEC is the appropriate agency, the trustee can file a complaint at

Office of Investor Education and Advocacy
US Securities & Exchange Commission
100 F Street, NE
Washington D.C. 20549-0213
Fax: (202) 772-9295 http://www.sec.gov/complaint.shtml

Chapter 8 Summary

✓ The trustee has a duty to invest trust property, preserve trust assets, and make the assets productive.
✓ Part of the trustee's responsibility when taking over a trust is to invest assets within a reasonable time and protect them, diversify assets, keep trust assets separate from personal assets, consider beneficiary's interests, keep beneficiary reasonably informed of trust actions, and avoid conflicts of interest, impropriety, and self-dealing.
✓ Review the trust document: it may set up specific requirements for managing and investing assets and may be relied upon by the trustee.
✓ The trustee should make sure all trust assets are insured typically with homeowners, renters, automobile, and general umbrella policy.
✓ The trustee should be prepared to examine surety bond requirements and to post bond.
✓ The trustee should not forget to purchase liability insurance if caregivers, drivers, or related activities are going on in trust.
✓ The trustee must also store trust personal property if beneficiary is moved from home.
✓ The trustee is not allowed to invest trust assets anyway he or she wants; rather, the type of investment standard will be determined by a variety of factors: whether trust is court supervised and whether the trust document specifies the investment standard (if silent, the trustee must follow the Prudent Investor Act).

✓ If the SNT is court supervised, the trustee has very limited investment options; however, the trustee may petition the court to increase options.

✓ If the SNT is not court supervised, then the trustee should check SNT document to see if it sets forth investment standard and follow those terms.

✓ If the SNT is not court supervised and if the SNT document is silent or states that investments shall be made under California law, then the trustee must follow Prudent Investor Rule.

✓ The Prudent Investor Rule allows the trustee to invest as a prudent person would and looks at overall performance rather than reviewing individual investments.

✓ The trustee should develop an investment strategy that takes into account a variety of factors, including assets available, beneficiary's present and future needs, and the length of time assets may be needed.

✓ It is prudent (if possible) to limit trust expenditures during the establishment of the trust, because long-term investing will allow for better distributions later and preserve more capital so the beneficiary does not outlive the trust assets.

✓ Trustees who have little or no investment or asset management experience should delegate these functions to a professional money adviser. Proper delegation is an acceptable way to manage trust assets.

✓ The trustee should control selection process and interview several candidates before selecting a financial adviser.

✓ Appendix H has a list of questions that can be asked of a prospective financial adviser.

✓ The trustee should write prospective adviser's answers next to questions and keep responses as part of trust records.

✓ The trustee should do background check of the financial adviser, chapter discusses several low-cost (or no-cost) ways to obtain information.

✓ The trustee should enter into a comprehensive agreement with financial adviser.

✓ The trustee must still review financial adviser's ongoing performance or be held responsible if the adviser does something wrong.

CHAPTER 9

Filing SNT Tax Returns and Paying Taxes

by
Kevin Urbatsch and Sandy Kasten

One of the trustee's primary responsibilities is making sure that all applicable taxes are paid and proper tax returns are filed.[306] The SNT trustee is typically only concerned with income taxation, but there may also be potential estate, gift, employment, and property tax issues and filing requirements to consider. If the SNT owns a business or rental property, city or county business taxes may also apply.

> **Warning**: Tax law is complex and full of exceptions to general rules. Tax laws change frequently. This chapter is intended only as a basic introduction to the most common SNT tax filing requirements and related tax issues that may apply. It is not intended to be a substitute for professional advice related to a particular tax issue. Dollar amounts and other figures cited in this chapter are current as of the publication date but should not be relied upon without consulting one of the websites listed below.

---

[306]   I.R.C. §§6012(b)(4); Treas Reg §1.641(b)-2(a); Revenue & Tax Code §18508(a); 18 Cal Code Regs §18505-1.

The Internal Revenue Service (IRS), California's Franchise Tax Board (FTB), Employment Development Department (state employment taxes), the State Board of Equalization (real estate taxes) have many useful publications available for free on their websites. These can be downloaded or ordered by mail. The websites are

IRS	www.irs.gov
FTB	www.ftb.ca.gov
Employment Development Department	www.edd.ca.gov
State Board of Equalization	www.boe.ca.gov

> **Helpful Hint:** To avoid any argument that notices were not actually sent, all notices to both the IRS and Franchise Tax Board should be sent by certified mail, return receipt requested. The trustee should also request that a copy be sent back and provide a self-addressed stamped envelope.

SHOULD THE SNT TRUSTEE HIRE A TAX PROFESSIONAL TO HELP?

The trustee is strongly advised to hire a tax professional who is familiar with the taxation of trusts to handle the SNT's taxes. The trustee can use SNT funds to pay the tax professional. Rather than waiting until tax returns are due, the author recommends that the trustee notify the trustee's tax professional when the a new SNT is established, or when the trustee becomes the successor trustee of a preexisting SNT. The trustee should provide the tax professional with a copy of the trust document.

A tax professional that has an understanding of the beneficiary's needs and family situation, as well as some familiarity with the trust's income, expenses, and assets, can identify potential tax problems and help in planning future transactions to minimize their tax impact.

Even if a tax professional is hired, the trustee should remember that he or she is still responsible for any errors on the return that result in underpayment of tax and for any penalties for failure to file on time.[307] It is important that the trustee carefully screen the tax professional, review all tax documents before

---

[307] I.R.C. §§6901(a)(1)(B), (b); Revenue & Tax Code §§19071-19072, 19512.

they are filed, and review this chapter to make sure that all applicable taxes are reported and paid.

In this chapter, we discuss the considerations in hiring a tax professional. Further, in chapter 11, there are suggestions on how to locate an appropriate tax professional.

WHAT KIND OF TAX PROFESSIONALS SHOULD BE HIRED TO ASSIST THE SNT TRUSTEE?

An SNT trustee is allowed to hire an accountant or other professional to assist the SNT trustee.[308] However, the SNT trustee must use reasonable prudence in selecting the tax professional and periodically review the professional's performance.[309] If the SNT trustee fails to use reasonable prudence, he or she will be legally responsible for mistakes made by the accounting or tax professional.

Typically, the SNT chooses to hire an attorney, a certified public accountant (CPA), an enrolled agent (EA), or a California Tax Education Council (CTEC) tax preparer. An attorney's practice may include tax return preparation and planning. Attorneys are typically hired if there is a complex tax issue requiring a legal opinion or litigation in court. CPAs are qualified in all areas of public accounting, including taxation and auditing, and can assist in overall tax planning. EAs specialize only in taxation. A CTEC tax preparer is limited to filing a tax return and answering questions from the IRS on returns they filed. In addition to these tax professionals, there are payroll services that prepare employment tax returns and bookkeepers who specialize in the preparation of court accountings.

The most important factor in selecting a tax professional is that person's familiarity and experience with fiduciary taxation, and with the tax issues affecting SNTs in particular. Attorneys and CPAs will usually charge more than enrolled agents or CTEC preparers, but this is not always the case. Some tax professionals may limit their practice to preparing personal income tax returns, or may specialize in business taxation and have little or no experience with fiduciary tax matters. A tax professional's practice may or may not include bookkeeping or the preparation of court accountings. The trustee might hire

---

[308] Probate Code §16247.

[309] Probate Code §16401.

more than one tax professional to assist with the same SNT. For example, the trustee might hire an enrolled agent to prepare the SNT's fiduciary income tax returns, and a payroll service to prepare employment tax returns.

The main difference (although there are others) between an Attorney, CPA, an EA and a CTEC Tax preparer is their education and exams.

- Licensed California attorneys can legally prepare tax returns and assist a client with tax matters. An attorney in California must be licensed through the State Bar of California. To obtain a license, an individual must pass the two day California bar exam and ethics exam. There are ongoing continuing legal education requirements. Most attorneys also received a JD degree from a law school. While attorneys are allowed to prepare such returns, not many attorneys are competent to do so. The two types of attorneys who generally will prepare returns are tax attorneys or estate and trust attorneys. Typically, an attorney is the most expensive option. One real benefit in working with an attorney is that all communications between the attorney and SNT trustee are protected by attorney-client privilege.
- To earn the CPA designation in California, accountants must earn a four-year college or university degree with specific course requirements at a school recognized by the California State Board of Accountancy, successfully complete a rigorous, standardized uniform national examination, complete an ethics examination, and acquire two years of public accounting experience to meet the stringent licensing requirements of the State of California. To assure that they stay current on developments in the field and maintain their licenses in California, CPAs are required to complete a minimum of forty hours of continuing education each year. In addition, members of the California Society of CPAs are obliged to adhere to a code of professional ethics.
- An individual can become an EA in two ways. An individual can become an EA if he has worked for the IRS for five years, or if he has taken the Special Enrolment Examination, which consists of three parts. The first part consists of questions on tax codes for individuals, the second part on tax codes for business entities, and the last part on Circular 230 and the Treasury Department guide. To maintain this license continuing education is also required with a minimum of seventy-two hours every three years, including two hours of ethics each year.

- An individual can become a CTEC registered tax preparer by obtaining a license issued by the California Tax Education Council. The license requirements are to pass a sixty-hour course on tax preparation, including a final exam. The class covers most issues commonly found on an individual's tax return. The course does not cover partnerships, corporations, trusts, nonprofits, etc. (It generally does cover briefly sole proprietorships.) Furthermore, in order to renew this license the preparer must complete a minimum of twenty hours each year of continuing education on tax issues. (Generally the requirement for completing these courses is attendance, not demonstrated proficiency.)

To verify that an individual has the appropriate license:

- Attorneys, contact the State Bar of California www.calbar.ca.gov
- CPAs, contact the California Board of Accountancy www.dca.ca.gov/cba
- CRTPs, contact the California Tax Education Council www.ctec.org
- EAs, call the IRS Office of Professional Responsibility at (313) 234-1280.

HOW DOES AN SNT TRUSTEE FIND AND HIRE A TAX PROFESSIONAL?

There is no one place that is a clearing house for finding the best type of tax professional. One of the best ways to find a professional is to seek the advice of a special needs planning attorney. Oftentimes, the attorney has a relationship with one or more tax professionals who are familiar with the needs of an SNT trustee.

Below is a list of accountant associations that can provide some leads for an SNT trustee:

- AAA Association for Accounting Administration (http://www.cpaadmin.org/)
- AGNI Accountants Global Network International (http://www.agn.org/)
- AGN—North America (http://www.agn-na.org/)
- AICPA American Institute of CPAs (http://www.aicpa.org/)
- BBB The Better Business Bureau (www.bbb.com)
- BKR International (http://www.bkr.com/)

- CBA California Board of Accountancy (http://www.cba.ca.gov/)
- CPAAI CPA Associates International (http://www.cpaai.com/)
- Diamond Certified (www.diamondcertified.org)
- IAAER International Association for Accounting Education and Research (http://www.iaaer.org/)
- IGAF International Group of Accounting Firms (http://www.igaf.org/)
- IRS US Internal Revenue Service (http://www.irs.gov/)
- Polaris International (http://www.polarisinternational.org/)

Questions that should be asked of any tax professional:

- What is your operating credential?
- How many years have they worked in taxation?
- What is their educational background?
- Do they specialize in any areas of taxation?
- What accounting experience do they have with special needs trusts?
- Do they guarantee their work?
- What is the cost?
- Do they have references?

IS ADDING TO (OR FUNDING) AN SNT BY GIFT OR INHERITANCE A TAXABLE EVENT?

Generally no. The assets that are placed into an SNT typically come from an inheritance, gift, or similar type arrangement. In nearly every case, any tax owed would already have been paid by whoever was placing assets into the SNT. However, if a SNT receives a distribution or a series of distributions, from a deceased person's retirement plan, IRA, or annuity, the SNT will usually be subject to income tax on those distributions.

> **Example 1:** In her living trust, a mother left her entire estate to her daughter's third-party SNT. The entire net estate (after paying mother's final expenses) is valued at $300,000. The receipt of $300,000 from the mother's living trust by the daughter's third-party SNT is not a taxable event for the SNT. Thus, the entire $300,000 would be owned by the SNT and no tax would be immediately owed.

Example 2: Assume the same facts as in Example 1. The daughter's uncle names the SNT as the beneficiary of his IRA. After the uncle's death, the SNT begins to receive annual distributions from the uncle's IRA. The SNT must report these distributions as income and pay any income tax due as a result of receiving the distributions.

Critical Pointer: Anyone naming a SNT as the beneficiary of a retirement plan or annuity should consult with an estate planning attorney to ensure that the trust is properly drafted.

There could be a tax owed if persons or entities failed to pay all applicable taxes prior to transferring the assets to the SNT.

Example: A mother in her living trust left her entire estate to her daughter's third-party SNT. Mother died in 2011. Her entire estate is worth $6 million, after paying mother's final expenses other than the federal estate tax. The trustee of the mother's living trust transferred the full $6 million to daughter's third-party SNT. In 2011, an estate with a net worth of more than $5 million must pay a federal estate tax. The IRS could seek payment of the estate tax from either the mother's trustee or the third-party SNT assets.

If real property is transferred to the SNT, the property will be reassessed for property tax purposes unless exclusion applies. See discussion below about real property taxes.

If a trustee is uncertain whether all appropriate taxes were paid, he or she should consult with a tax professional. See chapter 11 for a discussion on finding appropriate tax professionals.

IS FUNDING AN SNT WITH A LITIGATION RECOVERY A TAXABLE EVENT?

Generally no. Any tax owed would already have been paid by whoever was placing assets into the SNT.

Example: A person with a disability was injured in an automobile accident. He received a net settlement of $300,000 for his physical personal injuries after paying his attorney's fees and court costs. The entire $300,000 would be added into his first-party SNT, and no tax would be immediately owed.

However, if the litigation recovery is taxable and taxes were not paid, then the SNT trustee may be responsible for the taxes.

Example: A person with a disability was injured in an automobile accident. He received a net settlement of $200,000 for his physical personal injuries and $100,000 for lost wages. The entire $300,000 was added into his first-party SNT and no taxes were paid. The $100,000 for lost wages is taxable. If the funds were transferred to the SNT without paying the taxes, the IRS could seek payment for those taxes from the SNTs assets.

A first-party SNT is often funded with the proceeds of a personal injury award or settlement. A litigation settlement or judgment compensating an individual for physical injury or sickness is not income[310], the subsequent earnings (usually interest or dividends) derived from the initial award may be taxable.

Example: An injured person receives a $3 million settlement, which is paid directly to her first party SNT. The funds are invested and earn $150,000 per year in dividends. The $3 million is not taxable income, but the $150,000 must be reported as income.

One issue that may arise in a first-party SNT is with a particular type of investment. Personal injury awards and settlements are often paid in the form of an annuity (often called a structured settlement annuity), so that the first-party SNT receives payments over a period of time rather than in a lump sum. These annuity payments will generally be nontaxable.[311] Thus, the SNT

---

[310] I.R.C. §104(a)(2).

[311] I.R.C. §104(a).

trustee should not worry about including these payments as part of the SNTs taxable income.

Often the SNT beneficiary because of his or her disability will have tax deductible medical expenses that can seriously reduce the taxes for an SNT. However, if the SNT beneficiary is under the age of twenty-four, his or her income may be subject to the "kiddie tax," which can have the effect of limiting available medical expense deductions.

It should also be noted that no medical expense deduction is allowed for payments to a caregiver who is a relative (spouse, parent or other ancestor, lineal descendant, brother or sister) of the disabled beneficiary, unless the relative has an appropriate professional license.[312]

WHAT TAX IDENTIFICATION NUMBER SHOULD A TRUSTEE USE FOR THE SNT?

Every SNT should have a tax identification number (TIN). A tax identification number may also be referred to as an employer identification number (EIN) or federal employer identification number (FEIN). This number, rather than the beneficiary's social security number, should be used on all SNT accounts. Keeping the SNT's taxable income separate from the beneficiary's taxable income will help the trustee when dealing with government employees who administer the public benefits programs.

It is possible the SNT already has a TIN. Either, the attorney who drafted the SNT will have already applied for at TIN, or an earlier trustee will have obtained one. The trustee should make sure that the trust does not already have a TIN before obtaining one. A successor trustee for an SNT that already has a TIN should not obtain a new one but should use the existing TIN.

The TIN is relatively easy to obtain online. Go to www.irs.gov and search for TIN. The trustee can then click through to "Apply for an TIN online." There will be a series of questions. Most of which are self-explanatory. In going through the online application process, the trustee should complete the following steps:

1.   Click on "irrevocable trust" when it asks which type of entity the trustee is seeking to obtain an identification number for.

---

[312]   I.R.C. §§152(d)(2), 213(d)(11).

2. The grantor of the trust will depend on whether or not it is a first—or third-party trust. If first party, the grantor is the beneficiary and if third party, the grantor is the person(s) putting assets into the trust, typically a parent or grandparent.
3. A social security number of the grantor will then be needed.
4. There are then questions on the trustee, including the trustee's address. It is important that the trustee keep address information current as this is the address the IRS will use to communicate with the trustee on tax issues.

As an alternative, the trustee can also use IRS form SS-4 to apply for a tax identification number for the SNT by telephone, fax, or mail.

If not already done, the trustee should let all financial institutions know the TIN number for all trust assets.

SHOULD A TRUSTEE (OR SUCCESSOR TRUSTEE) NOTIFY THE IRS OR CALIFORNIA FRANCHISE TAX BOARD WHEN HE OR SHE BECOMES TRUSTEE?

Yes. The trustee (or when a successor trustee takes control) should notify the IRS and California Franchise Tax Board that the trustee is taking control of the SNT.[313] This is done by filing a completed IRS Form 56 (Notice Concerning Fiduciary Relationship) for both the IRS and Franchise Tax Board.

To obtain a copy of the form, you can go to www.irs.gov and search for Form 56. Completing the form is fairly straightforward:

Part I: Name the person for whom trustee is acting. For a third-party SNT, the trustee is acting on behalf of the SNT. Thus, trustee should use the TIN number obtained as described in previous question. Then trustee enters his or her name and address information.

Part II: Check box C stating trustee is acting pursuant to valid trust instrument

---

[313] See I.R.C. §§6903, 7701(a)(6); Treas Reg §301.6903-1

Part III: On line 2, state income. On line 3, state 1041. On line 4, state date taken over as trustee going forward. On line 5, check box. On line 6, leave blank.

Part IV: Use these sections only if trustee is notifying IRS that he or she is no longer serving as trustee.

Part V: Leave blank

Part VI: Sign under Fiduciary's Signature, add title as "Trustee," and date form.

The trustee should send the form to the local IRS office. If unknown by the trustee, check on www.irs.gov and search for local offices. Enter the zip code where trustee is located.

While the California Franchise Tax Board does not have a similar form, it will accept a signed original IRS Form 56. The trustee should mail it to

Franchise Tax Board
PO Box 942840
Sacramento, CA 94240-0040

SHOULD A TRUSTEE NOTIFY THE IRS OR FRANCHISE TAX BOARD WHEN HE OR SHE IS NO LONGER SNT TRUSTEE?

Yes. The Form 56 should be filed again. However, the former trustee should complete Part V describing when his or her services ended on the SNT.

HOW DOES INCOME TAX APPLY TO TRUSTS?

For income tax purposes, trusts are considered to be either "grantor" or "nongrantor" trusts. It is very important to understand the distinction between the two types of trusts. Whether a SNT is considered a "grantor" or a "nongrantor" trust determines how it is taxed and what federal and state income tax forms must be filed for the trust.

A trust is considered to be a grantor trust if certain benefits or powers are held by the grantor, the trustee, or a third person. The term "grantor" is generally synonymous with the terms "settlor" or "trustor," meaning the person who creates a trust. A trust may be considered a grantor trust if the trust income can be used to benefit the individual who funded the trust. Nearly every first-party SNT—that is, a SNT funded with the disabled beneficiary's own assets (usually money received as a result of litigation or a settlement, or an outright inheritance)—is taxed as a grantor trust because the income may be distributed to or used for the benefit of the person who funded the trust.[314] The difference between a first-party SNT and a third-party SNT are discussed in chapter 2.

A summary of the difference in tax treatment between a "grantor trust" and "nongrantor trust" is as follows:

A. Grantor Trusts

A grantor trust is *not* considered a separate entity for income tax purposes. This means that a SNT that is a grantor trust does not pay its own income tax. The trustee still has tax return filing requirements, as discussed below. Instead, the person who is treated as the owner of the trust (the beneficiary with a disability in the case of a first-party SNT) will report the trust's income, deductions, and credits on his or her personal income tax returns and pay any income tax attributable to the trust income.

In many cases, it is advantageous for a SNT to be taxed as a grantor trust, because the beneficiary is likely to be in a lower income tax bracket than the trust would be if the trust were taxed as a separate entity.

B. Nongrantor Trusts

Any trust that is not a grantor trust is a separate entity for income tax purposes and is called a nongrantor trust. The nongrantor trust must pay any income tax due on its net taxable income. Like an individual, a nongrantor trust must file annual federal and California income tax returns, called "fiduciary income tax returns," to report the trust's income, deductions, and credits.

---

[314] I.R.C. §677,

A trust's taxable income is computed in much the same way as that of an individual.[315]

No standard deduction is available to a trust, unlike an individual; a trust must itemize its deductions. Federal tax law allows most trusts a very small personal exemption—$300 in the case of a "simple trust[316] "or $100 in the case of a "complex trust."

Because of public benefit eligibility requirements, no SNT will ever be a simple trust. Any nongrantor trust that does not come within the definition of a simple trust is a complex trust—therefore, a nongrantor SNT will be treated as a complex trust for income tax purposes.[317]

WHAT ARE A FIRST-PARTY SNT TRUSTEE'S REPORTING REQUIREMENTS?

As described above, if the first-party SNT is considered a "grantor trust," the income earned by the SNT assets is taxed to the SNT beneficiary.[318] Thus, for all practical purposes, the first-party SNT is invisible. All income is treated as the beneficiary's. This is so even if the income it is retained in the trust and never distributed for the benefit of the beneficiary.

> **Note:** The beneficiary is often the preferred taxpayer because his or her income tax brackets are usually much lower than the trust's tax brackets. In 2011, an individual will pay the highest income tax rate of 35 percent (federal) on taxable income over $379,150, while trusts (third-party SNTs with undistributed income) pay the highest income tax rate on taxable income over $11,350.[319]

The SNT trustee is required report information to the beneficiary. The standard method for doing this is by completing only the part of IRS Form 1041

---

[315] I.R.C. §641(b).

[316] A simple trust is one that is required by the trust document to distribute all of its current income.

[317] I.R.C. §642(b).

[318] I.R.C. §671; Treas Reg §1.671-4.

[319] Revenue Procedures 2011-12, IRB 2011-2 (12/23/2010).

and FTB Form 541 that includes identifying information (name, address, and tax identification number), with an attachment listing items of SNT income, gain, loss, deduction, and credit that will flow through to the SNT beneficiary's personal income tax returns (IRS Form 1040 and FTB Form 540).[320] This is filed with the IRS and the FTB. The trustee must give a copy of this attachment, referred to as a "grantor letter," to the beneficiary.[321]

> **Note**: In preparing the "grantor letter," the trustee should list tax deductible medical expenses paid on behalf of the SNT beneficiary so that the beneficiary can deduct these.

In lieu of the above method of tax reporting for a grantor trust, the IRS provides three optional methods. These optional reporting methods are discussed in the instructions to IRS Form 1041. In the author's opinion, the standard method described above is the simplest of the various reporting methods.

In order to minimize or eliminate the financial burden on the beneficiary, the SNT trustee can pay for the preparation of the trust's and the beneficiary's tax returns and can pay any tax that is due on the beneficiary's behalf.

WHAT ARE A THIRD-PARTY SNT TRUSTEE'S REPORTING REQUIREMENTS?

A third-party SNT is typically a nongrantor trust. This means that the third-party SNT trustee reports the SNT's income on the trusts own income tax return and pays, from trust income or principal, the taxes on its income.[322] A nongrantor third-party SNT is subject to the higher tax rates than an individual, so it will generally pay a greater tax on income than would a beneficiary under a grantor trust. However, as discussed in more detail below, there is a way to significantly reduce the overall taxes paid by utilizing the trust's deduction for distributions made for the benefit of the trust beneficiary.

---

[320] I.R.C. §6034A(a); Treas Reg §1.671-4(b)(2).
[321] I.R.C. §671. Revenue & Tax Code §17731.
[322] I.R.C. §671.

Note: In 2011, an individual will pay the highest income tax rate of 35 percent (federal) for taxable income over $379,150 while for trusts (third-party SNTs retained income) pay the highest income tax rate for taxable income over $11,350.[323]

Because the undistributed income of a nongrantor trust will typically result in higher taxes, many trustees will look for a way to reduce the trust's tax burden. One significant way to do so is by distributing income to the beneficiary (or on the beneficiary's behalf). If this is done, the trustee may take a deduction against the trust income, and taxes will be paid at the beneficiary's (often much lower) tax rate. The distribution deduction may not exceed the smaller of (1) the actual amount distributed; or (2) the trust's "distributable net income" (DNI).[324] Thus, most third-party SNT trustees attempt to make sure that all income is distributed each year.

Example: An SNT has $40,000 of dividend and interest income. The trust has $5,000 of tax deductible administration expenses. Its net income is $35,000. If it distributes $50,000 to or for the benefit of the beneficiary, its distribution deduction will be limited to $35,000. If, instead, it distributes $10,000 for the benefit of the beneficiary, its distribution deduction will be limited to $10,000. The additional $25,000 of income will be taxed at the (often higher) trust tax rate. (Note that although this example uses a simple fact situation for illustrative purposes, DNI is not always the same amount as the trust's net income after deductions.)

Warning: It is possible that a third-party can be taxed as a grantor trust—for example, when a parent has established a revocable third-party SNT while the parent is still living. Because the parent can still change the SNT's terms and provisions, the taxation of the SNT will be identical to the first-party SNT discussed in the prior question, except that the parent, rather than the beneficiary, will be treated as the grantor for income tax

---

[323] Revenue Procedures 2011-12, IRB 2011-2 (12/23/2010).

[324] I.R.C. §§651, 661.

purposes. If the trustee is not certain if his or her SNT is a grantor or nongrantor trust, the trustee should consult with an attorney. See chapter 11 for instructions on locating an attorney.

When appropriate, distributions made on behalf of the SNT beneficiary can be used to reduce the overall income tax.

> **Example:** A third-party SNT earns $25,000 of net income during 2011. As noted above, if this income were retained in the trust and no disbursements were made on the beneficiary's behalf, the trust would be paying income tax of 35 percent on net income over $11,350. However, if the third-party SNT trustee had made disbursements of trust income throughout the year of $25,000 on the beneficiary's behalf, the top tax rate paid would only be 15 percent, assuming the beneficiary had no other taxable income.[325]

> **Critical Pointer:** If it is appropriate, the third-party SNT trustee at the end of the year should make sure that all income was distributed, but if not, the trustee may make a tax election to make disbursements in the first sixty-five days of the following year and have those disbursements counted as being made in the prior taxable year.[326] Obviously, distributions should not always be made solely for tax purposes. However, if there are distributions that will enhance the quality of life of the beneficiary, and saves on taxes, it should be considered.

The taxable income of a nongrantor trust is computed in much the same manner as taxable income for individuals. There are specific differences, however, with respect to computing the taxable income of trusts. For example,

---

[325] See Revenue Procedures 2011-12, IRB 2011-2 (12/23/2010).
[326] I.R.C. §661(a); I.R.C. §663(b).

- the personal exemption is $100 for a complex trust.[327] However, as discussed below, a third-party SNT may qualify as a "qualified disability trust" and obtain a higher exemption,[328]
- expenses that would be miscellaneous itemized deductions for an individual taxpayer but that would not have been incurred absent the trust (i.e., trustee fees and attorney fees related to trust tax matters) may be deducted and are not subject to the 2-percent adjusted gross income floor;[329] and
- if the income is distributed in a given year (or if an election is made sixty-five days into the next year[330]) to the SNT beneficiary (or for his or her benefit), then the SNT receives a deduction and the beneficiary will be responsible to pay the tax on that income.

The trustee reports the beneficiary's share of a nongrantor trust's income, deductions, and credits on Schedule K-1, which is filed with the IRS and FTB as part of the trust's fiduciary income tax return. The trustee must provide copies of the federal and California Schedules K-1 to the beneficiary for use in preparing the beneficiary's personal income tax returns.

A detailed discussion of trust income taxation far exceeds the scope of this book. If an SNT trustee is unfamiliar with these rules, he or she is strongly encouraged to hire a tax professional familiar with filing fiduciary income tax returns. See chapter 11 for instruction on finding a competent tax professional.

---

[327] The term "complex" does not refer to the level of difficulty involved in trust administration. Rather, a "complex trust" is defined as any nongrantor trust that does not come within the definition of a "simple trust." A "simple trust" is required by the trust document to distribute all of its current income. All qualifying third party SNTs give the trustee discretion regarding distributions of income and principal, and are therefore complex trusts.

[328] I.R.C. §642(b).

[329] I.R.C. §67(e).

[330] I.R.C. §661(a); I.R.C. §663(b).

WHAT IS A QUALIFIED DISABILITY TRUST?

As noted in the previous question, a third-party SNT as a nongrantor, complex trust only has a $100 personal exemption. A trust may increase its personal exemption if it qualifies as a qualified disability trust (QDT). To be characterized as a QDT, the trust must be irrevocable and established for the sole benefit of a person under the age of sixty-five who is disabled, as defined by the SSI programs.[331] If the trust meets these requirements, a QDT is entitled to an exemption equal to the personal exemption for an individual ($3,700 in 2011[332]). Distributions from a qualified disability trust are not subject to the "kiddie tax."

> **Note**: Most third-party SNTs are not set up to be for the "sole benefit" of a beneficiary under age sixty-five. These are requirements of a first-party SNT and are generally not followed when establishing a third-party SNT. Thus, it would be the rare third-party SNT that would qualify as a QDT. However, the trustee should carefully review the terms of the SNT to see if it qualifies. If unsure, the trustee should meet with an attorney to see if the trust complies with the QDT requirements. To find such an attorney, check chapter 11 of this book.

HOW MUCH INCOME IS REQUIRED BEFORE A THIRD-PARTY SNT TRUSTEE HAS TO FILE A TAX RETURN? WHAT TAX FORMS NEED TO BE FILED? IS THERE A TIME LIMIT WHEN THE FORMS NEED TO BE FILED?

In general, the filing of tax forms by the trustee is similar to filing tax returns for an individual. Tax returns must generally be filed prior to April 15 of each year.[333]

---

[331] I.R.C. §642(b)(2)(C)(ii); 42 U.S.C. §1396p(c)(2)(B)(iv).

[332] See Revenue Procedures 2011-12, IRB 2011-2 (12/23/2010).

[333] I.R.C. §6072(a); Treas Reg §1.6072-1(a); Revenue & Tax Code §18566.

- **Federal Requirement:** The third-party SNT trustee must file an **IRS Form 1041** (US Income Tax Return for Estates and Trusts) if there is any taxable income for the tax year,[334] or if there is gross income of $600 or more, regardless of the amount of taxable income.[335]
- **California Requirement:** The third-party SNT trustee must file **FTB Form 541** (California Fiduciary Income Tax Return) if there is net taxable income of over $100; if the gross income exceeds $10,000, regardless of the net taxable income; or if the trust has alternative minimum tax liability (see Instructions for FTB Form 541 (General Information—Who Must File).[336] As a practical matter, a California fiduciary income tax return should be filed if there is a federal filing requirement.

Note: It is possible that the SNT trustee would be required to file FTB Form 541 and not an IRS Form 1041 depending on the amount of income. It is sometimes advisable to file even when filing is not required, as when the SNT has a loss that can be carried forward to a future tax year.

CAN A THIRD-PARTY SNT TRUSTEE SEEK AN EXTENSION OF TIME TO FILE RETURNS AND PAY TAXES?

Yes for an extension of time to file and *yes* (for good cause) for an extension of time to pay taxes. A trustee may request an extension of time to file both federal and California tax returns. However, as described below, this does not extend the time to pay the tax.

For federal IRS purposes, to receive an automatic six-month extension to file the federal (Form 1041) tax form, the trustee must

- submit IRS Form 7004 (Application for Automatic 6-Month Extension of Time to File Certain Business Income Tax, Information and Other

---

[334] I.R.C. §6012(a)(4).

[335] I.R.C. §6012(a)(4).

[336] Revenue & Tax Code §18505(e)-(f)).

Returns) or an application in any other manner prescribed by the commissioner;

- file the application on or before the date prescribed for filing the return with the appropriate IRS office; and
- show on the application the properly estimated tax amount for the taxable year.

For California FTB purposes, to receive an automatic six-month extension to file the California (Form 541) tax form, the trustee does not need to file a written application.[337] Even though no form is required, the trustee should use FTB Form 3563 to make an extension payment if it is estimated that there will be a state income tax balance due.

An extension of time for filing the tax return is not an extension of time for payment of either the federal or California tax due.[338] The trustee may request an extension of time to pay the trust's federal taxes by filing IRS Form 1127 (Application for Extension of Time for Payment of Tax).

In rare cases, the IRS or FTB may grant an extension of time to pay the income tax. Granting an extension of time for payment is discretionary with the IRS[339] and ordinarily is allowed only in cases of undue hardship.[340] For California purposes, the trustee may make a request to the FTB for a reasonable extension for payment of tax. However, the FTB will only grant if there is a very good reason the tax cannot be immediately paid.[341]

> **Critical Pointer:** The trustee should always make the best possible estimate of the trust's income tax liability and pay that amount on or before the original due date. If possible, the trustee should inform the beneficiary of the approximate amount of trust income that must be reported on the beneficiary's personal income tax returns, so that the beneficiary can calculate his or her personal income tax liability as accurately as possible. If the trust files on extension, the beneficiary should obtain an

---

[337] 18 Cal Code Regs §18567(a).

[338] Treas Reg §1.6081-1(a), Revenue & Tax Code §18567(b).

[339] I.R.C. §6161.

[340] Undue hardship is described in Treasury Regulations §1.6161-1(b)).

[341] Revenue & Tax Code §18567(c).

extension of time to file his or her personal income tax returns. If the beneficiary files before receiving a Schedule K-1 or grantor letter (discussed above) from the trust, he or she will likely have to file amended returns after receiving the trust's information.

IS THERE A PENALTY FOR FAILURE TO FILE AND PAY TAXES?

Yes. A late filing penalty will be imposed if the trustee fails to file a required tax return. A late payment penalty may be imposed if less than the full amount is paid on time. In general, for both federal and California purposes the penalty for late filing of a tax return is 5 percent of the tax due each month that the return is late, up to a maximum of 25 percent.[342] There may be exceptions if there was reasonable cause for delay, such as the death or serious illness of the responsible person. Penalties may be increased if the failure to file was intentional.

In general, the federal penalty for late payment of tax is described as follows:

- 0.5 percent of the net tax due for each month (or fraction of a month) the tax remains unpaid. This is calculated from the date the tax is due; the maximum penalty is 25 percent.[343]
- That penalty is doubled to 1 percent if payment is not made within 10 days after notice is given by the IRS.[344]

The California late payment penalty if 5 percent of the total unpaid tax plus.5 percent of the remaining tax for each month the tax remains unpaid, to a maximum of forty months.[345]. The total penalty may not exceed 25 percent of the total unpaid tax.[346]

---

[342] I.R.C. §665, Revenue & Tax Code §19131.

[343] I.R.C. §6651(a)(2).

[344] I.R.C. §6651(d).

[345] Revenue & Tax Code §19132(a)(2).

[346] Revenue & Tax Code §19132(a)(3).

As with the penalty for late filing, the penalty for late payment can be avoided if reasonable cause for the delay can be shown.[347]

DOES A THIRD-PARTY SNT NEED TO PAY AN ESTIMATED TAX?

Yes. As a general rule, third-party SNTs which are nongrantor trusts are required to pay quarterly estimated taxes for federal and California taxes.[348] As described in the previous questions on third-party SNT taxation, nearly all third-party SNTs are nongrantor trusts.

For federal purposes, SNTs that did not have a tax liability in the prior year or will have a tax less than $1,000 in the current year are exempt from paying estimated taxes.[349] In all other cases, the third-party SNT must make four equal estimated tax payments each year.

> **Example 1.** The trustee expects that the SNT's total income tax for the current year will be $3,300. The trustee expects that there will be about $2,500 of federal income tax withholding, leaving a balance due of $800. No federal estimated tax payments are required. If the withholding amount were less than $2,300, estimated tax payments would be required in this example.

> **Example 2.** The trustee expects that the SNT's total income tax for the current year will be $1,100. There is no withholding. Federal estimated tax payments are required.

The estimated tax payment must be calculated as follows:

- For trusts with adjusted gross income of $150,000 or less[350] in the preceding tax year, the required annual payment is the lesser of (i) 90 percent of the tax for the current taxable year or (ii) 100 percent of the

---

[347] I.R.C. §6651(a)(2); Revenue & Tax Code §19132(a)(1).
[348] I.R.C. §6654(l)(1); Revenue & Tax Code §19136(a).
[349] I.R.C. §6654(e).
[350] As determined under I.R.C. §67(e).

tax for the preceding taxable year, if it was a taxable year of twelve months and a return was filed.[351]

- For trusts with adjusted gross income in excess of $150,000[352] in the preceding tax year, the required annual payment is the lesser of (i) 90 percent of the tax for the current taxable year or (ii) 110 percent of the tax for the preceding taxable year, if it was a taxable year of twelve months and a return was filed.[353]

The third-party SNT trustee computes federal estimated taxes on IRS Form 1041-ES, which contains detailed instructions regarding payment dates and filing an early return, rather than paying a fourth installment of estimated tax. Payments are made with estimated tax voucher forms.

California trusts are required to make estimated tax payments in the same manner as individual taxpayers. However, a California estimated tax is not required if the prior year's tax was less than $500 or the current year's tax will be less than $500.[354] The third-party trustee calculates estimated taxes on FTB Form 541-ES, which contains detailed instructions regarding payment dates and filing an early return rather than paying a fourth installment of estimated taxes. Payments are made with estimated tax voucher forms.

Penalties for underpayment of estimated tax are imposed unless the estimated tax paid is more than the smaller of (1) 100 percent of the prior year's tax liability (110 percent if the SNT's adjusted gross income for the prior year was more than $150,000); or (2) 90 percent of the current year's tax liability.[355]

HOW IS A SNT BENEFICIARY TAXED?

It will depend on whether the individual with a disability is a beneficiary of a first-party SNT or a third-party SNT. If the trustee is unsure of the type of SNT that is being administered, a discussion of the differences is discussed in chapter 2.

---

[351]   I.R.C. §6654(d)(1)(B).

[352]   As determined under I.R.C. §67(e).

[353]   I.R.C. §6654(d)(1)(C).

[354]   Revenue & Tax Code §19136(c).

[355]   I.R.C. §6654(a), (e)(1); Revenue & Tax Code §19136.

Because a first-party SNT is generally taxed as a grantor trust, the trust is not treated as a separate entity for tax purposes. The beneficiary should report the trust's income, deductions, and credits on the beneficiary's personal tax return as if the trust did not exist.

Because a third-party SNT is generally taxed as a nongrantor trust, the trustee must provide the beneficiary with a Schedule K-1 showing the amounts of trust income, deductions, and credits that the beneficiary must report on his or her personal income tax returns.

Trust distributions to or for the benefit of the beneficiary are considered income of the beneficiary only to the extent of the trust's "distributable net income" (DNI). Distributions that exceed the trust's DNI are considered distributions of principal and are not taxed as income.

> **Example**: A SNT has $30,000 of interest income. The trust has $10,000 of tax deductible administrative expenses, leaving it a DNI of $20,000. If the trust distributes $25,000 on behalf of the beneficiary, $20,000 will be taxed as income to the beneficiary. The remaining $5,000 will be considered a nontaxable distribution of trust principal.

Income has the same "character" in the hands of the beneficiary that it had in the hands of the trust. "Character" refers to the type of income and affects how that income is taxed. For example, distributions to a beneficiary may include interest, which is taxed as ordinary income, and qualified dividends, which are taxed at a lower rate.

> **Note:** An issue that confuses many people when discussing the word "income" is that it may have different meanings depending on the situation. In this chapter, income is discussed as it is defined by the IRS and FTB in the context of taxation. In most other parts of the book, "income" is defined by public benefit programs, such as SSI, Medi-Cal, or Section 8. These public benefit programs define the word "income" much differently than does the IRS or FTB. For example, the Social Security Administration treats the receipt of food or shelter by the SSI recipient as a type of "income." The IRS or FTB would not do so. Thus, the trustee should remain diligent in knowing how the word "income" is being used in this book.

Often, distributions are made from a third-party SNT to pay the beneficiary's medical expenses that are not covered by public benefit programs. This can create a tax problem for the beneficiary if the amounts involved are large, because the beneficiary may not take a medical expense deduction for amounts paid by the nongrantor trust.

> **Example:** Suppose an SNT has $80,000 of "distributable net income" and the trustee employs a caregiver at a cost of $75,000 per year. The entire $75,000 is deductible by the trust and reportable as income by the beneficiary. Although the entire $75,000 was spent for a caregiver and would have been deductible as a medical expense if the beneficiary had paid the caregiver directly, the beneficiary may not take this deduction. Thus, the beneficiary would need to pay tax on the full $75,000 of "income."

> **Critical Pointer:** Regardless of who pays, there is no medical expense deduction allowed for a caregiver who is a relative (spouse, parent or other ancestor, lineal descendant, brother or sister) of the disabled beneficiary, unless the relative has an appropriate professional license.[356]

Another issue that may arise is when the SNT beneficiary is young and being claimed as a dependent on his or her parent's tax return. Distributions to the beneficiary may subject the beneficiary to the "kiddie tax." This tax applies to the "unearned income" (income that does not represent compensation for working) of a child under age nineteen, or aged twenty-four in the case of a student, unless the child's earned income equals at least half of his or her support. When the "kiddie tax" applies, the child is taxed at the parent's highest marginal income tax rate if this results in a larger amount than if the child were taxed at his or her own income tax rate.[357]

---

[356] I.R.C. §§152(d)(2), 213(d)(11).

[357] I.R.C. §1(g).

HOW ARE TRUSTEE'S FEES TAXED?

Fees earned by a trustee are taxable as income. How the trustee's fees are reported and taxed depends upon whether the trustee is considered a professional fiduciary under tax law.

In general, an individual (usually a family member or friend) who serves as a trustee on a single occasion is not considered a professional fiduciary. Someone who is in the business of serving as a trustee, executor, or conservator and does this kind of work on an ongoing basis is considered a professional fiduciary for federal tax purposes, regardless of whether or not he or she is licensed under applicable state law.

A nonprofessional trustee should report his or her trustee fees as miscellaneous income on page 1 of his or her federal income tax return (IRS Form 1040). Fees earned by nonprofessional trustees are not subject to self-employment tax.

The fees earned by a professional trustee are considered business income, and must be reported on Schedule C of the trustee's personal income tax return. A professional trustee's net business income is subject to self-employment tax.[358]

HOW SHOULD THE TRUSTEE HANDLE CAREGIVER AND OTHER SNT EMPLOYEES' TAXES?

Under federal and state tax laws, almost all caregivers are treated as employees subject to payroll tax, rather than as independent contractors. This is true whether the caregiver works full time or part time, and whether the caregiver is hired on a permanent or temporary basis. The caregiver may ask to be treated as an independent contractor rather than an employee, and the trustee may prefer to treat the caregiver as an independent contractor. However, the preferences of the caregiver and the trustee in this regard are not the controlling factor. For a thorough discussion on the factors in determining whether a caregiver is an employee or independent contractor, see discussion in chapter 6.

A caregiver who is hired through an agency may be an employee of the agency, rather than the SNT, where the trustee makes ongoing payments to

---

[358] Rev. Rul. 58-5, 1958-1 CB 322.

the agency for the caregiver's services. The trustee should ascertain that the agency does in fact treat the caregiver as an employee for tax purposes and that the agency carries a workers' compensation insurance policy.

Payroll tax rules are complex and confusing. Federal and state rules are not consistent with each other. The penalties for failing to pay required payroll taxes are severe. The authors recommend that the trustee utilize a payroll service or hire a tax professional who is familiar with payroll taxes.

A newly hired caregiver should be asked to complete IRS Form W-4, "Employee's Withholding Allowance Certificate," and US Citizenship and Immigration Services (USCIS) Form I-9, "Employment Eligibility Verification." The SNT trustee must verify that the caregiver may legally work in the United States.

Federal and state laws distinguish between "regular" and "household" employees. Different payroll requirements apply to these two types of employees. Federal and state rules are different; an employee may be considered a regular employee by one government entity and a household employee by the other. Federal law defines a household employee as a worker who performs domestic services in the private home of the employer.[359] Examples include private nurses and health aides.

When the employer is a nongrantor trust (typically a third-party SNT), the employee cannot be a household employee because the employer trust does not have a home. However, when the employer is a grantor trust (typically a first-party SNT), it is theoretically possible for the trust to have a household employee, because the grantor trust is generally ignored for tax purposes.

> **Critical Pointer**: Even in the case of a grantor trust, caregivers should never be treated as household employees for federal tax purposes. This is because payroll taxes are computed on the employer (beneficiary's) personal income tax returns, and the payroll taxes are paid as part of the beneficiary's personal tax liability. The trustee usually has no control over the preparation and filing of this return. In addition, the payroll tax liability may give rise to an estimated tax requirement. If there is a tax overpayment, it is possible that the SNT beneficiary will receive a tax refund in his or her personal name. It is far

---

[359]   IRC §3510(c).

better to treat all caregivers as regular employees for federal tax purposes so that the trustee retains control of the payroll tax reporting and payments.

When a SNT becomes an employer, the trustee must register with the California Employment Development Department within fifteen days. A regular employer should use EDD Form DE1. A household employer should use EDD Form DE1-HW. The SNT will be assigned a state employer identification number.

Some employment taxes must be withheld from an employee's pay. These include the employee's share of social security and Medicare taxes and the California state disability tax. Other taxes must be paid by the employer. These include the employer's share of social security and Medicare taxes and the federal and California unemployment taxes. In addition, regular employers must withhold federal and state income taxes.

Household employers must withhold income taxes only if the employer and employee agree that the employer will do so. There are various exceptions to these requirements when the employer and employer are related.

The minimum wage and overtime laws are very complex and differ depending on the nature of the work. Generally, a live-in employee must be paid one and one-half times the regular rate for all hours worked over twelve hours (rather than over eight hours) in one workday (for five workdays; on the sixth and seventh day, the overtime rate for time worked in excess of nine hours per day is double the regular pay).[360] Special exemptions apply to domestic companions for the aged or infirm.[361] However, each worker's situation must be examined for proper compliance.

WHEN WOULD AN SNT BE SUBJECT TO AN ESTATE TAX?

As already discussed, the initial funding of an SNT from an estate should not require payment of any estate tax, unless the SNT was somehow funded from a taxable estate that failed to pay the tax.

---

[360] Wage Order No. 15-2001(3)(A)-(B) (8 Cal Code Regs §11150(3)(A)-(B)).

[361] 29 U.S.C. §213(a)(15).

An estate tax may be owed after the death of a first-party SNT beneficiary.[362] The taxable estate is calculated by subtracting certain deductions from the decedent's "gross estate."[363] This rarely happens, however, because the SNT would have to be funded with significant assets before an estate tax would be assessed.

Under current law, an estate tax will only be imposed on estates over $5 million in years 2011 and 2012. In 2013, this number changes to $1 million. However, it is expected this amount will be increased. Be sure to check the author's website (www.myersurbatsch.com) or another attorney or CPA to determine if the law has changed.

If the SNT beneficiary's estate is over the applicable exclusion amount, the beneficiary's trustee or executor must file an estate tax return (IRS Form 706) within nine months after the date of the beneficiary's death, unless an extension is obtained.[364]

> **NOTE:** California repealed its inheritance tax in 1982.[365] Thus, there is no separate estate tax for California.

WHEN WOULD AN SNT BE SUBJECT TO THE FEDERAL GIFT TAX?

A gift tax is imposed on lifetime transfers of property for less than full and adequate consideration.[366] The transfer of property constitutes a completed gift, and thus is subject to tax, to the extent that the donor has parted with dominion and control of the property so as to leave the donor no power to change its disposition.[367] The gift tax is imposed on the donor (the person or entity making the gift) rather than the recipient of the gift.

There are two main exceptions to the application of the gift tax. Under the gift tax laws, the first $13,000 of gifts to any person made during a calendar

---

[362] I.R.C. §2001(a).

[363] I.R.C. §2051.

[364] I.R.C. §6075(a).

[365] Revenue & Tax Code 13301.

[366] I.R.C. §§2501(a), 2512(b).

[367] Treasury Regs §25.2511-2(b).

year are not included in the total amount of gifts made during such year.[368] In addition, there is a lifetime gift tax exemption amount that can be given away to any number of people that will be free from gift taxes, but will reduce the amount that can be given away by the taxpayer tax-free on his or her death. In other words, the lifetime gift tax exemption is tied directly to the federal estate tax exemption. If an individual gifts away any amount of his or her lifetime gift tax exemption, then this amount will be subtracted from his or her estate tax exemption on death. For 2011, the lifetime gift tax exemption is $5,000,000, which is the same as the federal estate tax exemption discussed in the previous question. This also comes back down to $1 million in 2013.

The transfer of assets to a first-party SNT should not be subject to the federal gift tax. This is because the assets used to fund the SNT already belonged to the beneficiary before they were transferred to the SNT. The first-party SNT trustee is not allowed to make gifts to anyone. However, if a first-party SNT trustee breaches the terms of the trust and does make a gift to someone other than the beneficiary, a gift tax may be imposed. In this case, the trustee will be personally liable for any gift tax.

The transfer of assets to a third-party SNT may be subject to the federal gift tax. A transfer to an irrevocable trust is generally treated as a gift to the income beneficiary. In most cases, a transfer to a third-party SNT would not be eligible for the $13,000 annual exclusion. This is because the exclusion does not apply unless the trustee is required to distribute all income to the beneficiary currently, which would be inappropriate in the case of an SNT.

In the unlikely event that an SNT is subject to a gift tax, the trustee must file a gift tax return (IRS Form 709) no later than April 15 of the year after the calendar year in which the gift was made, unless an extension is granted.[369]

WHEN WOULD THE SNT TRUSTEE NEED TO BE CONCERNED WITH PROPERTY TAXES?

If the SNT holds real estate, the trustee is required to pay applicable property taxes during trust administration. California values real property for tax purposes at the lower of (1) fair market value on the date of the year in question, or (2) a base-year value determined under Proposition 13 guidelines, adjusted for

---

[368] I.R.C. §2503(b), Rev Proc 2008-66, 2008-45.

[369] I.R.C. §§6019, 6075(b)(1).

inflation. The property tax rate is generally 1 percent of assessed value.[370] The assessed value cannot be increased by more than 2 percent per year.[371]

Real property is generally reassessed when there is a change of ownership. A change of ownership can occur by sale, gift, or inheritance.[372] Thus, when real estate is transferred into a SNT, or purchased by a SNT, it will generally be reassessed as of the transfer date. This may result in a property tax increase.

Certain transfers are excluded from reassessment. In the context of SNTs, the exclusion most likely to apply is the parent-child exclusion. This exclusion applies to transfers of a principal residence, plus a maximum of $1 million (assessed value, not market value) of other real property.[373] When a parent transfers real estate to a SNT for the benefit of a disabled child (regardless of the child's age), the transfer may qualify for this exclusion.[374] The trustee must claim this exclusion by filing the appropriate forms with the Assessor's office in the county where the real property is located.

Chapter 9 Summary

- ✓ The SNT trustee should be prudent in selecting and hiring a tax professional.
- ✓ Typically, the funding of an SNT is a nontaxable event.
- ✓ Trustee should obtain a tax identification number from the IRS for the SNT.
- ✓ The SNT trustee should complete and file IRS Form 56 when taking over control of SNT and then file one when he or she is no longer serving as trustee.
- ✓ The SNT trustee is required to provide tax information to beneficiary of SNT.
- ✓ There is a significant difference in treatment of taxes for trusts treated as grantor trusts versus nongrantor trusts.

---

[370] Cal Const art XIIIA; Revenue & Tax Code §§50-51, 93, 110.

[371] Revenue & Tax Code §51(a)(1)(D).

[372] Revenue & Tax Code §60.

[373] Revenue & Tax Code §63.1.

[374] Revenue & Tax Code §63.1(a)(1), (c)(9).

- ✓ A first-party SNT is often treated as a "grantor trust," and taxes are paid by the SNT beneficiary at his or her tax rate.
- ✓ A third-party SNT is often treated as a "nongrantor trust," and taxes are paid at the more expensive trust tax rates; however, an SNT trustee may reduce the tax amount owed by distributing taxable income for the use of the beneficiary, and then taxes will be owed at his or her tax rate.
- ✓ A qualified disability trust may increase its personal exemption from $100 to an individual personal exemption amount, which is much higher (in 2011, $3,700). Of use only for third-party SNTs who meet certain requirements.
- ✓ A third-party SNT must file an IRS form 1041 and FTB from 541 if there is taxable income owed.
- ✓ A third-party SNT can seek an extension of time to file tax returns; however, the payment of tax should be made on time to avoid penalties and interest.
- ✓ There are significant penalties assessed for failure to pay a timely tax that increase significantly the longer the tax remains unpaid.
- ✓ A third-party SNT will need to pay estimated taxes the second year of its existence if its income is over a modest amount.
- ✓ The SNT beneficiary's taxes will depend on the type of SNT. The beneficiary may have some adverse tax consequences if caregivers are hired and paid for in a third-party SNT, or the beneficiary may be subject to kiddie tax in a third-party SNT if the beneficiary is young.
- ✓ Trustee fees will be taxed differently between professional and nonprofessional trustees.
- ✓ Employment taxes will need to be paid on any employees the SNT trustee hires to assist the beneficiary.
- ✓ Estate taxes are generally not an issue, unless there is a significant amount of assets held in trust on the death of the beneficiary in a first-party SNT.
- ✓ Gift taxes are not an issue in a properly administered first-party SNT.
- ✓ Real property taxes will need to be paid on any real property owned by the trust.

CHAPTER 10

Terminating The SNT

An SNT will end or terminate for several reasons. The most common events that result in SNT termination are the following:

1. Death of the beneficiary;
2. Triggering of termination event described in trust (for example, trust may terminate if beneficiary is able to work);
3. Assets in SNT are too small or SNT is uneconomical to administer; or
4. Failure of trust purpose (for example, beneficiary is no longer disabled).

On termination, the SNT trustee has an obligation to wrap up the affairs of the trust. This obligation includes the normal trustee responsibilities of doing final accounts, paying taxes, paying creditors, and making final distributions. However, this process is drastically different between a first-party SNT and a third-party SNT.[375]

The biggest difference is that a first-party SNT includes a payback to all State's Medicaid agencies, including California's Medi-Cal agency, the Department of Health Care Services (DHCS) for all Medi-Cal services received by the SNT beneficiary. This can be problematic if there is not enough money

---

[375] See, Chapter 2 for a discussion on how to tell the difference between the two types of SNTs.

left in the SNT to pay the Medi-Cal amount. A third-party SNT has no such payback requirement to DHCS and is terminated like most trusts referring to basic rules.

> **Warning:** In 2010, the SSA added a new wrinkle to "early termination provisions" in first-party SNTs. Early termination means an SNT terminates prior to the beneficiary's death typically because the beneficiary is no longer disabled or there is very little money left in the trust. This rule only applies to first-party SNTs and not to third-party SNTs. Some first-party SNTs include a provision that allows early termination with no payback to a State's Medicaid agency or that all remaining funds can be distributed to someone other than the beneficiary. The SSA now states that first-party SNTs that include this type of provision are not valid unless they include the payback provision to the State Medicaid agency and all funds remaining after the payback will go to the beneficiary.[376] While first-party SNTs that include these provisions are now not considered exempt for SSI eligibility purposes, it does not mean that the beneficiary will immediately lose his or her SSI if an SNT includes a nonqualifying early termination provision. Once the SSA discovers that a first-party SNT includes a nonqualifying early termination provision, it will issue a notice to the beneficiary that the SNT is no longer valid and provide a 90-day right for the beneficiary or trustee to amend the SNT to remove the disqualifying provision. If an SNT trustee or beneficiary receives such a notice, he or she should contact a special needs attorney immediately to assist with this procedure.[377]

The chapter will go into the specific requirements of terminating a first-party SNT and a third-party SNT. See Appendix L for a checklist on things that should be considered on the death of the SNT beneficiary.

---

[376] POMS SI 01120.199

[377] See chapter 11 on instructions on how to find a special needs planning attorney.

WHAT ARE SNT TRUSTEE'S LEGAL RESPONSIBILITIES ON SNT TERMINATION?

A trustee must continue his or her administration of an SNT even though the trust has terminated.[378] This means that even though a beneficiary has died or the money has run out, the trustee still has a legal obligation to wrap up the final affairs of the trust. Before acting, the trustee should be satisfied that the terminating event has occurred. For example, if death is the triggering event, the trustee should obtain a certified copy of the death certificate for the beneficiary.

On termination, the trustee's activities are generally divided into three categories

1. Paying the final expenses of the trust and perhaps the expenses of the beneficiary or his or her estate
2. Making a final accounting to the remainder beneficiaries (or the court if SNT is court supervised)
3. Distributing any remaining assets to the appropriate people or entities

Before making any payments from the SNT, the trustee must understand which claims and debts should be paid first. The consequences of making the wrong payment is that the trustee may be required to pay out of his or her personal assets any claims that were not properly paid from the trust. Likewise, if the trustee pays creditors who were not authorized to be paid, the trustee may have to reimburse that payment to the beneficiary who would have received it. Thus, it is important that the SNT trustee know the proper priority before making any payments from the trust.

In order to understand the proper priority among creditors of the SNT, the trustee must first determine whether the SNT is a third-party or a first-party SNT. This issue is very important, because a first-party SNT requires that any assets remaining in the trust upon the death of the beneficiary be used to pay back the state before third-party debts can be paid from trust assets.

If the trust is subject to continuing court jurisdiction, the trustee should prepare a final accounting on termination of the trust, and his or her attorney

---

[378] Probate Code §15407(b).

should prepare a petition to settle the final account and to distribute the estate. The notice of report and account and petition for distribution will inform the beneficiaries that the trust has terminated. The trustee may also wish to send letters to the beneficiaries informing them of termination. Preparation of the trustee's final accounting may take a substantial amount of time depending on the length of time the trust was administered and the date of any prior accounting. These issues are discussed in more detail later in this chapter.

WHAT ARE THE SNT TRUSTEE'S RESPONSIBILITIES IN TERMINATING A FIRST-PARTY SNT?

The legal obligations upon termination of a trust of any trustee is to pay creditors and claims of the SNT, pay any taxes, prepare account, and make any final distributions to remainder beneficiaries. In the case of a first-party SNT, determining the priority of payment of debts and claims is critically important due to the Medi-Cal payback provision. Improperly paying a debt prior to Medi-Cal receiving its claim may lead to a claim against the SNT trustee by the state for the amount owed.

> **Note:** The only first-party SNT payback requirement is for Medi-Cal (or other state's Medicaid). There is no payback required for SSI, SSDI, Social Security, Medicare, HUD ("Section 8") housing programs, or other similar type governmental programs.

Below are the basic steps necessary for terminating a first-party SNT:

_____ Step One: Send Notice to Government Agencies and Remainder Beneficiaries
_____ Step Two: Review Payback Report from State Agencies
_____ Step Three: Check to See if Exceptions to Medi-Cal Payback Apply
_____ Step Four: Determine Priority of Authorized Creditors
_____ Step Five: Pay Allowable Funeral Expenses
_____ Step Six: Pay Authorized Creditors
_____ Step Seven: Prepare Final Accounting
_____ Step Eight: Make Final Distributions

Step One: Send Notice to Government Agencies and Remainder Beneficiaries

When the SNT terminates, the trustee must notify all state agencies that provided Medi-Cal (or in other states called Medicaid) assistance to the beneficiary in order to obtain a detailed report of expenses paid on behalf of the beneficiary during that individual's lifetime. The trustee should also check to determine whether the beneficiary received, or might have received, Medicaid services out of state. If so, then notice should also be sent to the other states' Medicaid agency to determine if there is a potential claim against the first-party SNT.[379]

Notice to state agencies should be sent as soon as possible after the SNT terminates to start the claims period running. DHCS must reply within four months of the date the SNT trustee provided notice to it with a claim for payback.[380] If it fails to do so, it may not make a claim for recovery.[381] If the SNT trustee fails to provide appropriate notice, DHCS has three years to make a claim for recovery.[382]

Notice should be sent to the following California agencies as well as to any other state agencies where the beneficiary may have received medical services and to any agency which has filed a request for notice.

Office of Director
Department of Mental Health
1600 Ninth Street, Room 151
Sacramento, CA 95814

Office of Director
Department of Developmental Services
1600 Ninth Street, Room 240
Sacramento, CA 95814

---

[379] A trust is obliged to reimburse any state that provided medical assistance, and for any period of time, including assistance received before the trust was created. POMS SI 01120.203(B)(1)(h).

[380] Probate Code §§3605(a), 9202, and see *Shewry v Wooten* (2009) 172 Cal App 4th 741.

[381] Probate Code §9201.

[382] Code of Civil Proc §338; *Shewry v. Begil* Cal App 4th 639.

Department of Health Care Services
Third-Party Liability and Recovery Division
Estate Recovery Section—MS 4720
PO Box 997425
Sacramento, CA 95899-7425

The SNT trustee also has a duty to keep the beneficiaries[383] reasonably informed of the trust and its administration.[384] The SNT trustee should consider sending out a notice of SNT termination to the remainder beneficiaries. The SNT trustee may (or may not) have to provide a copy of the trust and an account to the remainder beneficiaries. However, because the SNT trustee has an obligation to provide both information[385] and a copy[386] of the trust on request of a beneficiary, he or she may want to provide them at the outset to avoid any later issues.

Step Two: Review Payback Report from State Agencies

If DHCS or other Medicaid agency provides a timely response, the trustee should carefully review the report it receives to determine the accuracy of the services and costs for which the agency is claiming reimbursement. If the trustee does not have sufficient expertise or information about the beneficiary's circumstances to personally conduct this review, then members of the beneficiary's family as well as a care manger should be consulted to go over the itemized bills in detail. Billing errors are frequent. Oftentimes there are duplicate entries, entries for services never provided or even entries that show a payment that was made at times when the beneficiary was not even alive.

> **Practice Pointer:** There are professionals who can be hired to review Medi-Cal's bills to determine if the report provides an

---

[383] A "beneficiary" of a trust refers to any person who has any present or future interest, vested or contingent. Probate Code §24(c). This would include the people who would inherit the trust funds after the death of the SNT beneficiary.

[384] Probate Code §16060.

[385] Probate Code §16061.

[386] Probate Code §16060.7.

accurate summary of expenditures. See chapter 11 on finding a public benefits expert.

The cost of conducting the review, whether conducted internally or by an outside expert, is an "administrative expense," which is paid before the Medi-Cal reimbursement. (See Step Four for description of priority of payments.) The amount of the reimbursement must be approved by the state Medicaid agency. If the SNT was funded with the proceeds of a personal injury settlement, the claims report may identify expenses that were already reimbursed by an insurer or were the subject of a lien waiver at the time of the settlement. Therefore, the trustee should make sure they are not paying twice for the same claim.

If there are sufficient errors and DHCS refused to negotiate the payback amount down, the SNT trustee should consider filing a Probate Code §17200 petition as described in chapter 11.

Step Three: Check to See If Exceptions to Medi-Cal Payback Apply

In California, an appellate court has stated that no payback to DHCS for Medi-Cal services paid an SNT beneficiary of a first-party SNT is required in certain circumstances.[387] DHCS has no right to a payback of Medi-Cal services if the first-party SNT terminates and the SNT beneficiary has a surviving spouse; the SNT beneficiary has a disabled child; the SNT beneficiary has a child under age twenty-one; or the SNT beneficiary was under age fifty-five when non long-term Medi-Cal services were received.[388]

> **Note:** Before relying on these exceptions, the SNT trustee should check the author's website to see if this exception still applies. DHCS has attempted to change this law by legislation. Thus far it has been unsuccessful, but this may change in the future. To make sure that the exceptions still apply, review www. myersurbatsch.com.

---

[387] *Shewry v Arnold* (2004) 125 Cal.App.4th 186.

[388] 42 U.S.C. §1396p(b)(1)(B), (b)(2)(A); Welfare & Institutions Code §14009.5.

In the case that described the exception, the first-party SNT beneficiary died but left a child with a disability. In analyzing whether exceptions apply to Medi-Cal's right of recovery in this situation, the court stated that all the recovery exceptions (described above) apply regardless of whether assets were held in a first-party SNT or not. DHCS does not agree with this decision. Since this decision came out, it has limited its interpretation to only those situations when the SNT beneficiary died and left a child with a disability. However, DHCS clearly is wrong on this issue. The case stood for the proposition that if any of the exceptions apply then there is no payback to DHCS. Many attorneys, including this author, have successfully challenged DHCS on this issue.

Thus, if the trustee runs into a situation where there may not be a payback because the beneficiary only received community based Medi-Cal services while under the age of fifty-five, he or she should consult with an attorney to assist in negotiating with DHCS on the Medi-Cal recovery. See chapter 11 on how to find a special needs planning attorney's help during SNT administration.

> **EXAMPLE:** A first-party SNT beneficiary dies leaving a child age twenty. DHCS is notified and issues a request that it be paid back $150,000 for Medi-Cal services. The trustee does not have to pay DHCS, because in this situation if the SNT beneficiary left a child under age twenty-one, which is an exception to the recovery requirements. DHCS will not simply agree with this so it may take a court petition or suitable negotiation with DHCS before the trustee can be reasonably confident that no future problems will arise.

If an exception applies, the trustee can skip Steps Four and Five and go right to Step Six.

Step Four: Determine Priority of Authorized Creditors

If no Medi-Cal payback exception applies (see Step Three), there are only a few things that may be paid from a first-party SNT prior to paying Medi-Cal's recovery claim. In order to better understand the authorized disbursements prior to Medi-Cal's recovery, it is necessary to understand where the rules on Medi-Cal recovery come from.

There are two different government public benefit programs that are typically associated with first-party SNT planning, Supplemental Security Income (SSI), and Medi-Cal. Both SSI and Medi-Cal agree that a first-party SNT is entitled to pay certain expenses from the SNT's assets before paying the Medi-Cal recovery claim. The problem that arises is that SSI and Medi-Cal's rules are in conflict over the categories of payments that are allowed.

The SSI program allows the SNT trustee to pay the following two types of items prior to the Medi-Cal payback:

- Taxes due from the trust to the State or Federal government because of the death of the beneficiary
- Reasonable fees for administration of the trust estate such as an accounting of the trust to the court, completion and filing of documents, or other required actions associated with termination and wrapping up of the trust[389]

The SSI program specifically excludes the following things from being paid by the SNT trustee before the Medi-Cal payback:

- Taxes due from the estate of the beneficiary, other than those arising from inclusion of the trust in the estate
- Inheritance taxes due for residual beneficiaries
- Payment of debts owed to third parties
- Funeral expenses
- Payments to residual beneficiaries[390]

The Medi-Cal program allows the SNT trustee to pay the following two types of items prior to the Medi-Cal payback:

- The cost of the individual's remaining management and investment fees
- Outstanding bills for the benefit of the disabled individual or spouse that fall within the terms of the trust; or burial/funeral expenses of the disabled individual or disabled spouse[391]

---

[389] POMS SI 01120.203(B)(3)(a).

[390] POMS SI 01120.203(B)(3)(b).

[391] Medi-Cal Eligibility Procedures Manual Letter No. 192, p 9J-75.

Reasonable fees for administration of the SNT include fees for the following:

- Trustee, attorney, or public benefit expert who reviews the Medi-Cal claims
- Cost of accounting
- Completion and filing of documents in connection with wrapping up of the SNT including tax returns and appropriate notices

The SSI rules expressly prohibit two common kinds of expenditures expressly permitted by Medi-Cal's rules: debts owed to third parties and funeral expenses.[392] What makes this unusual is that the rules for SSI are far more restrictive than those for Medi-Cal, but there is only a recovery for Medi-Cal and not one for SSI. It would typically be expected that the agency receiving the funds would set the rules, not an agency that receives nothing. As a result, to have a qualifying first-party SNT that qualifies for SSI purposes, a California SNT must preclude paying for things that would otherwise be allowed.

Because of the difference in rules, the SNT trustee is left in a bit of a quandary to pay for remaining third-party creditor claims or to pay for a funeral. It is not uncommon for an SNT beneficiary to have no assets (other than an SNT) to pay for a funeral. The good news is that in California, the Department of Health Care Service (DHCS), the agency that administers Medi-Cal in California, will let an SNT trustee pay for a funeral even if there is not enough money left in the SNT to pay all of Medi-Cal's lien. See Step Five for procedure in getting a funeral paid from trust assets.

> **Example:** An SNT beneficiary dies at age eighty-five and his trust still has $100,000. After the SNT beneficiary's death, the SNT trustee is presented with a bill of $3,000 for a wheelchair, a bill of $2,000 from the SNT trustee's attorney for trust administrative expenses, federal and state income taxes of $1,000. The remainder beneficiaries of the SNT are the SNT beneficiary's two adult children aged forty-five and forty-eight.

---

[392] (SSI) POMS SI 01120.203(B)(3)(b); (Medi-Cal) Medi-Cal Eligibility Procedures Manual Letter No. 192, p 9J-75.

The SNT trustee sends notice to DHCS of the death of the beneficiary. DHCS sends a timely notice to trustee requesting $300,000 as the payback amount. The SNT trustee reviews the Medi-Cal bills and determines that it is valid.

The SNT trustee may pay the $2,000 bill for the attorneys' expenses in wrapping up trust estate and the $1,000 for taxes. However, the SNT trustee may not pay the $3,000 bill for wheelchair expenses, and the two children will receive nothing. The rest of the trust estate goes to DHCS.

Practice Pointer: The SNT trustee should never make disbursements to family members before knowing whether there are sufficient assets to pay back the state Medicaid agencies. Doing so may result in the SNT trustee being responsible for paying the Medi-Cal payback out of his or her own assets if the distributes do not have sufficient assets to pay back Medi-Cal.

Step Five: Pay Allowable Funeral Expenses

A common SNT termination event is the death of the SNT beneficiary. Within days of the death of an SNT beneficiary, the beneficiary's family or friends may call the trustee to ask whether funeral expenses can be paid from the first-party SNT. Until a determination is made on whether there are sufficient assets to pay the Medi-Cal recovery claim, the general rule is that funeral expenses cannot be paid. This is because the SSI rules only allow the trustee to pay funeral expenses for an SNT beneficiary after the Medi-Cal reimbursement is paid. See explanation in Step Four. If there is no money left after the Medi-Cal payback, then no funeral expenses can be paid.

Note: SSI's prohibition against paying funeral expenses has been strongly criticized by a number of commentators, and has famously been described as the "stinking dead body rule" by Florida social security and special needs attorney David L. Lillesand. He has often suggested that if there is no money to bury the person with a disability to have the body delivered to the local Social Security office for disposition.

However, in California, the DHCS agency is much more lenient probably because Medi-Cal rules expressly authorize payments for a funeral prior to Medi-Cal's payback. Remember that even though SSI has these more restrictive rules, it is not receiving any payback money from the SNT. Thus, on the SNT beneficiary's death, it is common to contact DHCS to seek permission to pay the deceased beneficiary's funeral expenses even when the Medi-Cal payback is greater than the assets remaining in the first-party SNT.

In the author's experience, the DHCS worker will allow the disbursement as long as the expenses are "reasonable." The author has taken this to mean that expenses can be paid for the funeral but not a large party for family, friends, or caregivers.

> **Practice Pointer:** If the first-party SNT document expressly disallows funeral expenses to be paid because of SSI reasons, the SNT trustee may wish to request instructions through a Probate Code §17200 petition to authorize the disbursement for funeral expenses despite the plain language of the SNT. Courts will generally authorize this disbursement despite the trust's language because DHCS will consent to the distribution and often there is no one else left in the SNT beneficiary's life to pay for the burial. For more information about utilizing a Probate Code §17200 petition, see chapter 11.

> **Practice Pointer:** Because the SSA rules state that funeral expense do not have priority over the Medi-Cal lien, it is good practice to have the SNT trustee fund a prepaid burial plan or an irrevocable burial trust for the beneficiary during the individual's lifetime. There is no prohibition against the SNT trustee paying for such a funeral. See chapters 5 and 6 on how to pay for a prepaid funeral.

Step Six: Pay Authorized Creditors

After all allowable SSI and Medi-Cal fees and expenses have been paid and the Medi-Cal payback has been paid as described in Step One through Step Five, the first-party SNT trustee may pay any remaining debts of the trust. Trust debts may include expenses incurred for case management, services for the beneficiary, investment advice, legal advice, or tax preparation that remain unpaid when the beneficiary died.

> **Example:** After the SNT beneficiary death, the SNT trustee paid all taxes, allowable debts, and the Medi-Cal payback amount. There still remains $80,000 in trust assets. The SNT trustee has received bills of $3,000 for wheelchair expenses, $5,000 in remaining care giving expenses, and $2,500 for public benefit advocacy work. The SNT trustee is authorized to pay these expenses from the remaining funds.

Step Seven: Making Final Distributions

If there are funds remaining in the SNT after the payment of all administrative expenses, taxes, and valid Medi-Cal reimbursements, the remainder should be distributed according to the terms of the SNT. Generally, the document will specify who should receive the funds after payment of all expenses.

> **Example:** The SNT trustee has paid all taxes, expenses, and the Medi-Cal payback provision. There remains $200,000 in trust. The SNT document says that all remaining assets will go to the beneficiary's then living children. On the death of the beneficiary, he had four surviving children. The SNT trustee will make disbursements to all four children. It is a good idea to have each child sign a receipt showing they received their disbursement.

The SNT trustee should carefully review the SNT document to see if the beneficiary was left with something called a power of appointment. An example of a type of power of appointment is as follows:

> **Sample Power of Appointment:** The trustee shall distribute the undistributed balance of the trust estate as the beneficiary may direct by exercise of a special power of appointment to any one or more persons or entities, or trusts for their benefit, other than the beneficiary's estate, the beneficiary's creditors, or creditors of the beneficiary's estate.

If there is a power of appointment, the SNT trustee should check to see if, while the beneficiary had legal capacity, he or she executed a separate will, a living trust, or a writing that exercised the power of appointment. In this case, the assets would no longer be distributed as set forth in the SNT document but rather by the document the SNT beneficiary executed. If the SNT trustee is unsure whether such a power of appointment exists or if one was properly exercised, he or she should check with an experienced estate planning attorney. See chapter 11 on locating an experienced special needs attorney.

> **Example:** The SNT states that the remaining trust assets shall be distributed to the SNT beneficiary's then living children. The SNT beneficiary has two living children at the time of his death. The SNT has $500,000 in assets after all expenses and taxes were paid. However, the SNT also states that the beneficiary has a power of appointment to alter distribution through a valid will.

The SNT trustee finds a document that purports to be the last Will and Testament of the beneficiary leaving all the assets to a charity. The SNT trustee should determine if the power of appointment was validly executed (for example, making sure beneficiary had legal capacity when he signed the document and the will meets California legal requirements). If the power of appointment was validly executed, the SNT trustee would distribute the $500,000 to the selected charity.

Step Eight: Prepare a Final Accounting

Once the correct expenditures have been determined and made, the SNT trustee should prepare a final accounting. (See chapter 7 for the form of account.) If the SNT has been under court jurisdiction, a final accounting and report will need to be filed and set for hearing in the local probate court. A court account must be filed in a very specific format that is discussed in more detail in chapter 7.

If the SNT has not been court supervised, the trustee will generally not need to file an account with the court. However, he or she may still want to provide a final accounting to all interested parties, including the remainder beneficiaries and the DHCS to begin the running of the time that these parties could file a lawsuit against the trustee. See Step Two above for addresses to send account to DHCS.

Note: Some SNTs will waive the accounting requirement. Even if it does, it may still be prudent to send one so that the running of the statute of limitations begins immediately.

What Are the SNT Trustee's Responsibilities in Terminating a Third-Party SNT?

While third-party SNT administration is typically not done with court oversight and is managed privately by the SNT trustee, it is still a good idea to formally wrap up the SNT. Unlike the first-party SNT, the third-party SNT does not have a Medi-Cal payback requirement on trust termination which makes termination that much simpler for the trustee.

Many SNT document will provide written instructions on what is required when the trust terminates. If it does not, then the SNT trustee must utilize the California Probate Code that provides authority for wrapping up the trust. Typically, this includes paying final expenses including last illness, burial, and administrative expenses, and taxes. If the trustee is uncertain or unfamiliar with trust termination, he or she may wish to hire an experienced estate planning attorney. In order to find such a qualified attorney, see chapter 11.

Step One: Payment of Fees and Expenses

In most well drafted third-party SNTs, the trust document may authorize, *but not require*, payments of fees and expenses. The trust should specifically state that any payment made for fees and expenses is within the discretion of the trustee so that an outside third-party cannot enforce a claim or right against the trust. Expenses typically include payment of any expenses of last illness, funeral, and burial or cremation, including memorials and memorial services. Thus, the trustee has the option of paying most of the bills of the beneficiary or not.

> **Note**: The SNT trustee should check the trust language to make sure that the SNT does not require payments of these bills. The trust may have been drafted without the benefit of an attorney's advice and the trust would require payment of these bills by trustee.

The SNT trustee must still pay those expenses that he or she entered into as trustee of the SNT. For example caregiver expenses, attorney's expenses, CPA expenses, or other service providers. Below is a summary of the types of expenses the SNT trustee will generally be expected to pay:

- **Professionals' Fees**. Professional fees are generally those for persons who provide advice and assistance to the trustee. They include fees for legal advice, accounting and tax advice, and other professional services needed to properly administer the trust.
- **Funeral Expenses**. An SNT beneficiary will generally not have sufficient resources to pay for a funeral. It is appropriate to authorize, but not require, payment of burial or cremation and other funeral expenses—including removal, transportation and disposition of remains, memorials, and memorial services.
- **Debts**. One of the most important differences between third-party and first-party SNT is creditor rights. If the third-party SNT is properly drafted the beneficiary's creditors will have no claim to trust corpus. Creditors only have a claims against funds distributed outright to the SNT beneficiary. Thus, it will be up to the SNT trustee's discretion to pay for the beneficiary's bills he or she incurred personally.
- **Taxes**. During the lifetime of the SNT beneficiary, the third-party SNT should authorize the trustee to prepare and file returns and arrange for payment of all taxes applicable to the trust, including all local, state, federal and foreign taxes incident to the trust agreement. Upon death, the trustee should make sure that tax payments are current or reserved for prior to distribution of the remaining trust estate to beneficiaries. The third-party SNT may or may not be included in the beneficiary's estate. The trustee should work with a tax professional to determine what state and federal taxes are due because of the death of the special needs beneficiary.

Step Two: Final Distribution

Upon the termination of the SNT, the third-party trust should provide for distribution of the remaining trust estate. Since there is no payback requirement and a clause for payback should not be part of the third-party special needs trust, distribution can be made to any individual(s), or charity chosen as set forth in the trust document.

The SNT trustee can prepare a spreadsheet that will make sure that all assets were properly distributed. The document will cover the following:

- **Distribution provisions (as governed by the trust)**. This will generally be set up in the SNT. If not, or if left to "heirs" the SNT trustee may need to determine who the beneficiary's "heirs" are. This usually requires an understanding of the California Probate Code. If the trustee is unsure, he or she should retain an experienced estate planning attorney.
- **Date of distribution**. The dates the SNT trustee provides assets to beneficiaries should be documented so if questions arise later, the trustee will have the information ready to answer the questions.
- **Preliminary distributions**. The trustee may have some outstanding issues to resolve that may take time. He or she may allow an early distribution so beneficiaries can receive some distributions pending the resolution of other issues.
- **Consent to distribution by beneficiaries**. If there is some question as to who should receive what, the trustee may prepare a consent of distribution to be signed by all beneficiaries. This way, the trustee is protected if later questions arise as to the advisability of certain disbursements.
- **Waiver of accounting**. In the next step, the trustee can provide an account to beneficiaries. Instead, the trustee may seek a waiver of the accounting requirement.
- **Reserve amounts**. The trustee may decide to keep a reserve. This is an amount of money left in the trust after all disbursements are made. This is in case there are later tax or debt claims that will need to be paid. Typically, a reserve is maintained for less than a year.

Step Three: Final Account

While a final account is not necessarily required for a third-party SNT administration, it is often a good idea to prepare one so the statute of limitations period will begin to run on trustee's activities.

Ordinarily, an action for breach of trust has a four-year statute of limitations from the date the "cause of action shall have accrued."[393] If an adult beneficiary with capacity who receives a trust accounting[394] wishes to pursue a claim against the trustee for breach of trust, the claim must be filed within three years after receipt of the account or report.[395] This shortened three-year statute of limitations may also apply to incapacitated adult and minor beneficiaries if the account is served on the legal representative, guardian, or parents.[396] For a more complete discussion of the accounting requirement, see chapter 7.

Chapter 10 Summary

The chapter provides:
- ✓ A checklist of things to do on behalf of the SNT beneficiary after his death.
- ✓ A general discussion of the SNT trustee's legal responsibilities on trust termination (paying all valid debts and taxes, doing a final account, and making final distribution).
- ✓ Steps to terminating a first-party SNT:
    - ○ Send Notice to Medi-Cal and Medicaid agencies.
    - ○ Review timely claims (four months) from Medi-Cal and Medicaid agencies.
    - ○ Determine if exception to first-party SNT applies (SNT beneficiary leaves child with a disability, child under age twenty-one, surviving spouse, or only community-based Medi-Cal received prior to age fifty-five).
    - ○ Understand priority of creditor claims for first-party SNT.
        - • Taxes may be paid before Medi-Cal payback.
        - • Administrative expenses may be paid before Medi-Cal payback.
    - ○ Funeral expenses may be paid if permission received from DHCS.

---

[393] Code Civil Procedure §343.
[394] See Probate Code §16063.
[395] Probate Code §16460(a)(1); *Noggle v Bank of America* (1999) 70 Cal App 4th 853.
[396] Probate Code §16460(b).

- o Pay off remaining debts.
- o Make final disbursements (watch out for power of appointment provisions).
- o Do a final accounting.
- ✓ Steps to terminate a third-party SNT:
  - o Termination is much easier than first-party SNT because there is no payback to DHCS for Medi-Cal payments.
  - o SNT trustee typically has discretion to pay (or not pay) the beneficiary's final debts.
  - o SNT trustee must pay remaining trust expenses and taxes.
  - o SNT trustee must make final disbursements.
  - o SNT trustee should do final accounting.

CHAPTER 11

Finding Help Administering SNT

The job of being an SNT trustee is hard. There are many rules and many ways to make mistakes. Thus, it is important that an SNT trustee know where to find help when needed. This chapter will guide the trustee in locating the appropriate person, entity or court procedure to obtain assistance.

CAN AN SNT TRUSTEE ASK A CALIFORNIA PROBATE COURT FOR HELP IN ADMINISTERING AN SNT?

Yes. Attorneys call this petition a "17200 Petition" based on the statute that authorizes it.[397] Typically, the filing of a 17200 Petition would be done only when there is a significant question that needs answering; such as the trustee is being asked to make a disbursement that may be objectionable by someone. The individuals and entities that are notified of the 17200 Petition who do not object to the petition will later be barred from objecting to the trustee's actions or expenditure of funds described in the petition. Many SNT trustees use this petition during administration to authorize a purchase of a home or modified van; to pay for experimental treatments requested by beneficiary or his or her legal representatives; to pay for a lengthy vacation; or to invest in a business. The options are really limitless.

> **Example:** Beneficiary's family wants SNT trustee to use trust funds to buy a new primary residence for the beneficiary. The

---

[397] Probate Code §17200.

family is looking at a home that costs over $800,000. The SNT trustee may not be willing to make such a large purchase without some assurance that he or she will not be personally liable if someone disagrees with his or her decision later. The SNT trustee hires an attorney to bring a 17200 Petition seeking the court's instructions on whether trustee should purchase home. Trustee notifies beneficiary, beneficiary's family, all remainder beneficiaries, and the state agencies that run SSI and Medi-Cal of the time and place of the hearing. At the hearing, no one appears to object and the court authorizes the disbursement. For all those properly noticed with the petition, they cannot later sue the trustee if they disagree with the decision.

The statute lists several ways in which a 17200 Petition can be used by an SNT trustee:

- Determining questions of construction of a trust instrument
- Determining the validity of a trust provision
- Settling accounts and passing on the trustee's acts, including the exercise of discretionary powers
- Instructing the trustee
- Granting powers to the trustee
- Fixing or allowing payment of the trustee's compensation or reviewing its reasonableness
- Appointing or removing a trustee
- Accepting the resignation of a trustee
- Compelling redress of a breach of the trust
- Modifying or terminating the trust
- Transferring a supervised testamentary trust between counties[398]

A trustee should retain an attorney to assist with the filing of a petition. They can be complicated to bring if not experienced with probate court procedures.

---

[398]   Probate Code §17200(b).

WHERE CAN AN SNT TRUSTEE FIND A SPECIAL NEEDS PLANNING ATTORNEY FOR ADVICE?

The best sources of help for SNT trustees are attorneys who specialize in this area of law. Not every attorney can provide the advice that a special needs trustee will need. The trustee should make sure that the attorney he or she seeks assistance from truly understands special needs planning. The attorney should really understand the public benefit issues that arise when administering an SNT. Not every estate planning attorney will understand these issues; even ones who help set up SNTs may not understand all the unique public benefit issues.

The following websites can help you find a special needs planning attorney and allows you to join the author's special needs news monthly brochure:

- **Myers Urbatsch, P.C.** is the law firm of Kevin Urbatsch, the author of this publication. It is recommended that the readers of this publication review the website for any updates to this book. It also includes general information about special needs trust administration and a trustee can sign up to receive the Special Needs News, a monthly e-mail update on information and services available to persons with disabilities. The website also includes Kevin Urbatsch's upcoming seminar schedule on many special needs issues. Myers Urbatsch, P.C.'s website is http://www.MyersUrbatsch.com.
- **Academy of Special Needs Planners** (ASNP) is a nationwide attorney organization dedicated to special needs planning. It has general information for nonmembers, including a list of California attorneys who specialize in special needs planning. ASNP's website is http://www.specialneedsplanners.com.
- **California Advocates for Nursing Home Reform** (CANHR) is a statewide organization that includes attorneys who can assist with special needs planning. Its primary focus is assisting elders obtain eligibility for nursing home eligibility; however, there are lots of special needs planners who belong to the organization. CANHR website is http://www.canhr.org.
- **Professional Fiduciary Association of California** (PFAC) is not an attorney organization but rather a statewide trade association for the state's private professional fiduciaries. The website

has lots of great information on how to be a trustee of a trust. PFAC's website is http://www.pfac-pro.org.

WHERE CAN AN SNT TRUSTEE FIND GENERAL INFORMATION ABOUT CALIFORNIA'S PUBLIC BENEFIT PROGRAMS?

An SNT trustee who wishes to become more familiar with California's laws and regulations concerning public benefit programs can do so through the following websites:

- **Disability Benefits 101** offers easy-to-understand, practical information on California public and private benefits (including SSI, SSDI, Medi-Cal and Medicare), employment services (different right to work programs), and other programs (food stamps or CalWorks). See http://www.disabilitybenefits101.org.
- **Program Operations Manual System (POMS)** consists of the internal rules used by the Social Security Administration to process Supplemental Security Income (SSI) claims. Once familiar with the format of these rules, an SNT trustee can find lots of valuable information on SSI and how SNTs are evaluated by the Social Security Administration. The POMS is available for free online at https://secure.ssa.gov/apps10/poms.nsf/partlist!OpenView.
- **All County Welfare Director Letters** (ACWDLs) are letters issued by the Department of Health Care Services (DHCS) to its staff with its interpretation of California Medi-Cal laws, rules, and regulations. These are not organized in a particularly easy to understand format, but a careful, diligent search can provide plenty of information on how California's Medi-Cal rules are interpreted by DHCS. For online access to the ACWDLs, see DHCS' website at http://www.dhs.ca.gov/mcs/mcpd/MEB/ACLs/LetterIndex/1978-2006_Letter_Index/A%20thru%20C%20Index.htm.
- **Technical Assistance Collaborative** (TAC) has helpful information on Section 8 housing for individuals with disabilities, including a thorough and informative free guide entitled "Section 8 Made Simple." See http://www.tacinc.org.
- The **California Probate Code** and the **Welfare and Institutions Code** are the two most commonly used codes for

special needs administration. The California codes are available for free online at http://www.leginfo.ca.gov/calaw.html.
- **California Code of Regulations** includes the regulations for various public benefit programs in California and California's authority for special needs trusts. The state regulations are available online for free at http://ccr.oal.ca.gov/linkedslice/default.asp?SP=CCR-1000&Action=Welcome.
- **Code of Federal Regulations** (CFR) includes the regulations on various federal public benefit programs such as SSI and Section 8 that are important when planning for persons with disabilities. The CFR is available online at http://www.gpoaccess.gov/cfr/index.html.

WHERE CAN AN SNT TRUSTEE FIND INFORMATION ON NOT-FOR-PROFIT AGENCIES THAT PROVIDE SERVICES AND RESOURCES TO PERSONS WITH A DISABILITY?

There are many nonprofit organizations that provide services and resources to enhance a person with a disability's life. Below (in alphabetical order) is a small sample of some of the ones that the author has worked with, or whose services he has great respect for:

- The **Arc of California** is a not-for-profit group dedicated to advocacy for individuals with disabilities. This advocacy includes providing employment opportunities for persons with disabilities, securing appropriate housing and leisure activities, and numerous other items of support for both family of persons with disabilities and the persons themselves. See http://www.arccalifornia.org.
- **California Disability Community Action Network** (CDCAN) by Marty Omoto provides cutting-edge information on legislative action that affects individuals with disabilities. The website also offers periodic e-mail updates. See http://cdcan.us.
- **California Foundation for Independent Living Centers** (CFILC) is a statewide organization of twenty-five independent living centers that promote independent living by individuals with disabilities. The centers provide counseling on public benefits, housing, and access to services. See http://www.cfilc.org/site/c.ghKRI0 pDIoE/b.695113/k.CB59/Home.htm.

- **Californians for Disability Rights, Inc**. is a longstanding advocacy group representing the rights of persons with disabilities. See http://www.disabilityrights-cdr.org.
- **Disability Resources** is a website that includes links to other websites around the nation that provide information for individuals with disabilities. The following link shows a lengthy list of California websites for a host of issues, including autism, assistive technology, speech disorders, and vocational rehabilitation through sports and recreation. See http://disabilityresources.org/CALIFORNIA.html.
- **Disability Rights Education & Defense Fund** (DREDF) provides advocacy on behalf of individuals with disabilities. See http://www.dredf.org.
- **Janet Pomeroy Center** provides recreational, vocational, and educational opportunities for people with disabilities through programs and services that encourage self-expression, promote personal achievement, and lead to greater independence. Their website is http://www.janetpomeroy.org/index.html.
- **Matrix Parent Network & Resource Center.** Matrix was founded upon the belief that parents can and must be the primary managers and advocates on behalf of their child with special needs. Parent-to-parent support and networking is central to the Matrix philosophy. It is powerful, effective, and allows us to continue expanding our services in the community, particularly to populations who are historically underserved. See http://www.matrixparents.org.
- **National Alliance on Mental Illness** (NAMI) is a national nonprofit association that provides information and assistance to individuals with mental illness. There are NAMI organizations throughout the country. See http://www.nami.org.
- **Protection and Advocacy, Inc**. (PAI) is an advocacy group that provides numerous services to individuals with disabilities. See http://www.pai-ca.org.
- **Star Academy** is a school that provides an intensive, individualized education program for students with disabilities. Their website is http://www.staracademy.org.
- **Support for Families** is a San Francisco—based organization to ensure that families of children with any kind of disability or special health-care need have the knowledge and support to make informed choices that enhance their children's development and well-being.

Through fostering partnership among families, professionals and the community our children can flourish. There are numerous resource fairs and seminars to help understand how to help a person with a disability. The website is http://www.supportforfamilies.org/index. html.

WHAT GOVERNMENT AGENCIES ARE THERE TO ASSIST PERSONS WITH DISABILITIES?

A complete list of federal government agencies that provide services to persons with disabilities can be found at www.disabilityinfo.gov. This website details the programs and services available from the federal government regarding employment, education, housing, transportation, health, benefits, technology, community life, and civil rights.

A list of the most common government agencies that provide services and support to persons with disabilities is provided below:

- **California Department of Developmental Services** (DDS) is the state agency providing services and support to children and adults with developmental disabilities. These disabilities include mental retardation, cerebral palsy, epilepsy, autism, and related conditions. See http://www.dds.cahwnet.gov.
- **California Department of Health Care Services** (DHCS), formerly known as DHS, was reorganized in 2007. This agency administers Medi-Cal. See http://www.dhcs.ca.gov/Pages/default. aspx.
- **California Department of Mental Health** (DMH) provides information on services available in California for individuals with mental health issues. See http://www.dmh.cahwnet.gov.
- **Centers for Medicare and Medicaid Services** (CMS) is the Department of Health and Human Services website, which provides information on the federal government's participation in providing health care. See http://www.cms.hhs.gov.
- **Social Security Administration** includes helpful and plentiful information on the federal government assistance programs for individuals with disabilities. See http://www.ssa.gov.

- **Department of Veterans Affairs**' website includes information on benefits available to veterans with disabilities. See http://www.va.gov.

WHO CAN AN SNT TRUSTEE HIRE TO ASSIST WITH PUBLIC BENEFIT ELIGIBILITY FOR PERSONS WITH DISABILITIES?

There are certain individuals who will provide advocacy and advice any time a person with a disability's public benefits are cut and advocacy is needed.

James Huyck is a consultant/advocate to trustees, families, consumers, attorneys, organizations, and others in successfully "navigating the regional center system" and other state agency services, which can be difficult and frustrating at times. He currently assists families with disabled members and all professionals who administer special needs trusts in accessing services from California's Regional Centers for the Developmentally Disabled and other government benefits programs. This includes assistance dealing with issues related to both eligibility and/or the receipt of needed services. He can be contacted at jfhuyck@yahoo.com or (916) 529-5300.

WHO CAN AN SNT TRUSTEE HIRE TO ASSIST WITH FINANCIAL PLANNING FOR A PERSON WITH A DISABILITY?

There are a host of financial advisers who will claim they have specialized knowledge in helping persons with disabilities. However, the SNT trustee should make sure that the selected financial adviser truly understands the unique planning needs of persons with disabilities. Chapter 8 describes in detail how to find an appropriate financial adviser. Below are the names of two financial advisers the author has worked with.

Scott MacDonald of **Merrill Lynch.** Scott MacDonald is a first vice president and certified special needs adviser. He has over twenty-four years of industry experience, joining Merrill Lynch in 1987. Mr. MacDonald has been featured in a variety of publications on serving clients with disabilities, including the *Oakland Tribune* and a cover story in *On Wall Street* magazine. He was a special consultant of Special Needs Trusts: Planning, Drafting, and

Administration through the California Continuing Education of the Bar and has lectured extensively for various Bar and Consumer Attorney Associations, the Special Needs Alliance, the National Guardianship Association and the Professional Fiduciary Association of California. Scott MacDonald can be contacted at scott_m_macdonald@ML.COM or (800) 260-2919.

Daniel Cutter of **Merrill Lynch.** Daniel Cutter is a certified special needs adviser at Merrill Lynch and a partner of a group focused on serving special needs families. Daniel has been in the financial industry since 1999. He earned his MBA in Finance from the University of San Francisco. Daniel is a special consultant of Special Needs Trusts: Planning, Drafting, and Administration through the California Continuing Education of the Bar (CEB). He serves on the board of the YMCA in Berkeley. Daniel Cutter can be reached at daniel_cutter@ml.com or (415) 955-3902.

Scott and Daniel provide customized financial planning and asset management for families with special needs loved ones, including special needs trusts, pooled special needs trusts, conservatorships, guardianships, charitable trusts, generational skipping trusts, and a variety of family trusts.

WHO CAN AN SNT TRUSTEE HIRE TO ASSIST WITH TAX FILING AND PLANNING FOR A PERSON WITH A DISABILITY?

In order to select an appropriate tax adviser, the SNT trustee should make sure that the professional understands fiduciary income tax. Chapter 9 discusses the different types of licenses that a tax professional can obtain. The author recommends two tax professionals whom he has referred clients to in the past:

Sandy Kasten, Esq. Ms. Kasten is an Oakland attorney with a special interest in the tax issues of trusts and conservatorships. She is a graduate of Hastings College of the Law and received her MBA in taxation from Golden Gate University. She works closely with fiduciaries and their attorneys, doing tax return preparation and planning. She also writes for California Continuing Education of the Bar and is a frequent lecturer for the Professional Fiduciary Association of California. Sandy can be contacted at (510) 295-5321 or at arnoldtax@yahoo.com.

Jeffrey Glick, CPA. Thirteen years of experience in public accounting specializing in trust and estate tax, tax planning for high net worth individuals, mid to upper level executives and closely held business owners. Experience in assisting entrepreneurs build, grow, maintain, and pass on their ventures through pro-active business and tax planning. Jeffrey can be contacted at (415) 887-4222 or jglick@gaatp.com. His website is http://www.gaatp.com.

Appendix A

Twelve-Step Summary To Begin Adminstering an SNT

STEP ONE: READ TRUST INSTRUMENT

Read the trust instrument thoroughly to become familiar with the terms of the SNT and to determine if there are any immediate tasks that need to be accomplished.

STEP TWO: DETERMINE TYPE OF SPECIAL NEEDS TRUST

Determine whether this is a first-party SNT or third-party SNT, as administration will be slightly different depending on the type of SNT.

A first-party SNT is funded with the beneficiary's property and is sometimes referred to as a "self-settled" trust. This type of SNT typically arises when the beneficiary with a disability has had an accident and received a civil settlement or judgment or the beneficiary receives an inheritance or gift in his or her own name and transfers the property to an SNT.

A third-party SNT is funded with property that belongs to a third person who is not the beneficiary. This is typically done through a parent or grandparent's estate plan.

STEP THREE: COMPLETE TRUST SUMMARY FORM

A Trust Summary Form should be completed and placed in the front of the file for the trust. A Trust Summary Form can be found at Appendix D. It is recommended that a different color paper is used so it can be immediately reviewed. The form should be a quick reference guide to the type of trust, distribution standard, type of public benefits, and related information.

STEP FOUR: EVALUATE BENEFICIARY'S CONDITION

Evaluate the beneficiary's living and personal care situation and determine whether any immediate action needs to be taken. For example, a person with a disability may require drug therapy each month. If the parent gave the drugs to his or her child but is now deceased, a replacement needs to be located immediately who is willing and able to help. The beneficiary evaluation should be conducted at least yearly.

The evaluation should include (at least) the following items:

An evaluation of the beneficiary's contact with family members and whether continuing and facilitating such contact is part of the trustee's responsibility.

An evaluation of the beneficiary's disability, including an evaluation of the beneficiary's physical and mental condition.

An evaluation of the beneficiary's rehabilitation and training programs in which he or she participates (or should be participating).

An evaluation of the beneficiary's current living situation and whether it is still appropriate, including (when appropriate) an evaluation of the caregivers for the beneficiary.

An evaluation of the beneficiary's financial condition, including available government benefits, to determine the beneficiary's needs and the effect of distributions from the SNT on the beneficiary's eligibility for public assistance.

An evaluation of the beneficiary's exercise of his or her civil rights. For example, is the beneficiary receiving a fair wage for work performed or being denied his or her right to vote or marry?

An evaluation of the beneficiary's current and future educational needs and programs.

An evaluation of the beneficiary's recreational activities, leisure time, and social needs, and the appropriateness of existing program services.

STEP FIVE: DETERMINE BENEFICIARY'S PUBLIC BENEFITS

The beneficiary's public benefits will drive the administration. It is important to know whether the beneficiary is receiving SSI, SSDI, Medicare, Medi-Cal or any of the other benefits. Thus, it is imperative that the trustee know exactly what benefits are being received and how much is being received from the various programs.

STEP SIX: KNOW THE OTHER FIDUCIARIES INVOLVED

These are typically other fiduciaries, such as a conservator of the person or estate, representative payee, and/or agent acting under a power of attorney. Be familiar with the extent and limits of the authority for each and the trustee's responsibility as it concerns the beneficiary.

A representative payee receives the social security benefits of another, for the use and benefit of that person, and must complete an annual report to the Social Security Administration detailing the use of the funds. See 42 USC §405(j)(1)(A), (j)(3)(A).

STEP SEVEN: DETERMINE WHETHER TRUST ADVISORY COMMITTEE OR TRUST PROTECTOR ARE INCLUDED IN THE SNT

Many trusts also include a trust advisory committee and trust protector. It is important to get everyone's name, contact information and the extent of his or her authority over the beneficiary.

STEP EIGHT: UNDERSTAND DISTRIBUTION PROVISION

Read and understand the distribution standard of the SNT. The distribution provision will inform the trustee whether it is acceptable for a distribution to cause a loss or reduction in benefits. A distribution standard that allows a trustee the discretion to make a distribution that may or may not cause a public benefit reduction is often called a discretionary distribution standard. A distribution standard that does not allow a distribution that will cause any reduction in public benefits is often called a supplemental distribution standard.

STEP NINE: PROVIDE A SYSTEMATIC PROCEDURE FOR REQUESTING DISTRIBUTIONS

Develop a system for the beneficiary (or advisory committee members) to contact the trustee requesting that a distribution be made. The disbursement procedure should determine whether disbursements can be made, e.g., only during business hours, on weekdays, or after twenty-four hours from a written request.

It is in the trustee's interest to clearly communicate these policies to the beneficiary. This will go a long way in eliminating future friction during the administration. One good suggestion is for the trustee to purchase a fax machine for a beneficiary or his or her caregiver. This way, disbursement requests can be faxed directly to the trustee's office and the trustee will have a written record of requests.

STEP TEN: PREPARE A BUDGET FOR EXPECTED DISTRIBUTIONS

Prepare a budget for expected expenditures of SNT assets. A monthly budget should be established from this meeting so that monthly expenses may be paid without constant requests.

Many entities such as Merrill Lynch or Mass Mutual have sample budget worksheets for persons with disabilities on their websites. The trustee should meet with the beneficiary, any legal guardians, and those friends and family willing to participate.

STEP ELEVEN: SET ACCOUNT DATE

Schedule an account on an annual basis for non-court supervised trusts and for court supervised trusts, schedule account one year after establishment and every two years thereafter.

STEP TWELVE: COMMUNICATE QUICKLY AND CLEARLY

The biggest complaint about trustees is not returning calls or communicating with beneficiary and those entitled to notice. It is important that these concerns are addressed immediately and that the trustee provide clear instructions on how communications will be conducted.

APPENDIX B

Summary of California Laws Concerning Trustee Duties

Duty	Prob Code §	Brief description
Duty to administer trust	§16000	You have a duty to follow the terms of the trust and the law governing the administration of trusts.
Duty of loyalty	§16002	You have a duty to administer the trust solely for the benefit of the beneficiaries of the trust.
Duty to deal impartially with beneficiaries	§16003	You have a duty not to favor the interests of one beneficiary over another, except to the extent trust provides to the contrary.
Duty to avoid conflict of interest	§16004	You have a duty to avoid transactions with the trust that benefit you personally.
Duty not to require beneficiary to relieve the trustee of liability	§16004.5	You cannot require a beneficiary to waive rights as a condition of distribution.
Duty not to undertake as trustee an adverse trust	§16005	You may not act as trustee of any other trust that has a competing interest with this trust.

Duty to take control and preserve trust property	§16006	You must marshal trust assets and take reasonable steps to preserve them.
Duty to make trust property productive	§16007	Subject to certain exceptions, you have a duty to make the trust assets profitable.
Duty to keep trust property separate and identified	§16009	This is one of the most important duties. You have a duty to keep the assets and debts of the trust separate from your own. In other words, you must not commingle funds.
Duty to enforce claims	§16010	You must take reasonable actions to pursue amounts that may be owed to the trust.
Duty to defend actions	§16011	You have the duty to take actions to prevent a loss to the trust, such as by defending a lawsuit.
Duty not to delegate; exception	§16012; §16052	Subject to certain exceptions, you must perform actions on behalf of the trust yourself rather than having others act on behalf of the trust.
Duty with respect to cotrustees	§16013	If you serve with a cotrustee, you each have a duty to participate in the administration and prevent the other from committing a breach of trust.
Duty to use special skills	§16014	In managing the trust property, you must use at least ordinary business ability. However, if you have special skills, you will be held to a higher standard of care.

Duty to comply with Prudent Investor Rule	§16045	You have a duty to invest as a prudent investor would considering purposes, terms, distribution requirements and circumstances of the trust.
Duty to diversify	§16048	In making investment decisions, you have a duty to diversify the investments unless it is not prudent under the circumstances
Duty to provide information to beneficiaries	§16060	There are duties relative to providing financial and other information to beneficiaries (and in some cases, the settlor's family members).
Discretionary powers to be used reasonably	§§16080; 16081	Even if trust says a particular action is entirely within discretion, trustee's duty is to act reasonably

Appendix C

SSA and DHCS Reporting Guidelines

SOCIAL SECURITY ADMINISTRATION (SSA)

1. **Persons Responsible for Reporting:** The person responsible for maintaining the special needs trust (SNT) beneficiary's eligibility for public benefits will have the responsibility for making certain disclosures to the Social Security Administration (SSA). It is nearly always the public benefits recipient who is responsible for making these reports to the SSA. However, if that person lacks the capacity to manage his or her own financial matters, a "representative payee" may be appointed by the SSA to be the person responsible for reporting. The representative payee is the person designated by SSA to receive the Supplemental Security Income (SSI) payment on behalf of the SNT beneficiary. In certain cases, if a special needs trust, by its terms, requires the trustee to make sure that beneficiary maintains eligibility for public benefits. If the SNT's terms so require a trustee may have this requirement.

2. **Basic Requirements:** The reporting party has an obligation to report to the SSA the existence of the SNT if the SNT beneficiary is receiving SSI benefits. The report should note that the SNT beneficiary is not receiving trust income unless the trustee decides to distribute income, which is in the absolute and sole discretion of the trustee. The SSI computer system will pick up any income generated by the SNT. This comes from the K-1 issued by the SNT. Medi-Cal has a computer match with the IRS and will learn of these income distributions. It will be incumbent upon the reporting party to show that payments were

made to third-party providers and not directly to the SNT beneficiary. SSI has a right to inquire as to the amount and purpose of distributions from the SNT. The SNT trustee must respond honestly and completely to any such inquiries. SSI is concerned that income *not* be used to provide food or shelter. The trustee should keep excellent records and receipts for SSI and Medi-Cal.

3. **What Must Be Reported:** The individual responsible for reporting must report all of the following to the SSA:

   a. **Address.** Change in SNT beneficiary's address.
   b. **Employment.** Change in employment status.
   c. **Living arrangements.** Change in the arrangements (such as adding or losing a roommate).
   d. **Income.** All income (including the receipt of any direct income or ISM from the SNT).
   e. **Resources.** Any change in countable resources.
   f. **Marital status.** Any change in the SNT beneficiary's marital status.
   g. **Physical or medical condition.** Changes or improvements in the SNT beneficiary's physical or mental condition (for example, the SNT beneficiary improves so much that he or she is no longer considered disabled).
   h. **Medical facility.** Admission to or discharge from any health facility or public facility (such as a hospital or nursing home).
   i. **Travel.** Any trip outside the United States.

4. **How and When to Make a Report:**

   a. **Submit it in Writing.** The report must be in writing to the Social Security Administration. See https://secure.ssa.gov/apps6z/FOLO/fo001.jsp to obtain the local SSA office by inputting the SNT beneficiary's zip code.
   b. **Provide Name.** The report must include the SNT beneficiary's name.
   c. **Include Social Security Number.** The report must include the SNT beneficiary's Social Security Number.

d.   **Describe the Event.** A description of the event that triggered the report and the date of the event. The report is due within ten days after the month in which the event took place.

5.   **Penalty for Not Filing Report.** If reports are not made on a timely basis, SSA may seek reimbursement for benefits incorrectly paid and assess a penalty for up to $100 for a late filing. Failure to respond to correspondence from SSA may result in a loss of benefits.

6.   **Appeals.** If SSA or Medi-Cal notifies the SNT beneficiary that it intends to reduce or eliminate benefits, there is a ten-day right of appeal. The appeal must be in writing. If the appeal is filed within ten days, the benefits continue. If the appeal is not filed within ten days, there is a sixty-day window to appeal an SSI decision and a ninety-day period to appeal a Medi-Cal notice of action or decision. However, benefits will be discontinued if the appeal is not filed within ten days.

DEPARTMENT OF HEALTH CARE SERVICES (MEDI-CAL)

1.   **Medi-Cal.** Notice must be given to the Department of Health Care Services or a division thereof if the trust is self-settled.

2.   **Timing of Notice.** Recipients must report any changes in status within ten days of the event. This is different from SSI's reporting requirement.

3.   **What Must Be Reported.** The benefits recipient is under a general duty to report any change in circumstances such as,

(A) Change of address
(B) Change in property or income
(C) Change in family composition
(D) Change in other health-care coverage
(E) Change in residence from one county to another within the state and apply for a redetermination of eligibility within the new county of residence (promptly notify the county department that initially established Medi-Cal eligibility in this case)

4.   **Establishment or Funding of Trust.** When the SNT is established or funded the local Medi-Cal agency that provided funding

must be notified of the establishment of the SNT. A copy of the signed trust must also be sent to this agency.

5. **Death of SNT Beneficiary.** The local Medi-Cal agency that provided medical assistance must be notified upon the death of the beneficiary. The addresses are as follows:

> Office of Director
> Department of Mental Health
> 1600 Ninth Street, Room 151
> Sacramento, CA 95814
>
> Office of Director
> Department of Developmental Services
> 1600 Ninth Street, Room 240
> Sacramento, CA 95814
>
> Department of Health Care Services
> Third-Party Liability and Recovery Division
> Estate Recovery Section—MS 4720
> PO Box 997425
> Sacramento, CA 95899-7425

6. **Notification of Accounting.** Trustee should furnish DHCS with accountings.
7. **Change of Trustee.** The DHCS must be notified of any change of trustee.

APPENDIX D

Special Needs Trust Summary

1. Name of Trust: _____

2. Date of Trust: _____

3. Beneficiary's Contact Information _____

4. Beneficiary's Disability: _____

5. [circle one]   First-party SNT-Assets from beneficiary
                          Third-party SNT-Assets from anyone but beneficiary

6. Beneficiary's Public Benefits:

    SSI $_____per month   **SSDI** $_____per month

    Medi-Cal Yes/No [circle one]   **Medicare** Yes/No [circle one]

    Medicaid Yes/No [circle one] (Medi-Cal program in other States). If received Medicaid list other States _____

    Veteran Benefits Yes/No [circle one] **Section 8** Yes/No [circle one]

    Regional Center Benefits Yes/No [circle one]

    Other Benefits describe _____

7. Date of Accounting_____

   Court Account Required Yes/No [circle one]

8. Bond   Required   Yes   or   No   [circle   one]—Amount   of   bond
   $_____

9. Trust Advisory Committee Yes or No [circle one]. If Trust Advisory Committee, list the names and contact information for Advisory Committee

Name	Relationship	Address and phone number

10. Trust Protector Yes or No [circle one]. If Yes Name and Contact Information
    _____

11. Distribution Standard—[circle one]

    a. Supplemental Standard—Only allows disbursements that do not reduce or eliminate public benefits
    b. Discretionary Standard—Allows disbursements that may reduce or eliminate public benefits if in beneficiary's best interests

12. If First-Party SNT established by Court Order (get copy of Court's Order), any specific distributions authorized in Court Order
    _____
    _____

13. Memorandum of Intent Yes or No [circle one]

14. Responsibility To Report To SSA or DHCS For Beneficiary's Eligibility for Public Benefits Trustee/Beneficiary/Other _____ [circle one]

15. List Successor Trustees

Name	Relationship	Address and phone number

16. List Remainder Beneficiaries

Name	Relationship	Address and phone number

17. Power of Appointment—Allows Beneficiary to Change Remainder Beneficiaries Yes or No [circle one]
18. If Yes, who may be appointed Anyone/Relatives Only/_____ [circle one or add unique appointment power]

COMMENTS

APPENDIX E

Budget Planning Worksheet

INCOME   Monthly Amount

Salary and Wages	$_____
Child support	$_____
Tax refund	$_____
Interest on savings	$_____
Investment income	$_____
Rental income	$_____
Unemployment compensation	$_____
Public assistance	$_____
Sources of funding related to the beneficiary's disability:	
State programs	$_____
Public benefits, such as SSI or SSDI	$_____
Assistance from fraternal and civic organizations	$_____
Other	$_____
Total Monthly Income:	$_____

EXPENSES

House payment or rent	
Property taxes	$_____

Homeowners' or renters' insurance	$_____
Homeowners' association fees	$_____
Home repairs/improvements	$_____
Household goods/furniture	$_____
Lawn care/snow removal	$_____
Natural gas or heating fuel	$_____
Electricity	$_____
Water	$_____
Telephone (cell and land line)	$_____
Computer and internet services	$_____
Computer hardware and software	$_____
Other Electronic devices	$_____
Groceries	$_____
Meals eaten out	$_____
Automobile payments	$_____
Automobile insurance	$_____
Gas and Oil	$_____
Automobile repair	$_____
Costs for disability-related adaptations to vehicle	$_____
Bus/Taxi/Train/Air/Public transportation	$_____
Other transportation	$_____
Clothing costs	$_____
Dry cleaning	$_____
Life insurance premiums	$_____
Pet care	$_____
Camps	$_____
Memberships/Club Dues	$_____
Movies, Netflix, books, newspapers, magazines	$_____
Vacation costs	$_____

Sports/Hobbies	$_____
Other Entertainment	$_____
Church or charitable donations	$_____
Loan payments	$_____
Credit card payment(s)	$_____
Personal (toiletries, allowances, etc.)	$_____
Miscellaneous (classes, etc.)	$_____
Dental bills (non reimbursable)	$_____
Care giving Costs	$_____
Medical costs (non reimbursable)	$_____
Medical insurance co-payment	$_____
Prescription medications (non reimbursable)	$_____
Therapy (e.g., physical, not covered by insurance)	$_____
Lodging and meals incurred during treatment away from home	$_____
Child care/nursing care (if not covered by insurance)	$_____
Adaptive technology	$_____
Legal fees	$_____
Other costs	$_____
Total Monthly expenses	$_____
	$_____

Budget Totals:
Total income
(Total Monthly expenses) $_____
Monthly Amount $_____

APPENDIX F

Beneficiary Disbursement Request Form

When Completed Fax to ( ) _____
Today's Date _____

Beneficiary's Last Name _____ First Name _____

Requester's Last Name _____ First Name _____

Relationship to Beneficiary _____

Requester's Contact Information _____

Payee Name _____ Payee Account #_____

Payee Address _____ Amount $ _____

Distribution Purpose _____

Original invoices from payee/creditors "must" be faxed with this form
All disbursements must be payable to a 3rd party

Today's Date _____

Beneficiary's Last Name _____ First Name _____

Requester's Last Name _____ First Name _____

Relationship to Beneficiary _____

Requester's Contact Information _____

Payee Name _____ Payee Account #_____

Payee Address _____ Amount $ _____

Distribution Purpose _____

Original invoices from payee/creditors "must" be faxed with this form
All disbursements must be payable to a 3rd party

APPENDIX G

SNT Distribution Public Benefit Decision Tree

1. SNT Beneficiary makes a request to buy item or service[399]

2. SNT Trustee determines if item or service is illegal

   If No, go to Step 3
   If Yes, stop and deny request

3. SNT Trustee checks terms of trust to see if item or service is acceptable

   If No because of specific prohibition, then stop and deny request
   If Yes because trust is silent or specifically allows then go to Step 4

4. SNT Trustee determines if SNT is Third-Party or First-Party SNT

   If Third—Party go to Step 5
   If First-Party, consider whether item or service is for sole benefit of beneficiary

---

[399] This list was inspired by David Lillesand, Florida special needs and elder law planning attorney

              If No stop and deny request
              If Yes go to Step 5

5.   SNT Trustee determines effect of item or service on beneficiary's public benefits

        If Beneficiary receives SSI consider if item or service will be counted as an available resource or as unearned income of beneficiary

            If No, go to next sentence
            If Yes, stop and deny request

        If Beneficiary receives SSI consider if item or service is considered food or shelter

            If No, go to Step 6
            If Yes, consider In-Kind Support and Maintenance (ISM) Rules and whether loss of Presumed Maximum Value (PMV) amount of SSI is okay

                If No, stop and deny request
                If Yes, go to Step 6

        If Beneficiary does not receive SSI but receives Medi-Cal consider if item or service is equipment or service that Medi-Cal will purchase

            If No, go to Step 6
            If Yes, stop and deny request

        If Beneficiary receives In-Home Supportive Services (IHSS) consider if request is to supplement IHSS workers' pay

            If No, go to Step 6
            If Yes, stop and deny request

        If Beneficiary does not receive either SSI or Medi-Cal go to Step 6

6.   SNT Trustee determines whether purchase of item or service is within SNT budget

            If No, stop and deny request
            Yes, go to Step 7

7.   Purchase Item or service

APPENDIX H

Checklist for Interviewing a Financial Adviser

The best approach in hiring a financial adviser is to talk to multiple candidates, check backgrounds, call references, and maintain objectivity.

Below, are some sample questions and general advice in the selection of a financial adviser.

Prior to meeting with a prospective adviser, the trustee should review the adviser's website and review any promotional material the adviser has. The website and written packet should include:

* information on the advisory firm

* financial planning and investment approaches and philosophies

* the adviser's résumé

* compensation methods and fee schedules

* registration Form ADV

There are certain types of advisers that must be licensed to sell different financial products.

Planner's Name: _____
Company: _____
Address: _____
Phone: _____
Fax: _____
E-mail: _____
Website: _____

1. Please tell us about your education and credentials.
2. Tell us about your experience in serving Fiduciary & Trust Clients. How many years have you served?
3. Do you have experience in providing advice on Special Needs Financial Planning? If yes, indicate the number of years.
4. How long have you been offering financial planning advice to clients?

   o   Less than one year
   o   One to four years
   o   Five to 10 years
   o   More than 10 years

5. How did you get involved in Special Needs Financial Planning as a profession?
6. What are your total Assets Under Management (AUM)? What is your AUM related to specialized trust/fiduciary clients? What percentage does that represent of your total client base?
7. What professional financial planning designation(s) or certification(s) do you hold?

   o   CERTIFIED FINANCIAL PLANNER™ or CFP®
   o   Certified Public Accountant-Personal Financial Specialist (CPA-PFS)
   o   Chartered Financial Consultant (ChFC)
   o   Other

8. Have you produced any publications, presentations or training seminars related to this market?

9. What financial planning continuing education requirements are you required to attend?

10. Are you or your firm licensed as a Registered Investment Adviser? Will you provide me with your disclosure document Form ADV Part II or its state equivalent?

   o Yes
   o No, If no, why not?

11. How are you paid for your services?

   o Fee
   o Commission
   o Fee and Commission
   o Salary
   o Other

12. What do you typically charge?

   A) Fee:
   Hourly Rate $_____
   Flat Fee *(range)* $_____ to $_____
   Percentage of AOM _____ percent

   B) Commission:

13. Are there any hidden internal fees related to mutual funds or other products?

14. What is the cost to exit your program?

15. Do you have open architecture for various investment products?

16. Do you receive disparate compensation for any particular products?

17. What restrictions preclude you from any particular product area, type or vendor?

18. Who/What institution stands behind you and what is their financial strength?

19. What insurance covers you and to what limits?

20. Explain your firm's supervision and oversight process.

21. Explain your firm's Legal and Compliance review process and supervision methods.

22. Do you provide a written client engagement agreement?

   ○ Yes
   ○ No. If no, why not?

23. Can you provide 3 families as a reference that you have provided Special Needs Financial Planning advice to? May I contact them?
24. Can you provide 3 other professionals in the disability community as a reference? May I contact them?

Unspoken questions:

- Do you "rationally trust" this person to advise you on your financial affairs?
- Do you believe that this person is among of the best advisers available?
- If not, you should keep looking, until you find one who is.
- Are you comfortable with the manner of your interactions?
- Do you always understand what the adviser says? Is he or she able to explain things to you clearly?
- Do you feel that you could learn something valuable from working with this adviser?
- Every adviser will have a direct or indirect cost to you. Your adviser's value to you must be substantially greater than his cost.

APPENDIX I

Sample Accounting Letter

_____, Trustee
(Address)
(Address)

(Date)

(Beneficiary Name)
(Address)
(Address)

        Re: _____Special Needs Trust Accounting

Dear_____:

As a beneficiary of the _____Special Needs Trust, you are entitled to a periodic accounting that contains a report of the receipts and distributions of principal and income that have occurred over the past year. Additionally, you are entitled to know the assets and liabilities of the trust as of the beginning and the end of the accounting period, as well as the names of those agents that I, as trustee, have hired to assist me in my duties as trustee, or you in your daily life. I have also included a list of all named remainder and contingent beneficiaries with their last known addresses. Enclosed with this letter are the schedules that reflect all of this information.

348

[Information regarding the status of trust activities (i.e., claims, major transactions, relationship w/ agents and/or beneficiary(ies), unusual events, termination, etc.) should be included here.]

The specific information regarding fees paid to agents hired by me can be found in the "disbursements" schedule. Unless indicated otherwise, agents of the trustee are neither related to nor are affiliated with the trustee.

I should also advise you that you are entitled to petition the court under Probate Code Section 17200 to obtain a review of the account and of the acts f the trustee. Claims against the trustee for breach of trust may not be made after the expiration of three (3) years from the date you receive an account or report disclosing facts giving rise to the claim. Please refer to Probate Code Section 16063.

[Trustee may insert the following if SNT document allows it, otherwise it should not be included (See chapter 7 for a discussion of this additional provision):]

"Please note that this three-year period is shortened under Probate Code 16461(c) by the following:

YOU HAVE [180 DAYS [*or longer if specified in the trust instrument*] FROM YOUR RECEIPT OF THIS ACCOUNT OR REPORT TO MAKE AN OBJECTION TO ANY ITEM SET FORTH IN THIS ACCOUNT OR REPORT. ANY OBJECTION YOU MAKE MUST BE IN WRITING; IT MUST BE DELIVERED TO THE TRUSTEE WITHIN THE PERIOD STATED ABOVE; AND IT MUST STATE YOUR OBJECTION. YOUR FAILURE TO DELIVER A WRITTEN OBJECTION TO THE TRUSTEE WITHIN THE PERIOD STATED ABOVE WILL PERMANENTLY PREVENT YOU FROM LATER ASSERTING THIS OBJECTION AGAINST THE TRUSTEE. IF YOU DO MAKE AN OBJECTION, THE 3-YEAR PERIOD PROVIDED IN SECTION 16460 OF THE PROBATE CODE FOR COMMENCEMENT OF LITIGATION WILL APPLY TO CLAIMS BASED ON YOUR OBJECTION AND WILL BEGIN TO RUN ON THE DATE THAT YOU RECEIVE THIS ACCOUNT OR REPORT."

Kevin Urbatsch

Should you have questions or concerns, please feel free to contact me at your convenience. Please be advised that if you wish to discuss your rights as a beneficiary, you should contact your own attorney.

Best regards,

Trustee

APPENDIX J

Checklist for Hiring and Managing a Caregiver

A trustee should review the list below to review the overall responsibilities of hiring and managing a caregiver:

Who is the caregiver's employer?
_____ HOME CARE AGENCY
Caregivers are employed by the home care company.
_____ REGISTRY
Depending on the arrangement, the trustee will likely have employer responsibilities.
_____ TRUSTEE HIRE
Caregivers are employed by the SNT trustee.

Who screens the caregiver's references and performs criminal background checks?

_____ HOME CARE AGENCY
Company does all screening. SNT trustee should ask for copy of any and all background check documents of specific employees.
_____ REGISTRY
Some registry agencies will do background check this and other will not. Trustee should make sure.
_____ TRUSTEE HIRE

Trustee must do all screening.

Who pays the caregiver?

_____ HOME CARE AGENCY
Caregivers are paid by the company.
_____ REGISTRY
Trustee usually pays a combined referral agency fee and caregivers' wages into a trust account of the referral agency, or separately pays the referral fee to the agency and wages to the caregiver. Trustee and caregiver negotiate wages and raises.
_____ TRUSTEE HIRE
Caregivers are paid by the SNT trustee.

Who handles caregiver's overtime and vacation pay?

_____ HOME CARE AGENCY
Caregivers are paid by the company.
_____ REGISTRY
SNT trustee is responsible.
_____ TRUSTEE HIRE
SNT trustee is responsible.

Who is responsible for withholding and paying Federal and State Income taxes?

_____ HOME CARE AGENCY
Company prepares and files quarterly and annual employer payroll tax returns.
_____ REGISTRY
Trustee is responsible for preparing and filing quarterly and annual employer payroll tax returns. Except when the registry does not use 1099 employees.
_____ TRUSTEE HIRE
Trustee is responsible for preparing and filing quarterly and annual employer payroll tax returns.

Who is responsible for withholding and paying Social Security and Medicare taxes?

_____ HOME CARE AGENCY
Company pays employer's share of these taxes.
_____ REGISTRY
Trustee is responsible for paying employer's cost of these taxes.
_____ TRUSTEE HIRE
Trustee is responsible for paying employer's costs of these taxes

Who is responsible for unemployment taxes?

_____ HOME CARE AGENCY
Company pays these taxes.
_____ REGISTRY
Trustee is responsible for paying these taxes.
_____ TRUSTEE HIRE
Trustee is responsible for paying these taxes

Who is responsible for providing insurance to cover the caregiver?

_____ HOME CARE AGENCY
Company will generally provide this, trustee should check to make sure agency will cover.
_____ REGISTRY
SNT trustee or homeowner where the beneficiary resides. SNT trustee should contact homeowner or renter's insurance carrier for details—may need to seek rider on policy for "household employee." Typical insurance should cover both when the caregiver is injured and if the caregiver injures another.
_____ TRUSTEE HIRE
SNT trustee or homeowner where the beneficiary resides. SNT trustee should contact homeowner or

renter's insurance carrier for details—may need to seek rider on policy for "household employee." Typical insurance should cover both when the caregiver is injured and if the caregiver injures another.

Who is responsible for providing workers compensation insurance to cover the caregiver?

_____ HOME CARE AGENCY
Company will generally provide this, trustee should check to make sure agency will cover.
_____ REGISTRY
SNT trustee or homeowner where the beneficiary
resides. SNT trustee should contact homeowner's insurance carrier for details.
_____ TRUSTEE HIRE
SNT trustee or homeowner where the beneficiary resides. SNT trustee should contact homeowner's insurance carrier for details.

Who coordinates services, including replacements when caregivers are sick or need time off?

_____ HOME CARE AGENCY
Company will provide this service.
_____ REGISTRY
Day-to-day coordination is worked out between the caregiver and the SNT trustee. A substitute may be available through the agency.
_____ TRUSTEE HIRE
Day-to-day coordination is worked out between the caregiver and the SNT trustee.

Who resolves any issues with the caregiver?

_____ HOME CARE AGENCY
Company's supervisors or case managers usually do this will provide this service.

_____ REGISTRY

SNT trustee and caregiver generally need to resolve day-to-day problems themselves.

_____ TRUSTEE HIRE

SNT trustee and caregiver generally need to resolve day-to-day problems themselves.

APPENDIX K

Sample Caregiving Agreement

Note: Personal Care Contracts can take many approaches. Terms will vary with individual circumstances. The following Form represents one approach.

PERSONAL CARE AGREEMENT

This Agreement is entered into by and between [*name of SNT trustee*] ("EMPLOYER") and [*name of caregiver*] ("CARE PROVIDER") this [date]. It sets forth the terms under which CARE PROVIDER will provide personal assistance to [*name of SNT beneficiary*] BENEFICIARY.

    1.   *DUTIES OF CARE PROVIDER.* CARE PROVIDER will provide care-giving services for BENEFICIARY at BENEFICIARY's residence or other facility where BENEFICIARY is living. [*Include specific details of type of care to be provided. Some suggested functions are indicated below.*]

    1.1 EMPLOYER contracts to pay and CARE PROVIDER agrees to provide the following lifetime services on an "as needed" basis for benefit of BENEFICIARY:

    (1) Attend to needs of BENEFICIARY, including preparation of nutritious, appropriate meals and snacks; house cleaning; laundry;

    (2) Assist BENEFICIARY with grooming, bathing, dressing, laundry, and personal shopping, as needed;

    (3) Purchase, with funds made available by EMPLOYER, or assist BENEFICIARY in purchasing clothing, toiletries, and other personal

items for BENEFICIARY as needed, taking into account EMPLOYER's ability to pay for such items;

(4) Purchase, with funds made available by EMPLOYER, or assist BENEFICIARY in purchasing hobby, entertainment or other goods for BENEFICIARY's use and enjoyment, as needed, taking into account EMPLOYER's ability to pay for such items;

(5) Monitor BENEFICIARY's physical and mental condition and nutritional needs on a regular basis in cooperation with health-care providers;

(6) Arrange for transportation to health-care providers and to the physician of BENEFICIARY's choice. CARE PROVIDER will also arrange for assessment, services and treatment by appropriate health-care providers, including but not limited to, physicians, nurses, nursing home services, physical therapists, and mental health specialists as needed for BENEFICIARY;

(7) Assist BENEFICIARY in carrying out the instructions and directives of BENEFICIARY's health-care providers;

(8) Arrange for social services by social service personnel as needed by BENEFICIARY;

(9) Even if additional services are not needed, visit at least weekly with BENEFICIARY and encourage social interaction;

(10) Arrange for outings and walks in keeping with BENEFICIARY's lifestyle, if reasonable and feasible for BENEFICIARY;

(11) Interact with and/or assist any agent of BENEFICIARY in interacting with health professionals, long-term care facility administrators, social service personnel, insurance companies, and government workers in order to safeguard BENEFICIARY's rights, benefits, or other resources as needed.

1.2 The privacy of BENEFICIARY shall be preserved and respected as to visitors, telephone conversations and personal mail. Family members shall be permitted to visit BENEFICIARY.

2. *DURATION*. The services indicated above shall be provided to BENEFICIARY by CARE PROVIDER for the lifetime of BENEFICIARY or until terminated with 30 days notice by either party.

3. *COMPENSATION*. The parties stipulate that as of the execution of this Agreement, BENEFICIARY is [age] years of age. EMPLOYER agrees to pay, and CARE PROVIDER agrees to accept, in payment for the aforesaid services to be rendered by CARE PROVIDER, the compensation set forth below, which compensation the parties stipulate and agree to be fair and

reasonable and commensurate with the quality and extent of the services and their fair market value.

3.1 The parties stipulate that court appointed conservators or guardians who render the aforesaid services in this county, generally receive $[amount] per hour under Court order. Professional geriatric care managers typically receive $[amount] per hour for performance of the services noted above. The parties stipulate and agree that the CARE PROVIDER shall receive $[amount] per hour.

3.2 The parties agree and stipulate that compensation to the CARE PROVIDER shall be computed as follows: $[specify hourly rates] per hour, multiplied by [specify average weekly hours] hours, multiplied by [life expectancy] years, multiplied by 52 weeks (or [hourly rate] x [average weekly hours] x 52 = [total compensation]).

4. *NONASSIGNABILITY.* This agreement is for services unique to BENEFICIARY. CARE PROVIDER agrees to personally perform the above services. CARE PROVIDER shall have no obligation to render services or otherwise be liable to any other person or entity.

5. *PERSONAL DAY/VACATION.* In the event that CARE PROVIDER decides to take a personal day or vacation, he or she will only do so if such an absence is feasible, practical, and responsible. Additionally, CARE PROVIDER will contact EMPLOYER to ensure that BENEFICIARY does not experience a lapse in care while CARE PROVIDER is away.

5. *LIABILITY.* Medical care is to be provided at the expense of EMPLOYER. CARE PROVIDER shall not be liable for the cost of BENEFICIARY's care. EMPLOYER agrees to reimburse CARE PROVIDER for any reasonable out-of-pocket expenses incurred on BENEFICIARY's behalf.

6. *EFFECTIVE DATE.* This Agreement shall take effect and be binding on the parties hereto upon payment of the agreed upon compensation set forth above for CARE PROVIDER.

7. *ARBITRATION CLAUSE.* The parties agree that any dispute between them regarding the services under this Agreement or any other aspect of this Agreement, will be determined by submitting it to arbitration under the laws of the State of [state], rather than by a lawsuit through the court process. [It may be desirable to be more detailed in identifying the arbitration mechanism, or it may be preferable to preserve the option of jury or court trial for the client.]

8. *REPRESENTATIONS.* The CARE PROVIDER represents to the EMPLOYER as follows:

a. The CARE PROVIDER's [state] Driver's License Number is [number]. It expires on [date].
b. The CARE PROVIDER has never been, and is not now, the subject of any claim or court action (civil or criminal) alleging criminal or dishonest activity.
c. The CARE PROVIDER has no known medical condition (such as being subject to seizures or blackouts) which could result in risk to BENEFICIARY.

9. *MISCELLANEOUS.*

9.1 This Agreement contains the entire Agreement and understanding between the parties, surpassing all prior communications, either written or oral, concerning the subject matter of this Agreement. This Agreement may be changed only by a written instrument executed by both parties hereto.

9.2 This Agreement shall be governed by and construed in accordance with the laws of the State of California.

THIS IS A LEGALLY BINDING AGREEMENT. EACH PARTY HAS READ THE ABOVE AGREEMENT BEFORE SIGNING IT. EACH PARTY UNDERSTANDS THE AGREEMENT HE OR SHE IS MAKING, HAVING HAD THE OPPORTUNITY TO ASK TO HAVE EACH TERM THAT THE PARTY DOES NOT UNDERSTAND FULLY EXPLAINED.

We, the CARE PROVIDER and the EMPLOYER, having read this Agreement, agree to its terms and sign it as our free act and deed on the date(s) set forth below.

EMPLOYER:
[name typed or printed]
[signature]
[date signed]

CARE PROVIDER:
[name typed or printed]
[signature]
[date signed]

[Notarial Acknowledgment]

APPENDIX L

Checklist on Death of Beneficiary

It is not necessarily the SNT trustee's responsibility to manage the personal decisions on the death of the person with a disability. However, someone (often the SNT trustee) should take the following actions after the death of a beneficiary.

The following checklist was modified from a checklist prepared by special needs planning attorney Diedre Wachbrit Braverman with her permission.

- ☐ Review the beneficiary's Advance Health Care Directive and Memorial Instructions form to discover any expressed wishes by the beneficiary or his parents or guardians/conservators regarding burial, cremation, services or other preferences.
- ☐ Work with the surviving family and the health-care agent to provide an appropriate funeral or other service.
- ☐ Notify the beneficiary's employer, if applicable, and obtain benefits forms if life insurance, retirement planning or other survivor's benefits are in place.
- ☐ At least 12 death certificate should be obtained.
- ☐ Determine whether an estate tax return must be filed. Choose a trust attorney to prepare this return.
- ☐ Retain an experienced CPA to file the final income tax return.
- ☐ Make payments due if you are able to confirm their validity. Keep track to ensure that the trust does not pay twice. If you are unable to confirm the validity of a debt, ask the creditor for evidence.

☐ Ensure that the trust authorizes you to pay the beneficiary's final expenses. Remember that medical expenses are deductible on the final income tax return if the estate pays them within one year of death.

☐ Do not distribute funds from the trust until you fully understand the terms of distribution.

☐ Prepare annual accountings on the financial status of the trust.

APPENDIX M

No-Brainer SNT Distribution List

The following is an alphabetical list of generally permissible distributions from an SNT that will not reduce or eliminate SSI. It is not meant to be an exhaustive list.

- Automobile/van;
- Accounting services;
- Acupuncture/acupressure;
- Appliances (TV, VCR, DVD player, stereo, microwave, stove, refrigerator, washer/dryer);
- Bottled water or water service;
- Bus pass/public transportation costs;
- Camera, film, recorder and tapes, development of film;
- Clothing;
- Clubs and club dues (record clubs, book clubs, health clubs, service clubs, zoo, advocacy groups, museums);
- Computer hardware, software, programs, and Internet service;
- Conferences;
- Cosmetics;
- Courses or classes (academic or recreational), including books and supplies;
- Curtains, blinds, and drapes;
- Dental work not covered by Medi-Cal, including anesthesia;
- Downpayment on home or security deposit on apartment;
- Dry cleaning and/or laundry services;
- Education expenses including tuition and related costs;
- Elective surgery;

- Eye glasses;
- Fitness equipment;
- Funeral expenses;
- Furniture, home furnishings;
- Gasoline and/or maintenance for automobile;
- Haircuts/salon services;
- Hobby supplies;
- Holiday decorations, parties, dinner dances, holiday cards;
- Home alarm and/or monitoring/response system;
- Home improvements, repairs, and maintenance (not covered by Medi-Cal), including tools to perform home improvements, repairs, and maintenance by homeowner;
- Home purchase (to the extent not covered by benefits);
- House cleaning/maid services;
- Insurance (automobile, home and/or possessions);
- Legal fees/advocacy;
- Linens and towels;
- Magazine and newspaper subscriptions;
- Massage;
- Musical instruments (including lessons and music);
- Nonfood grocery items (laundry soap, bleach, fabric softener, deodorant, dish soap, hand and body soap, personal hygiene products, paper towels, napkins, Kleenex, toilet paper, and household cleaning products);
- Over-the-counter medications (including vitamins and herbs);
- Personal assistance services not covered by Medi-Cal;
- Pet and pet supplies, veterinary services;
- Physician specialists if not covered by Medi-Cal;
- Pornography (as long as legal);
- Private counseling if not covered by Medi-Cal;
- Repair services (*e.g.*, for appliances, automobile, bicycle, household, or fitness equipment);
- Snow removal/landscaping/gardening (lawn) services;
- Sporting goods/equipment/uniforms/team pictures;
- Stationery, stamps, and cards;
- Storage units;
- Taxicab;
- Telephone service and equipment, including cell phone, pager;

- Therapy (physical, occupational, speech) not covered by Medi-Cal;
- Tickets to concerts or sporting events (for beneficiary and an accompanying companion, if necessary);
- Transportation (automobile, motorcycle, bicycle, moped, gas, bus passes, insurance, vehicle license fees, gas, car repairs);
- Tuition and expenses connected with education
- Utility bills (satellite TV, cable TV, telephone—but not gas, water, or electricity);
- Vacation (including paying for a personal assistant to accompany the beneficiary if necessary)

APPENDIX N

Sample Investment Policy Statement

[TRUST OR CLIENT's NAME][400]

1. *Introduction/Background*

BENEFICIARY is a 48 year old female (DOB) with two young adult children. She is in good physical health, other than being recently diagnosed with schizophrenia. She is separated from her estranged husband and is currently going through a divorce. In the past she has not made good financial decisions, and she has a gambling addiction.

The trust was set up by her father as a third-party SNT before he died to provide for her special needs. Currently BENEFICIARY is not employed and is not very good about managing her finances. She lives a modest life in a rental house in the Sierra foothills.

Her son just graduated from high school and is living with her while attending a community college. (The son has a trust that is supporting him while he is in school.)

Based on the IRS Publication 590 Single Life Expectancy table, Ms. BENEFICIARY's life expectancy is 84 years (an additional 36 years).

---

[400] This sample investment policy statement was developed from a statement provided to the author by Scott MacDonald, Merrill-Lynch special needs financial advisor.

a. ***Income****:* Ms. BENEFICIARY's income comes from SSI at $830 per month. Ms. BENEFICIARY'S SNT estimated annual income is from interest income from 4 deeds of trust (estimated annual income $12,000) and whatever interest or dividend income we can get from her investable assets.

b. ***Expenses****:* Ms. BENEFICIARY's living expenses, i.e. rent, auto insurance, health insurance, and utilities will be paid from the trust, if possible. Trust fees include professional services fees consisting of fiduciary, legal and tax accountant fees (estimated $8,000 annually).

c. ***Assets:*** Ms. BENEFICIARY's assets are a piece of property in TOWN, CA (appraised value as of 1/17/11 $135,000). Her SNT's assets are 4 deeds (installment notes) valued at $205,000 (appraised value as of 1/17/09), and cash for a total asset portfolio of approximately **$1,100,000**.

d. ***Trust provisions:*** The BENEFICIARY'S NAME Special Needs Trust was established on DATE at the time of her father's death. Per the terms of the trust, BENEFICIARY is entitled to discretionary distribution of income and principal based on the assets in the trust. In the trustee's discretion, BENEFICIARY may have as much as necessary for her special needs.

e. ***Needs:*** Ms. BENEFICIARY has significant need for income from this trust due to the fact she is unemployed. The trustee is considering putting a mobile or prefab home on the TOWN property to provide BENEFICIARY with a permanent residence.

2. *Measurable Investment Objectives:*

The objectives are to provide the income needs to the degree possible for Ms. BENEFICIARY's lifetime. The goal is to earn the highest rate of return with the least amount of risk in a diversified portfolio. Ms. BENEFICIARY's will need monthly distributions from the trust to support her living expenses.

a. *Minimum portfolio returns:* A reasonable objective is an average of 4-6% rate of return for the next five years. Per the UPIA this return is for the whole portfolio, not individual investments.

d. *Maximum acceptable portfolio risk:* Risk is to be measured as the potential for loss, rather than simple volatility using a semi-standard deviation scatter plot. The average risk should not exceed a moderate, or "average" risk class based on Morningstar's risk score on performance. This risk score compares funds in the same peer group and is a weighted, average of three, five and ten year performance. Defining and managing the risk levels are a key duty of a prudent professional fiduciary. The goal is to have the funds all in the northwest quadrant of the scatter plot.

3. *Investment Management Procedures:*

As a prudent investor, day-trading and short sales would not be acceptable methodologies.

4. *Classes of Investments:*

Diversification is the key to successful investment portfolio management. No classes of investments are excluded if they meet the return and risk objectives. The UPIA specifically did not exclude certain types of investment, leaving it up to particular risk versus return goals set forth in the trust.

5. *Asset Manager/Fund Hiring and Firing Criteria:*

A careful analysis of the asset manager or fund should be conducted prior to investing. Criteria includes tenure (at least 5 years with the fund), local references (at least two, and one from another professional fiduciary or attorney), and better than the peer group benchmark (S&P 500, EAFE, Barclay's Intermediate Government/Corporate Index, 3-month T-bill) for the prior 5 years. Not meeting the minimum acceptable earnings objective or the maximum acceptable risk objective over the previous year will be the criteria for firing.

6. *Investment Adviser:*

As a professional fiduciary it is my duty to thoroughly review and evaluate an investment adviser before delegating the investment responsibilities. Normally, an investment adviser would be chosen based on a review of their investment approaches, their knowledge and experience with the UPIA, their past performances, their years in the field and their professional degrees. Also, the adviser would be expected to inspire confidence in what they do, and be readily available to answer questions from the professional fiduciary. Fees and/ or transaction costs would be evaluated compared to their value versus return. A substandard performance that doesn't meet the average minimum earnings objective and maximum risk tolerance over a year timeframe would be grounds for dismissal.

7. *Reporting:*

Periodic reviews include receiving monthly statements of accounts and quarterly summary reviews of the performance compared to the appropriate benchmark. The reviews should include a breakdown by asset class, sector and size. Twice a year in-person meetings will be conducted so there is a direct opportunity to discuss questions or issues. The adviser is to add the notes from the meeting in the file.

8. *Rebalancing:*

From time to time rebalancing the portfolio is required to continue to meet the return/risk objectives. This reallocation should be reviewed at a minimum of once a year.

Acknowledged by:

_____

Investment Manager   Date

Prepared by:
[FIDUCIARY FIRM NAME]
LICENSED FIDUCIARY
DATED _____

APPENDIX O

Sample Petition for Court Account

KEVIN URBATSCH SBN 168380
MYERS URBATSCH, PC
100 Spear Street, Ste. 1430
San Francisco, CA 94105
Telephone: (415) 593-9944
Fax: (415) 896-1500

Attorneys for Trustee
Roger Zelazny

IN THE SUPERIOR COURT OF THE STATE OF CALIFORNIA
IN AND FOR THE CITY AND COUNTY OF SAN FRANCISCO

In re the matter of:		CASE NO.: 1-11-PR-123456
	)	FIRST ACCOUNT & REPORT OF TRUSTEE;
	)	PETITION TO SETTLE ACCOUNT; TO
THE CORWIN AMBER SPECIAL	)	REDUCE BOND; AND TO FIX & ALLOW
NEEDS TRUST	)	TRUSTEE AND ATTORNEY FEES (Probate
	)	Code § 1060)
	)	
	)	DATE:
	)	TIME:
	)	DEPT:
	)	

ROGER ZELAZNY, trustee of the CORWIN AMBER SPECIAL NEEDS TRUST, presents his verified First Account and Report and Petition to Settle the Account; to Reduce Bond; and to Fix and Allow Trustee and Attorney Fees and Costs; (Probate Code § 1060). Petitioner alleges:

1. **Jurisdiction and Venue.** This Court has jurisdiction over this matter pursuant to Probate Code §17000, et seq.
2. Venue is proper in that this court approved the underlying settlement, under case number1-08-CV-105511 and established the trust in this jurisdiction.
3. **Parties.** Pursuant to an Order of the Superior Court of San Francisco dated April 14, 2009, the Corwin Amber Special Needs Trust was established for Corwin Amber.
4. ROGER ZELAZNY (hereinafter referred to as "Trustee") is the current Trustee of the Trust.
5. CORWIN AMBER, the beneficiary of the Trust, is 14 years of age (Date of Birth 10/04/1995). He suffers from a disability that impairs his ability to provide for his own care and constitutes a substantial handicap.
6. **First Account & Report of Trustee.** Petitioner's account of the Corwin Amber Special Needs Trust covers the period from April 14, 2010 through April 30, 2011. A Summary of Account is attached hereto, and a full, true and correct account setting forth all credits and charges of petitioner as trustee is attached as **Exhibit A.**
7. During the account period, all cash of the trust estate was invested and maintained in interest bearing accounts or investments authorized by law or the governing instrument, except for an amount of cash that is reasonably necessary for the orderly administration of the estate.
8. **Unusual Disbursements**.

   a. **Caregiver Fees.** Throughout this account period, the trustee disbursed trust funds to Fred Saberhagen for caregiver fees. Mr. Saberhagen is the employer of the caregivers. Payments were made directly to him, and he then disbursed the funds accordingly to the caregivers. True and correct copies of the invoices submitted to the trustee for payment of caregivers are attached hereto as **Exhibit B.** Pursuant to the court order establishing the special needs trust (which was filed under this case number on May 11, 2009, as an attachment to the Declaration of Kevin

Urbatsch Regarding Establishment of Special Needs Trust) the trustee is authorized to hire a caregiver for Corwin Amber for $35/ hours. As noted by his doctor reports, Corwin requires 24-hour care. He functions at a level of a small infant, yet he continues to grow physically making his care increasingly difficult for his family. While the cost of care is large, finding safe and reliable people from a private agency would cost even more than is being expended by the trust now.

9. No capital changes occurred during the account period.
10. The trust has no liabilities.
11. Petitioner has managed and administered the beneficiary's estate frugally and without waste, collecting income and principal, investing the sums available for investment, retaining and disposing of property and investments, and applying or disposing of the income or corpus of the trust estate as required by law, the governing instrument and the orders of this Court, as detailed in the schedules attached to this petition.
12. The original bank statements will be filed prior to the hearing on this matter.
13. **Bond.** Per court order dated April 15, 2010, petitioner filed a bond in the amount of $1,008,982.82. Based on the ending value of the estate ($653,770.74), the estimated annual annuity payments ($120,000), the estimated annual income to be earned ($15,475-based on a 2% return), and the reasonable amount for the cost of recovery on the bond ($84,709), petitioner requests that the amount of bond be reduced by $134,982.80, for a total bond amount of $874,000,000. (Probate Code section 2320 (c)(4); Calif. Rule of Court 7.206.)
14. **No Affiliate Relationships.** During the accounting period, neither the trustee nor her attorney of record, KEVIN URBATSCH, Esq., had any family or affiliate relationship with any agent hired by petitioner as trustee.
15. **Fix and Allow Attorney Fees.** Petitioners retained the services of KEVIN URBATSCH, Esq., as their attorney in all matters concerning the trust administration in which it was necessary to have advice of counsel in the proper administration and conduct of the trust and in connection with preparing the First Account and Report of petitioner as trustee. Mr. Urbatsch received $4,922.00 in attorney's fees during

this account period, pursuant to an order made by this court on April 15, 2010. Petitioner now seeks an order of this court to authorize and direct the Trustee of the CORWIN AMBER SPECIAL NEEDS TRUST to pay to Kevin Urbatsch the amount of $3,397.50 for his attorneys' fees all as set forth in the Declaration of Kevin Urbatsch attached hereto as **Exhibit B**.

16. **Fix and Allow Trustee Fees.** Pursuant to an order made by this Court on April 15, 2010, Petitioner is entitled to receive payment of interim fees based upon his then yearly rate to be divided equally throughout the year. During this account period, the trustee received a total of $7,029.00. Interim fees were based upon 1% of the trust assets under management, as allowed in this court's order approving this trust. Petitioner asks the court to confirm these fees, and to approve additional fees, based on the trustee's actual services provided. During this account period, the trustee has spent a total of 112.40 hours in managing the trust estate. Based on an hourly rate of $100.00, the trustee is entitled to $11,240. Therefore, Petitioner asks the court to allow payment of additional trustee fees in the amount of $4,211 (the difference between $11,240 and $7,029.00). In support of this request, the trustee's itemized time sheets are attached hereto as **Exhibit C.** By endorsing his name to this Petition, Petitioner represents that this is a reasonable value of the services as Trustee. In the management of the Trust estate during the period of this account, Petitioner has performed the following services:

Petitioner has managed and administered the trust estate frugally and without waste, collecting income and principal, investing the sums available for investment including investing in interest-bearing accounts, retaining and disposing of property and investments, and applying or disposing of income or corpus of the estate as required by law.

17. **Notice.** The persons entitled to notice of hearing on this petition include the beneficiary and members of the trust advisory committee, as follows:

Corwin Amber, Beneficiary, 125 Logos, Amber, CA 95111

John Baptsits, Father of Beneficiary and Trust Advisory Committee member, 125 Logos, Amber, CA 95111

Harry Dresden, Trust Advisory Committee Member, 125 Logos, Amber, CA 95111

Department of Health Services, Director, MS 0000, P.O. Box 997413 Sacramento, CA 95899-7413

Department of Mental Health, 1600 9th Street, Room 151, Sacramento, CA 98614

Department of Developmental Services, P.O box 944242, Sacramento, CA 94244-2020

18. There are no requests for special notice on file.

WHEREFORE, Petitioner requests that:

1. The court find that notice of hearing has been given as required by law;
2. The court make an order approving, allowing, and settling the attached first account and report of the CORWIN AMBER SPECIAL NEEDS TRUST as filed;
3. That bond be reduced by $134,982.80, for a total bond amount of $874,000;
4. The court confirm payment of interim trustee fees in the amount of $7,029.00;
5. The court authorize and direct petitioner to pay Leo Bautista, as trustee, $4,211 for trustee services.
6. The court authorize and direct petitioner to pay KEVIN URBATSCH, Esq., $3,397.50 for legal services rendered to the petitioner during the account period; and
7. For such other relief that the Court deems proper.

Date: _____, 2011 By: _____

ROGER ZELAZNY,
Petitioner and Trustee

Date: _____, 2011 By: _____

By: KEVIN URBATSCH
Attorney for Petitioner

VERIFICATION

I, ROGER ZELAZNY, declare:

I am the petitioner in the above-entitled matter and I declare that I have read the foregoing account and petition, and the requests designated therein, and know its contents. The account, which includes the report and the supporting schedules, is true of my own knowledge, except for the matters stated therein on our information and belief, and as to those matters, I believe them to be true. The account contains a full statement of all charges against us and all credits to which we are entitled in the estate during the account period.

I declare under penalty of perjury under the laws of the State of California that the foregoing is true and correct. Executed in the City of _____, California.

Date: _____, 2011

_____

Roger Zelazny

GLOSSARY OF COMMONLY USED SNT ADMINISTRATION TERMS

250% California Working Disabled Medi-Cal. This program provides full-scope Medi-Cal to persons with disabilities who work and have income that is too high to qualify for other Medi-Cal categories such as Categorically Eligible, Medically Needy or Aged & Disability Federal Poverty Level Medi-Cal. For this program, the recipient may have up to 250 percent of the federal poverty level in countable income and still receive Medi-Cal benefits. Enrollees pay a monthly, sliding-scale premium for this health coverage.

Accounting (Account) (See Also Simplified Account and Standard Account): A trustee must account for the trustee's actions. Generally, an account may be done informally at least once a year and a copy provided to the beneficiary or his or her legal representatives. An account will include all actions taken by the trustee including an explanation of all disbursements, investments, and purchases made by trustee. If the trust is court supervised, this account is a much more formal procedure and requires a petition and hearing in a local probate court. The petition must follow a set procedure. It is recommended that an attorney assist with all court accounting filings.

Aged & Disability Federal Poverty Level Medi-Cal: This program provides free Medi-Cal services for persons with disabilities who meet the income and asset requirements of the A&D FPL program. It covers individuals and couples whose income is slightly higher than the SSI eligibility requirements.

Agent: An agent is typically someone who has been appointed by the person with a disability to manage his or her own personal or financial care under a power of attorney or an advance health-care directive. The person with a disability can only sign such a document when the person with a disability has legal capacity.

Basis (sometimes called Cost Basis): The amount of money used to purchase an asset. For example, if a home was purchased for $50,000 its cost basis in the property is $50,000. It is important for the trustee to keep this information in its records. The basis is typically most important when a trust asset is being sold because it will set the capital gains tax on that asset.

Beneficiary (Primary, Remainder and Contingent): This is the person or persons who are to receive the benefit of the trust. The primary beneficiary of a SNT is the person with a disability. Oftentimes, they will only be called a "beneficiary." There may also be named "remainder beneficiaries" or sometimes "contingent beneficiaries", these are the persons who would receive the trust assets once the primary beneficiary either dies or there is a provision in the trust that would cause the assets to go to someone else. For example, an SNT could say, I leave my assets to be administered for the benefit of my child with a disability for as long as he is alive but on his death or upon his no longer being disabled, the assets of the trusts shall be distributed to my grandchildren. In this example, the remainder beneficiaries would be the grandchildren.

Bond: A bond is in essence an insurance policy purchased using trust assets that will pay the trust back if the trustee steals the money from the trust. Most trusts do not require a bond of a trustee because the trustee is someone who the beneficiary respects. However, if a court order established the trust, a trustee bond may be required. To qualify the trustee must have excellent credit and a decent sized net worth or enough of a net worth to cover the amount of the bond which is based on the amount of assets in the trust. If interested in being bonded, check http://www.phillipsbonding.com/ to see if the trustee would qualify.

Breach of Trust: A breach of trust is a violation by the trustee of any duty that the trustee owes the SNT beneficiary.

CalWORKS (TANF)-linked Medi-Cal: This program provides free, full-scope Medi-Cal services for California residents who qualify for CalWORKS (California Work Opportunity and Responsibility to Kids Program), i.e. individuals who care for financially needy children, grandchildren, or other minor relatives. Individuals who are over 60 or disabled are exempt from the Welfare to Work requirements. (CalWORKS is also known under its federal name as Temporary Aid to Needy Families or TANF (formerly known as Aid to Families with Dependent Children or AFDC.

Categorically Eligible Medi-Cal: Categorically needy individuals are automatically eligible for Medi-Cal if they receive Supplemental Security Income (SSI) or California Work Opportunity and Responsibility to Kids (CalWorks).

Conservator: This is a person who has been appointed by a court to manage the personal or financial care of a person with a disability who lacks the legal capacity to manage it themselves. Generally, the roles are divided between Conservator of the Person (who is responsible for things like making medical decisions or deciding where the person with a disability will live) and the Conservator of the Estate (who is responsible for managing the person with a disability's assets not in the special needs trust).

(d)(4)(A) SNT: Another name for an individual first-party special needs trust named after the federal statute that authorizes it, 42 U.S.C. 1396p(d)(4)(A).

(d)(4)(C) SNT: Another name for a pooled first-party special needs trust named after the federal statute that authorizes it, 42 U.S.C. §1396p(d)(4)(C).

Deeming (SSI): A concept where a minor's parents' assets and income are counted as the minor's when trying to qualify for SSI. Likewise, if an SSI eligible person is married, the spouse's assets and income are counted as the SSI eligible person. See chapter 4 for further discussion.

Department of Health Care Services (DHCS): This is the California agency that runs Medi-Cal in California. They issue All County Welfare Letters that provide guidance on how the agency interprets its role in running the Medi-Cal program.

Disbursement: This is the process by which money or assets are spent from the trust for the benefit of the person with a disability who is the beneficiary of an SNT.

Distributable Net Income (DNI): DNI is a tax term that is generally applicable on third-party SNTs. Third-party SNTs are taxed at trust tax rates (rather than at individual tax rates) which are much harsher (meaning that more tax is paid on smaller amounts of income). DNI allows the trustee to make distributions of trust income for the benefit of the beneficiary and lower the amount of tax paid to the beneficiary's tax rate rather than the trust tax rate.

Earned Income (SSI): An SSI type of income that results in one dollar reduction of SSI for every two dollars earned after the first $65 received of income earned by the SSI recipient.

Estate Tax: The tax owed by an individual's estate or trust on death. This may arise in situations where an SNT is funded with significant assets. There are generally large exemptions that may pass estate tax free. For example, in 2011 and 2012 an individual may pass $5 million estate tax free. In 2013, the current law reduces the exemption to $1 million (however check the latest news because this will likely change before it is implemented). Note, in California there is no estate tax.

Fiduciary Duty: This is the legal definition for the type of duty a trustee owes to the beneficiary. It is the highest duty one person can owe another under the law. It is much like the duty a parent owes to a minor child. Thus, the trustee must take better care of trust property and look out for the interests of the beneficiary better than they would take care of their own money or person.

Financial Planner: A financial planner evaluates the finances and helps develop a financial plan to meet both the immediate needs of a beneficiary of a special needs trust and his or her long-term goals. Some, but not all, planners have credentials from professional organizations. Some well-known credentials are certified financial planner (CFP), chartered financial consultant (ChFC), certified investment management analyst (CIMA), and personal financial specialist (PFS). A PFS is a certified public accountant (CPA) who has passed an exam on financial planning. Some planners are also licensed to sell certain investment or insurance products. Fee-only financial planners charge by the hour or collect a flat fee for a specific service, but don't sell products or earn sales commissions. Other planners don't charge a fee but earn commissions on the products they sell to you. Still others both charge fees and earn commissions but may offset their fees by the amount of commission they earn.

First-Party SNT: A first-party SNT is funded with the assets of the person with a disability.

Franchise Tax Board: The California version of the IRS. It is responsible for collecting the amount of tax revenue in California.

Funding: The process of placing money or assets into a trust. Generally this is done by either changing the title to property to the name of the trust or making a beneficiary designation to the name of the trust if for example the asset is a life insurance policy or retirement account.

Grantor Trust: A tax term that defines how a trust will be taxed. In SNTs, a first-party SNT is nearly always a grantor trust, meaning that it will be taxed at the beneficiary's tax rate. See chapter 9 for a further description and **nongrantor trust** on alternative way to tax trusts.

In-Kind Support and Maintenance (ISM): An SSI type of income that results (in 2011) of $244.67 reduction of SSI payment if the SSI recipient receives food or shelter from a third-party or SNT. The amount of reduction will be based on the presumed maximum value (PMV) rule or the value of the one-third reduction rule (VTR). For further discussion, see definitions of PMV and VTR in this glossary and see chapters 2 and 4.

Impairment-Related Work Expenses (IRWE). An IRWE is an out-of-pocket expense related to an impairment that is needed to be able to work. These expenses paid for by the individual may be deducted from earnings when Social Security calculates the SSI payment. See chapter 4.

Irrevocable Trust: A trust that cannot be terminated or modified except in certain very narrow circumstances which usually requires a court order.

Judicial Council Form: The Judicial Council is a part of the California judiciary that creates sample form documents to be used in court filings. Sometimes these forms are mandatory and sometimes they are optional. Many times when trustees go to court they can find relatively easy simple fill in the blank forms for their court filings. The forms are located at http://www. courtinfo.ca.gov/forms/.

Medi-Cal: The Medicaid program (called Medi-Cal in California) is the primary provider of medical benefits for low-income persons with disabilities. In addition to the optional services Medi-Cal covers, California's Medi-Cal program must provide:

- Primary medical care coverage, such as outpatient hospital services and emergency services, physician services, diagnostic testing, emergency services, laboratory and X-ray services, surgery, inpatient hospital services, pregnancy-related services, and family planning.
- Ongoing care and recovery, such as in-home medical care services, personal care services, nursing facility stays, and adult day health care.
- Early and Periodic Screening, Diagnosis, and Treatment (EPSDT) for children under the age of 21.
- Other related costs, such as medical supplies, durable medical equipment, and transportation for doctor visits.

Medi-Cal Waiver Program: A Medi-Cal Waiver allows the Department of Health Care Services (DHCS) to waive Medi-Cal criteria for persons who would not be able to receive these Medi-Cal benefits otherwise. Services provided under a waiver are typically not part of the available benefit package under Medi-Cal or may be an extension of an existing benefit when there are predetermined limits such as with therapy services. An example is the Home and Community Based Service (HCBS) waivers which are creative alternatives, allowed under the federal law for states participating in Medi-Cal, to be implemented in the home community for certain Medi-Cal beneficiaries to avoid hospitalization or nursing facility placement.

Medically Needy Medi-Cal (sometimes called Share-of-Cost Medi-Cal): This program provides full-scope Medi-Cal services to aged, blind, or disabled people with income above the eligibility levels of no-cost

Medi-Cal programs (such as SSI and A&D FPL). The program usually requires that individuals incur a monthly share of cost, which functions like a monthly copayment.

Medicare: Medicare is a federal program with no income or resource requirements. It provides health insurance for individuals who are age 65 or over, disabled, or have end-stage kidney disease or amyotrophic lateral sclerosis. Medicare does not provide complete coverage for all health-care needs. It only covers medically "reasonable and necessary" services. For example, it will not pay for many routine or preventive services such as annual physical exams, eyeglasses, dental care, hearing aids, or long-term care at home or in a nursing home.

Memorandum of Intent: Sometimes called a Letter of Understanding, is a document prepared by a parent (or grandparent) of a person with a disability that may describe the person with a disability, provide a summary of their disability and ongoing care and advocacy, give guidance on the best way to work with the person, and discuss how the parent or grandparent intends the trustee to use trust assets to enhance the quality of life of a person with a disability. It is generally not legally binding, meaning that a trustee can ignore it and not be sued, but most trustees will review the document when deciding if an SNT distribution should be done.

Miller Trust: A type of first-party SNT that is not in use in California. See chapter 2 for more information.

Negligence: Negligence is the failure of the trustee to meet the applicable standard of care set forth under California law or by the trust document.

Nongrantor Trust. A tax term that defines how a trust will be taxed. In SNTs, a third-party SNT is nearly always a nongrantor trust, meaning that it will be taxed at the more onerous trust tax rates rather than at the individual tax rates. However, using **distributable net income (DNI)** a trustee is allowed to shift the burden of taxes to the typically lower beneficiary tax rate by making distributions on beneficiary's behalf. See chapter 9 for a further description and **grantor trust** on alternative way to tax trusts.

Overpayment (SSI). An SSI overpayment occurs when the SSA determines that it has been improperly paying SSI benefits and seeks to have its money returned. For example, if the SSA has been paying SSI benefits of $600 per month for two years and then determines that it should not have been paying $300 of that amount, it will seek repayment of $7,200 ($300 times 24 months) by overpayment. This can be repaid either in a lump sum or (more typically) the SSA will reduce the ongoing SSI payments until the amount is repaid.

Pickle Amendment. The 1976 Pickle Amendment to the Social Security Act requires states to maintain SSI-linked Medi-Cal eligibility for SSI recipients who lose their SSI due to Social Security cost of living allowance. Eligibility extends to those who would have been eligible for SSI in the past, even if they never received it.

Pooled SNT: A type of first-party SNT that is already in existence that is managed by a nonprofit or charity. A person with a disability who has capacity can join this type of trust. Generally, the costs of pooled SNTs are very expensive. An individual will not be a trustee of an SNT. See chapter 2 for more information.

Presumed Maximum Value (PMV): An SSI applicant will lose a certain amount of his or her SSI check if someone pays for his or her food or shelter and doesn't live in the home. This type of income is called "in-kind support and maintenance." The amount of reduction in 2010 is $244.67 per month or the actual amount if less than this amount. If both food and shelter are paid for by someone living in the home then the reduction is under the value of the one-third reduction rule (VTR). See VTR in this glossary and a further discussion in chapters 2 and 4.

Prudent Investment Standard: The investment standard required in most trusts which states that a trustee shall invest and manage trust assets as a prudent investor would, by considering the purposes, terms, distribution requirements, and other circumstances of the trust. In satisfying this standard, the trustee shall exercise reasonable care, skill, and caution.

Qualified Disability Trust (QDT). This is a tax term that means if a trust qualifies it will increase the personal exemption of a trust (currently $100) up to the personal exemption amount of an individual (currently $3,700). This really only applies to third-party SNTs because first-party SNTs typically are grantor trusts and do not need to utilize the exemption increase. However, unless specifically drafted this way, the third-party SNT may not qualify unless it was established for the "sole benefit" of the person with a disability who is under age 65 which is rarely the case for a third-party SNT. For a further discussion see chapter 9.

Registered Investment Adviser (RIA). Investment advisers who register with the Securities and Exchange Commission (SEC) and agree to be regulated by SEC rules are known as registered investment advisers. Only a small percentage of all investment advisers register, though being registered is often interpreted as a sign that the adviser meets a higher standard.

Representative Payee: A person who has been appointed by the Social Security Administration to manage a person with a disability's SSI or SSDI's monthly checks.

Revocable Trust: A Trust that can be modified or amended by the settlor. An example of a revocable trust is a living trust designed for the purpose of avoiding probate.

Seed Trust: A type of first-party SNT that is established by a parent or grandparent using the assets of the person with a disability for a person with a disability who has legal capacity to manage his or her own financial affairs. See chapter 2 for more information.

Settlor, Trustmaker, Grantor, Trustor: These are different names for the person or entity that created or established the trust. For example, if a parent created a trust for a child with a disability, then the parent would be named the settlor, grantor, trustmaker, or trustor of the trust depending on the drafting attorney's own convention of use. In California law, the term *settlor* is used however there is no difference in treatment if a trust document uses a different name.

Share-of-Cost: The amount of money that an individual needs to pay in order to qualify for medically needy Medi-Cal. The share of cost is all income over the "monthly maintenance need" level (MMNL), *i.e.*, the minimum amount necessary to meet basic living expenses as determined by DHCS and based on federal poverty level figures.

Share-of-Cost Medi-Cal: See Medically Needy Medi-Cal.

Shelter: SSI defines shelter to include room, rent, mortgage payments, real property taxes, heating fuel, gas, electricity, water, sewerage, and garbage collection services.

Simplified Accounting: A type of account that may be used for a SNT that is under continuing court jurisdiction. It lists transactions chronologically. If this method is used, the accounting must use the Judicial Council form as described in chapter 7. There are certain types of trusts that may not use the simplified account method and instead must use the standard account method described below.

Social Security Administration (SSA): The federal agency that runs the Social Security system. This includes running the Social Security Disability Income (SSDI) and the Supplemental Security Income (SSI) programs.

Sole Benefit: A legal requirement for the type of disbursement that can be made from a first-party SNT. It means that disbursements must be made for the benefit of the person with a disability only and that disbursements cannot be made to third parties. California has interpreted to mean that others may derive some benefit from the disbursement but the primary benefit is derived by the person with a disability.

Standard Accounting: A type of account that may be used for a SNT that is under continuing court jurisdiction. It lists transactions by subject matter. There are certain SNTs that must use the standard accounting—for example, if the trust estate includes real estate. If this method is used, the accounting must use only one Judicial Council form but may use the remaining 33 forms as described in chapter 7. The alternative is that the trustee may create his or her own forms but they must substantially be similar to the Judicial Council forms.

Statute of Limitations: Laws setting deadlines for filing lawsuits within a certain time after events occur that are the source of a claim. For example, if a SNT account provides information to a beneficiary that shows the trustee was negligent, the beneficiary only has 3 years to sue on the claim or be forever prevented from filing a lawsuit. This example is called a 3-year statute of limitations. The length of time will vary depending on different statutes.

Substantial Gainful Activity (SGA): SGA is a level of work that is substantial and gainful. It is defined as "work activity that involves doing significant physical or mental activities" even if you only do it part-time. Monthly countable earnings of more than $1,000 (in 2010) usually demonstrate SGA. If the SGA is over this amount, it may affect eligibility for SSI and SSDI. The SSA uses SGA to determine the individual's initial and continuing eligibility for SSDI and initial eligibility for SSI (except for individuals who are blind). See chapter 4 for more information.

Surcharge: If an SNT trustee breaches his or her duty and it causes the SNT money damages, the trustee can be surcharged which is a monetary penalty the trustee must pay to the SNT from his or her own funds.

Third-Party SNT: A third-party SNT is typically part of a parent's or grandparent's estate plan for a child with a disability. However, it is not limited to them; any person other than the person with a disability can fund this type of trust. Such a trust is funded with the assets of a "third-party," that is, parents, grandparents, or anyone else other than the person with a disability whom the trust benefits.

Trustee: This is the person responsible for administering the trust once it is established. A trust may also name successor trustees who would be the persons responsible for managing the trust if the originally named trustee can no longer serve. A trust can have more than one trustee at a time. Be aware that a cotrustee can be held responsible for another cotrustee's breach of a fiduciary duty. Thus, it is important that all cotrustees pay close attention to everything that is done in the administration of the trust. If there is any question or problem, that should be communicated to the other cotrustee or cotrustees immediately. As a general rule, where there are two cotrustees, both have to agree on all matters of trust administration, and where there are three or more cotrustees, the majority rules. In order to minimize the chances of being held responsible for someone else's poor judgment or breach of duty, a cotrustee should be sure to make a written record of any points of disagreement about trust business. In extreme cases, a cotrustee may be required to blow the whistle on other cotrustees' activities.

Trust Advisory Committee: In some SNTs, there will be a group of persons called a trust advisory committee. Typically, the committee will have the authority to speak on behalf of the beneficiary and make requests for disbursements. They may also have the authority to remove and replace a trustee. As with nearly all questions surrounding trust administration, it is very important to read the document to understand what role the committee will serve.

Trust Protector: As with the trust advisory committee, a trust protector is used in some SNTs. The protector will be given a series of responsibilities as spelled out in the trust document. Typically, these include the right to remove and replace trustees and the right to amend the trust if there are changes in the law that will require an amendment to the trust to keep it current.

Unearned Income (SSI): A type of SSI income that results in a dollar for dollar reduction of SSI after the receipt of $20 of money by an SSI recipient. Unearned income is cash given to an SSI recipient that has not been earned.

Value of One-Third Reduction Rule (VTR): The VTR applies when the SSI recipient lives in another's house throughout a month, receives both food and shelter from inside the household, and does not meet his or her pro rata share of cost of the food and shelter expenses for the household. The SSI recipient will lose 1/3 of the federal portion of his SSI check. In 2010, the loss would be $224.67. See Presumed Maximum Value (PMV) and chapters 2 and 4 for further discussion.

INDEX

CPSIA information can be obtained at www.ICGtesting.com
Printed in the USA
LVOW011441150213

320282LV00002B/196/P

9 781462 060511